At the Water's Edge

At the Water's Edge

Defending against the Modern Amphibious Assault

Theodore L. Gatchel

Naval Institute Press • Annapolis, Maryland

The latest edition of this work has been brought to publication with the generous assistance of Marguerite and Gerry Lenfest.

Naval Institute Press
291 Wood Road
Annapolis, MD 21402

© 1996 by Theodore L. Gatchel

First Naval Institute Press paperback edition published 2011

All rights reserved. No part of this book may be reproduced without permission in writing from the publisher.

ISBN 978-1-59114-322-2 (paperback)
ISBN 978-1-61251-430-7 (eBook)

The Library of Congress has cataloged the paperback edition as follows:
Gatchel, Theodore L.
 At the water's edge : defending against the modern amphibious assault / Theodore L. Gatchel
   p. cm.
 Includes bibliographical references and index.
 ISBN 978-1-59114-322-2 (paperback : alk. Paper)
 1. Amphibious warfare—History—20th century. 2. Amphibious warfare—Case studies. 3. Defensive (Military science)—Case studies. I. Title.
  U261.G38 1996
  355.4'6—dc20
                                       96-38214

∞ Print editions meet the requirements of ANSI/NISO z39.48-1992 (Permanence of Paper).
Printed in the United States of America.
19 18 17 16 15 14   8 7 6 5 4 3

To Vance

Contents

List of Illustrations **IX**

List of Maps **XI**

Preface **XIII**

List of Abbreviations **XV**

1. Anti-Landing Defense:
   The Other Face of Amphibious Warfare **1**

2. The Search Begins:
   Gallipoli, 1915 **10**

3. Preparations for Invasion:
   Great Britain, 1940 **24**

4. German Mobile Defense:
   Sicily and Salerno, 1943 **39**

5. German Defense at the Water's Edge:
   Normandy, 1944 **59**

6. The Americans Try Their Hand:
   Wake and Midway, 1941–1942 **78**

7. Japanese Naval Defense:
   The Southwest Pacific Area, 1942–1944 **94**

8. Japanese Defense at the Water's Edge:
   The Gilberts and Marshalls, 1943–1944 **117**

VIII ~ Contents

9 Japanese Defense in Transition:
  Saipan to Iwo Jima, 1944–1945 **134**

10 The Ultimate Naval Defense:
  Okinawa and Japan, 1945 **153**

11 A Poor Man's Naval Defense:
  Inchon and Wonsan, 1950 **173**

12 Lessons Learned and Unlearned:
  The Falkland Islands, 1982 **186**

13 Anti-Landing Defense and the Implications for Future Amphibious Operations **203**

  Notes **219**

  Bibliography **235**

  Index **249**

Illustrations

German Panzer Mark IV tanks   **45**

USS *Savannah,* following bomb hit at Salerno, 1943   **56**

Casemate, part of Atlantic Wall, Normandy   **61**

Defense at the water's edge, Normandy   **67**

German remote-controlled Goliath demolition vehicles   **68**

Naval defense at Guadalcanal   **99**

Natural caves, Biak in the southwest Pacific   **105**

Kamikaze units, 1944   **114**

Japanese defense at Tarawa, November 1943   **124**

Death over dishonor, Tarawa, November 1943   **129**

Japanese tank out of action, Saipan, 1944   **141**

Modified LVT spewing flames into cave at Peleliu   **146**

The Oka, a rocket-propelled suicide bomb   **156**

The *Yamato,* largest battleship in the world   **162**

Koryu type D midget submarines, Kure Naval Base, Japan, 1945   **166**

Destruction of South Korean minesweeper *YMS-516,* 1950   **183**

Maps

Gallipoli, 1915 **19**

Southeast England, 1940 **36**

Sicily, 1943 **49**

Salerno, 1943 **54**

Normandy, 1944 **73**

Wake Island, 1941 **86**

Southwest Pacific Area, 1943–1944 **104**

Philippine Islands, 1944–1945 **112**

Tarawa Atoll, 1943 **126**

Saipan, 1944 **139**

Okinawa, 1945 **161**

Kyushu, 1945 **168**

Korea, 1950 **181**

Falkland Islands, 1982 **197**

Preface

Although I began writing this book when I retired from active duty in the U.S. Marine Corps in 1991, the thinking behind the work started much earlier. During my thirty-year career in the Marines, conventional wisdom held—correctly, I think—that the amphibious assault is the most difficult operation of war. At the same time, I wondered why the forces who defended against landings were almost universally unsuccessful.

My interest in the subject was heightened by the discovery that many officers, including some from the Marine Corps, seemed to believe that changes in warfare had made the amphibious assault infeasible. My purpose in writing this work is not to dismiss the obstacles to be overcome in conducting landings but, rather, to illustrate the difficulties experienced by commanders of the past in defending against amphibious landings. Some of my friends have reacted with surprise that I would write something that might help a future enemy defend against an American landing. My response is the classic "know your enemy." Only by fully understanding how to defend against a landing can our forces making future amphibious assaults hope to maintain the successful record of those who have made such landings in the past.

In writing this book, I have had a great deal of help. I especially thank five friends from the Naval War College (NWC), who patiently read each of the chapters and gave me the benefit of their expertise and advice: Dr. John Hattendorf, Ernest J. King Professor of Maritime History; Capt. Frank Snyder, USN (Ret.), professor emeritus of naval operations; Dr. Milan Vego, professor of naval operations; Frank Uhlig, Jr., editor emeritus of the *Naval War College Review;* and Col. Anthony Walker, USMC (Ret.), who participated in several of the landings described. Also, I extend my great appreciation to Rear Adm. Joseph Strasser, president of NWC during the period when I conducted most of my work, and to Dr. Robert Wood, dean of the Center for Naval Warfare Studies, for allowing me to do my research as an advanced research fellow.

Additionally, I thank Col. Joseph H. Alexander, USMC (Ret.), who shared his material that had been translated from Japanese sources for his book on Tarawa; Dr. Donald Bittner, Marine Corps University; Dr. Evelyn Cherpak, director of the NWC Archives; Dr. Edward Drea, U.S. Army Center of Military History; Evelyn Englander, head librarian at the Marine Corps Historical Center; Maj. Gen. Scott Grant of the British Army, who made arrangements for me to have access to the Ministry of Defence Library and the reading room of the National Army Museum; Robert Schnare, director of the NWC Library, whose superb reference section staff helped me to locate many unusual documents; Dr. Brian Sullivan, who provided material on the Italian armed forces; Kerry Strong, director of the Marine Corps University Archives; and Dennis Vetock, U.S. Army Military History Institute.

I am also in debt to my editor, Terry Belanger, for her help and for making the process of editing as painless as possible for a first-time author.

Abbreviations

ADM	Admiralty Records (United Kingdom)
ANZAC	Australian and New Zealand Army Corps
ATIS	Allied Translator and Interpreter Section (Southwest Pacific Area)
CAB	Cabinet Records (United Kingdom)
CinC	Commander in Chief
CinCPac	Commander in Chief, U.S. Pacific Fleet (during World War II); currently, Commander in Chief, U.S. Pacific Command
CinCPacFlt	Commander in Chief, U.S. Pacific Fleet (current usage)
CNO	Chief of Naval Operations (United States)
CO	Commanding officer
ComPhibGru	Commander, Amphibious Group
COS	Chiefs of Staff Committee (United Kingdom)
DD tank	dual drive (amphibious) tank
DUKW	U.S. 2.5-ton amphibious truck (World War II)
ETHINT	European Theater Historical Interrogations
GPO	Government Printing Office
HMSO	Her (His) Majesty's Stationery Office
JGSDF	Japanese Ground Self Defense Force
JIC	Joint Intelligence Committee
JICPOA	Joint Intelligence Center, Pacific Ocean Areas
KdK	Kleinkampfverbände (small German Navy battle units)
LCAC	landing craft, air cushion

XVI ~ List of Abbreviations

LDV	Local Defence Volunteers
LPD	amphibious transport, dock
LSL	landing ship, logistics
LST	landing ship, tank
LVT	landing vehicle, tracked
LVT(A)	landing vehicle, tracked (armored)
NA	National Archives
NATO	North Atlantic Treaty Organization
NTLF	Northern Troops and Landing Force
NWC	Naval War College
OKW	Oberkommando der Wehrmacht (High Command of the Armed Forces, Germany, World War II)
OP	Operations Plan
PRO	Public Records Office (United Kingdom)
RAF	Royal Air Force
RG	Record Group
SAS	Special Air Service
SBS	Special Boat Squadron
SNLF	Special Naval Landing Force
SWPA	Southwest Pacific Area
UDT	Underwater demolition team
UK	United Kingdom
USACGSC	U.S. Army Command and General Staff College
USSBS	U.S. Strategic Bombing Survey
VMF	Marine Fighting Squadron
WO	War Office (United Kingdom)

At the Water's Edge

Anti-Landing Defense:
The Other Face of Amphibious Warfare

Successful penetration of a defended beach is the most difficult operation in warfare.
Gen. Dwight D. Eisenhower

For most of the twentieth century, perceptions of the value of amphibious operations have undergone the equivalent of a roller coaster ride. These perceptions reached a historic low following the Anglo-French disaster on the Turkish peninsula of Gallipoli in 1915. After the problems that caused that disaster were overcome, however, perceptions steadily grew more favorable until the end of World War II. At that historic high, noted military analyst J. F. C. Fuller proclaimed that the amphibious tactics developed in the Pacific were, in all probability, "the most far-reaching tactical innovation of the war."[1]

Following World War II, the roller coaster ride continued with peaks at Inchon during the Korean War and the British landings in the Falkland Islands and valleys whenever a new type of weapon led commentators to predict the end of amphibious warfare as a serious military threat. Such predictions have resulted, in part, from perceiving the difficulties involved in a successful landing. Examined closely, this perception leads to an apparent historical contradiction. On one hand, the amphibious assault generally has been regarded as the most difficult of military operations. Gen. Dwight D. Eisenhower's comment (above) is typical. He did not make the comment in connection with the invasion of Normandy, as one might expect, but in a 1939 report on defense of the Philippines. British military historian B. H. Liddell Hart expresses a similar view: "A landing on a foreign coast in face of hostile troops has always been one of the most difficult operations of war."[2]

On the other hand, nearly all modern amphibious operations have been successful. Of the many landings attempted since Gallipoli, only a handful have been turned away by the defenders. In December 1941, U.S. Marines defending Wake Island repulsed an initial Japanese landing, and attacks by U.S. Army Air Force planes, combined with bad weather, forced the Japanese to withdraw from a landing at Pandan in the Philippines. In September of the following year, a combined force of U.S. and Australian soldiers forced a Japanese landing party to withdraw from a beach at Milne Bay, New Guinea, where they had landed ten days earlier. One other case, although not strictly a defeated landing, deserves mention. A combined Anglo-French landing at Dakar, French West Africa, in September 1940 was called off at the last minute when the attackers realized that they were unprepared for the expected resistance. With these exceptions, amphibious attackers in World War II won an unbroken string of victories against varying degrees of opposition in both European and Pacific theaters. These amphibious victories have been described in detail in official and other accounts. The apparent contradiction between the difficulties of conducting these operations and their unparalleled rate of success, however, has received little attention.

Previous attempts to resolve this contradiction have been either unsatisfactory or incomplete. Adm. Sergei Gorshkov, principal architect of the modern navy of the former Soviet Union, provides one example. Commenting on World War II landings, he attributes their almost universal success to "the general military-political conditions favorable for the invaders and also by the concentration of the strength of the invasion force outstripping the defence."[3] He goes on to note that, during the war, no amphibious operation was subject to continuous disruption from the point of assembly to the landing itself. Admiral Gorshkov attributes that failure either to inadequate intelligence or to the lack of means on the part of the defender to attack the landing force at all stages of the operation. To determine the validity of Gorshkov's assertions, one must examine the amphibious operation from an unconventional perspective: that of the defender. One way to begin such an examination is to explore the three basic approaches to opposing a landing: naval defense, defense at the water's edge, and mobile ground defense.

A naval defense involves the use of naval and air forces to defeat the invader's amphibious forces at sea before, during, or after the landing itself. In this sense, the term *naval* refers to the defender's target (the enemy's ships) rather than to the means of attacking that target. To be a true naval defense, as opposed to an interdiction of the invasion force at sea, the defensive action must take place in close proximity to the landing itself. A naval defense has several significant strengths. Because it uses forces separate from those required for a ground defense, a naval defense usually can be devised to complement a ground effort without competing for the same resources. A naval defense also deals with the attacker earlier than a ground defense, thereby giving the ground defender increased warning of the impending attack and time to prepare for it. Additionally, the ground defender will not have to deal with any of the attacker's forces destroyed at sea prior to the assault.

The principal disadvantage of the naval defense is the need for extremely close coordination among the defending ground, air, and naval commanders to prevent them from working at cross-purposes. A ground commander hoping to lure the enemy into landing over a particular stretch of beach, for example, would not want the naval commander to order heavy mining of that area regardless of naval considerations. In theory, this need for coordination might not appear to be a significant weakness. In practice, however, inadequate interservice coordination has resulted in the failure of many joint defensive efforts.

In *Some Principles of Maritime Strategy,* British naval strategist Julian S. Corbett raises another issue that has proved difficult for those attempting to implement a naval defense against amphibious operations. Because amphibious assaults are naval operations requiring at least local or temporary control of the sea and air, many naval forces, in addition to those that are strictly amphibious, might be involved. This factor, in turn, frequently creates the conditions for more general naval actions. Many of the great sea battles of modern times (e.g., Coral Sea, Midway, Savo Island, Philippine Sea, Leyte Gulf) were precipitated by, or related to, amphibious operations. Preoccupation with a more general naval engagement has caused more than one naval defender to lose sight of the objective, the invading enemy's landing force. Corbett cautions against this confusion of aims by noting that instructions in the Royal Navy traditionally insisted that commanders encountering an invasion fleet make the enemy's transports the "principal object."[4] Focusing on the enemy's transports has proved exceptionally difficult for some naval defenders, particularly the Japanese and others schooled in the view that the enemy's main battle fleet must always be the principal objective.

If a defender fails to destroy an invader's force at sea, the next option is to deny the attacker a foothold on the beach by a vigorous defense at the water's edge. The focus of this type of defense, like that of an area defense in ground warfare, is the defensive position itself, rather than the enemy force. The defender accomplishes the mission by holding terrain, thereby denying its use to the enemy. That action could, in fact, result in the destruction of the enemy's force, but the primary focus is on defense of the position.

The idea of defeating an attacker at the water's edge has an instinctive appeal. In his 1897 work, British author George Armand Furse makes the following points:

> The enemy's great difficulty is to land; we should not, therefore, trust to defeat him once he has got on shore, but should meet him as he quits the transports, and prevent his landing. The defenders should not renounce the predominance which they possess in a contest on the beach. . . . The ease with which it is practicable to defeat a landing should not be undervalued, and all the principles of tactics clearly point to a vigorous and determined resistance on the beach as the correct course to pursue.[5]

This comment clearly points out the greatest advantage of a defense at the water's edge. It counters the amphibious assault at the most vulnerable time, the ship-to-shore movement. This form of defense has the added advantages of allowing for the most detailed preparation and being the least susceptible to deception and surprise.

When a defender is confronted with any but the smallest of coastlines to protect, however, a defense at the water's edge is exceptionally costly in personnel and materiel. Rarely does a defender have the resources to be strong everywhere, so gaps are created in the defenses or combat power is dissipated. During World War II, the Germans chose not only to fortify the coast of Europe from Denmark to southern France but also to keep three hundred thousand troops in Norway to protect that country from an Allied invasion. By attempting to defend everywhere, the Germans created the conditions that eventually allowed the Allies to overcome the German defenses at a particular point.

Since World War II, technology has exacerbated this weakness of the defense at the water's edge. When troops and equipment were landed by conventional landing craft and wheeled or tracked amphibians, hydrographic conditions and obstacles to beach egress limited landings to 20 percent of the world's coastline or less. This reduced the problem for defenders by allowing them to plan area defenses only where a landing was technically feasible. The use of helicopters and air-cushion landing craft has reversed the situation by making landings possible over more than 70 percent of the world's coastline. Because of the difficulties of defending at the water's edge, some defenders have searched for other solutions to the problems of defeating a landing.

One alternative approach is to allow an enemy to land and then counterattack after determining that the landing is, in fact, the main attack and not a feint. This approach parallels the conduct of the mobile defense in land warfare. Accordingly, I refer to this form of defense against amphibious assault as a mobile ground defense. The objective of this type of defense is destruction of the enemy force, as opposed to holding a particular piece of ground. Because of its emphasis on maneuver, the mobile ground defense has been the instinctive preference of many soldiers.

In a short section on amphibious operations in *The Art of War*, Jomini sums up his thoughts on defending against a landing:

> I can only advise the party on the defensive not to divide his forces too much by attempting to cover every point.... Signals should be arranged for giving prompt notice of the point where the enemy is landing, and all the disposable force should be rapidly concentrated there, to prevent his gaining a firm foothold.[6]

In this short comment, Jomini alludes to both the advantages and disadvantages of the mobile defense. A major advantage is that the defender concentrates its force at the point of decision instead of dissipating it over a wide expanse of coastline. As a result, this form of defense makes the most efficient use of men and materiel. Another distinct advantage is that by eschewing the employment of fixed positions, the defender limits the ability of the enemy to plan supporting fires in advance.

Along with these advantages, there are some notable disadvantages. First, this form of defense allows an attacker, who is relatively unimpeded, to gain a foothold on the beach. Many defenders have found that, once established, even the most precarious beachheads can be impossible to dislodge. During the Italian campaign of World War II, for example, the Germans and Italians consistently employed this style of defense without success, but they came close to it on several occasions.

The second disadvantage of the mobile defense is that it requires the defender to have greater mobility ashore than the attacker has at sea. The battle becomes a race to concentrate at a specific point that only the attacker knows before the landing begins. When navies were powered by sail and armies marched on foot, the forces at sea had a clear advantage. Describing how ships could easily outrun forces ashore, Sir Walter Raleigh said, "And I know it to be true that a fleet of ships may be seen at sunset, and after it at the Lizard, yet by the next morning they may recover Portland; whereas an army on foot shall not be able to march it in six dayes."[7] In spite of the availability of modern ground and air transportation to defenders today, navies continue to maintain their traditional advantage in mobility. As the U.S. Marine Corps frequently points out, an amphibious task force off the Virginia Capes when the sun goes down could be landing the following morning anywhere from Long Island, New York, to Myrtle Beach, South Carolina. In the same time, no army could move the equivalent distance ashore with enough combat power to repulse a major amphibious assault before the landing force had established itself ashore.

This situation would hold even if the defender were allowed to move its forces without interference. In practice, however, the defender must count on its movements being delayed by a variety of enemy means, including air strikes, naval gunfire, and special operations forces. Enemy action notwithstanding, the defender faces a third set of problems regarding the ability to move.

Before beginning to use its mobility, the defender must first make the critical decision that the landing it is about to counterattack is the main attack and not a feint or diversionary landing. This decision is a critical one that requires timely and accurate information about the enemy and a command and control system available to disseminate this information quickly to all who need it. Because of these requirements, the mobile ground defense is highly susceptible to deception.

Although the defense against amphibious operations can be divided conceptually into naval, water's edge, and mobile ground forms, such neatness rarely exists in practice. Most defenders start with a concept built around one of the three basic defenses but finish with a combination of styles. Ideally, a defense would incorporate all three basic concepts into an integrated operation under the direction of a single commander. In practice, a variety of factors, including inadequate resources, lack of preparation time, absence of doctrine, and interservice rivalries, have prevented this goal of a balanced defense from being achieved.

In addition to these various types of defense, four complementary actions are closely related to defense against a landing: (1) blockading or attacking the enemy's amphibious forces in its embarkation ports, (2) interdicting those forces at sea before they arrive at the site of the intended landing, (3) denying the attacker the conditions of sea and air control necessary to initiate a landing, and (4) taking actions after an attacker has successfully landed to prevent achievement of the objectives for which it conducted the landing. The distinction between the first three of these complementary actions and a true anti-landing defense is one of location. A true defense takes place in the vicinity of the landing. Many operations needed to support a landing, such as escorting the amphibious force to the objective area and establishing air and sea control, take place away from the landing site and are not, strictly speaking, part of the amphibious operation. Likewise, many other complementary actions might be needed to support the defense against a landing without being part of the defense itself.

Blockading or attacking an enemy's amphibious forces in its embarkation ports has been carried out successfully in the past, particularly by the British in the days of sail. They continued that tradition in World War II by bombing and shelling German invasion forces marshalling in French ports in 1940 for the invasion of Britain. In more recent times, air-power advocates have added a new twist to blockade in the form of strategic bombing of the enemy's embarkation ports in order to prevent an amphibious operation from ever getting under way. Although directly complementary to the subject of anti-landing defense, the issues of blockade and strategic bombing are largely beyond the scope of this book.

Following blockade or strategic bombing, the next option available to a defender is interdicting the enemy's force at sea before it arrives in the objective area. Like blockade, interdiction has been both a longtime favorite of naval theorists and a course of action endorsed by the advocates of air power. The subject of interdiction, as discussed in this book, is limited to interdiction directly related to the defense against amphibious operations.

Air superiority and sea control in the objective area are of vital interest to a defender, and they are more directly related to the defense itself than either blockade or interdiction. Virtually all practitioners of amphibious warfare agree that at least local air superiority and sea control are required in the objective area to ensure the success of a landing. In the broadest sense, air superiority and sea control might be achieved by the strategic bombing of a nation's industrial base. For our purposes, discussion is limited to those tactical and operational measures taken by the defender in the vicinity of the landing to deny the attacker the needed degrees of air superiority and sea control.

One further complement to an anti-landing defense is available. Even if all defensive measures have failed and the attacker has gained and maintained a foothold on the beach, the defender has not necessarily lost the battle. Some action to prevent the attacker from achieving the landing objective still might be possible.

In his classic work on strategy, Clausewitz introduces the idea of a culminating point, an idea that has since found its way into U.S. operational doctrine.[8] In simplest terms, this concept holds that, as an attack progresses, it loses force until it reaches a culminating point, at which the attacker can no longer prevail over the defender. The secret of a successful attack is to achieve a decisive objective before reaching this culminating point. A defender, on the other hand, must strive to draw out the defense to such an extent that the attacker reaches the culminating point before achieving a decisive victory. The idea of a culminating point is particularly important in amphibious warfare because of the nature of a landing. When conducting a conventional ground attack, the attacker builds up combat power to the greatest achievable potential before starting the attack. From that point on, the attacker's power diminishes until the culminating point is reached or victory is achieved. An amphibious attack, on the other hand, presents a more complicated problem. A landing force must build up its combat power on the beach from an initial zero while the attack is in progress. This severe handicap would appear to increase the opportunity for a defender to deny an attacker a victory before reaching the culminating point.

In order to win, an amphibious attacker must also achieve a series of sequential victories. It must reach the objective area, get ashore, resist counterattack, and force a decision before reaching the culminating point. The defender, on the other hand, needs only to thwart the attacker at any one of these stages to be successful.

The apparent contradiction that arises from the study of amphibious operations—theory that would seem to favor the defender versus a historical record strongly biased toward the attacker—poses interesting questions about the nature of the attack and defense as forms of warfare. Unlike conventional ground combat, amphibious warfare normally does not involve meeting engagements that can cloud the issues of attack versus defense. The case studies in this book, for example, reflect situations in which a deliberate attack was planned and, in most cases, executed against an equally deliberate defense. As a result, the cases can provide some evidence about the relative strengths and weaknesses of the two forms of warfare themselves. Amphibious operations also provide a vehicle for examining two other important aspects of modern warfare: joint/combined operations and the issues of continental warfare versus naval warfare.

Amphibious operations are inherently joint in nature, even though a landing carried out by the U.S. Navy and U.S. Marine Corps would not be a joint operation in the strict sense of current Department of Defense terminology. In any case, amphibious operations involve the landing of ground forces from ships. Also, modern amphibious operations, almost invariably, have included the use of air forces. In addition, many modern amphibious landings have been combined operations in the American sense of the term, that is, forces from more than one nation have taken part. The British, at times, have used the term *combined operation* synonymously with the term *amphibious operation.* Regardless of terminology, the multiservice nature of amphibious warfare has forced its practitioners to reach some accommodation regarding the command and control of air, ground, and naval forces. Such has not always been the case with respect to those defending against a landing. A defender can choose to employ ground forces alone or use forces from different services independently. Lacking an inherent requirement to coordinate between services, defenders frequently have lagged behind attackers in this respect.

Related to the issues of joint and combined warfare are those involving continental warfare versus naval warfare. Amphibious warfare is the projection of naval force ashore. The commander of an amphibious operation has no choice but to deal with both the naval and land aspects of the assault. A ground commander charged with the defense of a coast against amphibious assault has no corresponding requirement to deal with naval aspects of the defense. As a result, many defenders appear to have had a less thorough grasp of the entire operation than did their amphibious opponents.

2

The Search Begins:
Gallipoli, 1915

> *When the question of dispatching a military expeditionary force to the Gallipoli Peninsula comes to be passed in review, the first point to be considered is the general one of whether a landing is possible at all, in the face of active opposition under modern conditions.*
> *In regard to this history affords no guide.*
> **British General Staff memorandum, 1906**

In the annals of war, the name Gallipoli has become synonymous with incompetence and failure, yet the amphibious operation that bears the ill-fated name is generally regarded as the starting point for modern amphibious warfare. Although the landing of armies from ships has been an operation of war for as long as military history has been recorded, the landings at Gallipoli differed from earlier landings. They constituted a major combined operation, during which many of the landings were heavily opposed assaults, not merely the uncontested delivery of an expeditionary force to a foreign shore. The landings at Gallipoli also involved all of the components of a modern amphibious operation. In addition to armies and navies, air forces made their presence felt in an indecisive way. Not surprisingly, therefore, Gallipoli became the focal point for the study of amphibious warfare, particularly in the United States and Great Britain, during the period between the two world wars. U.S. amphibious doctrine today can be traced back directly to various successes and failures at Gallipoli.

By the end of 1914, World War I had been in progress for less than six months, but movement on the western front in France and Belgium had ground to a halt. The great attrition battles of Verdun and the Somme were yet to come, but both sides were already searching for ways to break the deadlock. One possibility that appealed to Winston Churchill, Britain's First Lord of the Admiralty, was a campaign against

Turkey, which had entered the war on Germany's side in November 1914. Potential benefits of such a campaign ranged from opening a line of communications to the beleaguered Russsians through the Turkish Straits to reducing the Turkish threat to the Suez Canal.

In November 1914 and again the following February, ships of the Royal Navy shelled the Turkish forts guarding the entrance to the Dardanelles. Although these bombardments and the demolition parties that landed after the February shelling disabled some of the Turkish guns, the most important effect of these actions was a warning to the Turks of possible events to come. Turkish concerns about the vulnerability of their forts must be viewed in the context of a larger debate, then taking place, about the effectiveness of naval gunfire against fortifications.

During the nineteenth century, conventional wisdom on the subject had generally followed the dictum attributed to Adm. Horatio Nelson, "A ship's a fool to fight a fort." British Adm. John Fisher, first sea lord at the time of Gallipoli, had reaffirmed Nelson's view: "Any naval officer who engages a fort worthy of the name deserves to be shot."[1] By the start of the Gallipoli campaign, however, naval guns had been improved and spotting aircraft had been introduced, thus affording an unprecedented ability to adjust fire against targets ashore. The apparent ease with which German siege artillery had destroyed the fortifications around Liège and Namur, Belgium, and Maubeuge, France, earlier in the war had also indicated to many military theorists that the balance between fortifications and artillery had shifted dramatically in favor of artillery.

On 18 March 1915, the British attempted to run the Dardanelles with a combined fleet of French and British battleships without first landing an army to neutralize the forts protecting the straits. The arrival of a powerful Anglo-French naval force off Constantinople, Turkey, was expected to be enough to drive Turkey out of the war. Unfortunately for the British and French, the operation did not go according to plan. The operation began with sweeping efforts to clear Turkish minefields known to be blocking the straits, but the Turks had laid another line of mines parallel to the channel that remained undetected. The Allies discovered this line when the French battleship *Bouvet* struck one of the mines and sank within minutes. Before the day was over, the British battleships *Ocean* and *Irresistible* had been sunk by mines and the battle cruiser *Inflexible* put out of action. At this point, the Allied commander, Vice Adm. John de Robeck, withdrew his forces. Having exhausted most of their ammunition in the engagement with the Allied fleet, the Turkish defenders welcomed the respite.

Four days later, Admiral de Robeck announced that he would not attempt to force the straits again without a major supporting operation by the army. A sizable army force under Gen. Ian Hamilton embarked for the purpose of occupying Constantinople, but the troops had been loaded on board transports in such a way that they were unprepared to make an amphibious assault across a defended beach. The only answer was to unload the force and reload it accordingly. The closest friendly port with space to accommodate such a massive undertaking was Alexandria. On 23 March, the frustrated attackers sailed for Egypt. The Turkish defenders were both astounded and relieved to see their enemies depart.

The Situation at Gallipoli

The day after the British departed, Marshal Otto Liman von Sanders, a German cavalry general who had previously headed the German military mission to Turkey, took command of the Turkish Fifth Army, which had been formed to protect the Dardanelles. By 26 March, he had established his headquarters in the town of Gallipoli and was estimating the scope of his task. Certain that the British would return, he based this belief both on his personal assessment of the British national character and on intelligence reports from various sources.[2]

The force being reassembled by General Hamilton in Alexandria was a powerful one that included the 29th Division, a regular infantry unit originally slated for France, the Australian and New Zealand Army Corps (ANZAC), and the Royal Naval Division. The addition of French army forces brought Hamilton's command to just over seventy-five thousand men.[3]

During the process of reorganizing his force, Hamilton was unable to hide his actions from enemy eyes. Until he complained to London, his command was designated the Constantinople Expeditionary Force, a title hardly designed to keep its objective secret. Because Egypt was not technically at war, local newspapers regularly published details of the reloading operations. An advanced base on Lemnos Island off the Gallipoli coast that the British had acquired was equally accessible to Turkish agents and sympathizers. Aided by these various holes in British security, Liman von Sanders was able to make a reasonably accurate assessment of his enemy's strength, which he estimated to be between eighty and ninety thousand men.[4]

To oppose Hamilton's landing, the Turks built up the defending forces from two divisions in January 1915 to six by the time of the landing, for a total of about sixty thousand men.[5] To prevent the British from determining their strength and dispositions, the Turks took extraordinary security measures. They conducted all troop movements and construction of field fortifications at night.

In his diary, Hamilton paid tribute to his enemy's efforts: "Not one single living soul has been seen, since the engagement of our Marines at the end of February, although each morning brings forth fresh evidence of nocturnal activity, in patches of freshly turned up soil."[6] Hindered by the precautions of his foe and lacking adequate means for reconnaissance, Hamilton relied on reports from London, which estimated the strength of the Turkish defenders at forty thousand in the vicinity of Gallipoli with less than 10 percent south of Achi Baba.[7]

Responsibility for the defense of the straits was split three ways. Marshal Liman von Sanders commanded the ground forces of the Turkish Fifth Army on both sides of the straits. From his headquarters in Constantinople, German Adm. Guido Usedom commanded the forts along the straits, associated mobile artillery, minefields, and the only aircraft available to the Turks. Admiral Usedom exercised command of the Dardanelles forts through a Turkish officer stationed there. German Adm. Wilhelm Souchon from Constantinople commanded the Turkish navy. According to the Turkish constitution of the time, overall command of the armed forces was invested in the Sultan. In fact, Minister of War Enver Pasha, a powerful army officer who had assumed the title of deputy generalissimo, exercised ultimate command over the navy and army.[8] The lack of a unified commander for Gallipoli, other than Enver, would result in severe problems for the defenders. Referring to the three separate commanders for the Dardanelles, the Turkish General Staff stated after the war, "Liaison between them was not satisfactory, and the High Command at Constantinople had frequently to intervene to ensure coordination of effort between these three independent authorities."[9]

The geography of the region presented the attackers with a dilemma about where to land. In many respects, the Asian shore of the Dardanelles was preferable to the European side. More suitable beaches were available, maneuver room was unlimited once ashore, and the terrain was better for movement than the more broken ground of the Gallipoli Peninsula. A landing on the Asian side would also place the attackers in position to take the most troublesome forts from the rear, thus reducing the obstacles to another naval attempt to force the Straits.[10] Weighed against these advantages were two important disadvantages. First, a successful attack on the Asian side would leave the attackers on the wrong side of the straits to threaten Constantinople directly. Second, after landing, the attackers would be faced with a long march, with their flank exposed to the large Turkish armies in Anatolia.

Terrain on the Gallipoli side clearly favored the defenders, although this was not apparent to the Allies at the time. Maps available before the landing showed the ground between the southern beaches and the first day's objective, the high ground at Achi Baba, as a gentle slope. As the attackers were to learn the hard way, the ground was broken in a manner that impeded movement and provided the defenders with cover and concealment. Terrain also worked to the defenders' advantage in another fundamental way. The number of landing beaches on Gallipoli Peninsula was limited; even where suitable beaches existed, egress was often difficult or impossible because of high cliffs. The Allies located suitable beaches at the extreme southern end of the peninsula (Helles), on the western coast around the middle of the peninsula at Suvla Bay and at what would become known as Anzac Cove, and, finally, at the northern end of the peninsula along the shores of Saros Bay near Bulair.

Both sides generally agreed on the locations of the most likely beaches for a landing. Within the defending camp, however, there was disagreement over how best to deploy the defending forces. The Turkish General Staff considered the number of suitable beaches small enough to base the defense plans largely on terrain considerations.[11] Liman von Sanders, on the other hand, believed that there were more potential beaches than he could adequately defend and that plans, therefore, would have to be based on other considerations.[12]

The terrain at Gallipoli favored the attackers in only one way. The absence of an adequate road network on the peninsula hindered the ability of the Turks to move forces and supplies quickly from one threatened area to another. Unlike most terrain problems, however, this one could be corrected by building roads if the defenders would have enough time. Although Liman von Sanders was certain that the British would return, he did not know when. As a result, he immediately launched a crash program designed to take the maximum advantage of any respite allowed him.

The Turkish Plan

Liman von Sanders's initial step was to develop a concept for the defense, and he was quick to do this. His statement of the concept is a classic description of a mobile ground defense, in which he noted that, by trying to defend every possible beach, the Turks had lost the ability to strike a decisive blow at a landing. In summarizing his concept, he states, "Our success depended not on sticking tight, but on the mobility of our three battle groups."[13]

The Turkish General Staff, on the other hand, held a different view. Regarding the number of possible landing beaches as small in relation to the available defending forces, the general staff proposed assigning divisions to cover specific beaches, with the objective of preventing the enemy from establishing a foothold ashore.

Liman von Sanders's view prevailed, however, and he deployed the Fifth Army to cover three broad geographic areas. The 5th and 7th Divisions, along with an independent cavalry brigade and a gendarme battalion, were assigned to the northern part of the peninsula to guard against a landing from Saros Bay that would threaten Bulair. The 9th and 19th Divisions were placed farther down the peninsula, the 19th largely in reserve near Maidos. To complete the picture, the 3d and 11th Divisions were located across the straits in Asia, the 3d south of Kum Kale and the 11th in the vicinity of Besika Bay. Although the Turks had adopted a mobile defense concept, they nevertheless covered the most likely beaches with a defense at the water's edge. Along the stretch of coastline at Helles that the British called "W Beach," for example, the defenders had strung a deep belt of barbed wire, laid a minefield, and constructed machine-gun positions to enfilade the beach.[14]

The Landings at Gallipoli

On 25 April at about 0500, reports began arriving at the Turkish Fifth Army headquarters of landings in progress on both sides of the Dardanelles. Liman von Sanders notes in his memoirs that, although some members of his staff were shaken by the news, he was confident because he had accurately anticipated the general location of most of the enemy's landings. He also reasoned correctly that not all of these reported landings represented real threats. In his words: "It seemed improbable to me that extensive landings would take place at all of these places, but we could not discern at that moment where the enemy was actually seeking the decision."[15] This assessment appears to confirm that the British deception plan succeeded. The plan had called for demonstrations and diversionary landings on both sides of the straits to mask the main assault at the tip of the peninsula and a major supporting landing by the ANZACs near Ari Burnu. The objective of the ANZAC landing was to cut the peninsula, thereby preventing the Turkish forces facing the main landing to the south from escaping or being reinforced.

Liman von Sanders's most pressing concern on 25 April was the possibility that the main landing would take place at Saros Bay, the closest available landing site to Constantinople. On receiving word of activity there, he ordered the 7th Division to move in that direction and rode there himself with several members of his staff. Although he suspected the apparent landing at Saros Bay was a feint and had released several battalions to move south, he did not finally release the two divisions in the north until two days later. The demonstration at Saros Bay fixed significant portions of two Turkish divisions in the north while the Allied landing force established itself ashore far to the south. French landings and demonstrations on the Asian side of the straits had the similar effect of pinning down defending forces away from the site of the main landings.

Shortly after being told about the activity at Saros Bay and Cape Helles, the Fifth Army commander received word of a landing on the west coast of the peninsula near Ari Burnu. At 0430, the ANZACs had landed a mile north of their intended beach at a site that the Turks had neither mined nor blocked with obstacles. Caught by surprise, the Turks reacted with an extremely limited defense until the middle of the morning. By that time, Col. Mustafa Kemal, commander of the Turkish 19th Division, had begun limited counterattacks that eventually committed the entire division against the landing. Kemal's troops continued their counterattacks during the day. The broken terrain that had slowed the ANZAC advance also limited the effectiveness of the Turkish response, but the counterattacks prevented the ANZACs from accomplishing their mission of cutting the peninsula.

In the south, the Turks found themselves faced with landings on five separate beaches running in an arc from the west coast of the peninsula to Morto Bay at the mouth of the Dardanelles. At "Y Beach," the westernmost of the southern landing sites, two thousand men from several British battalions landed without opposition and remained in the beachhead for almost half a day before the Turks counterattacked. The British held out through the night, only to evacuate the beachhead the next day. The Turks claimed a victory, but the cause of the withdrawal appears not to have been their opposition as much as a lack of initiative on the part of the British commander and confusion among his subordinates.

Compared with their counterparts at Y Beach, the men who landed at "V Beach" below the old fortress at Sedd el Bahr met a hot reception. The Turks had built a strong defensive position there; it included trenches protected by two rows of barbed wire and machine guns sited to enfilade the entire beach. During the landing, naval gunfire initially kept the defenders' heads down, but when the bombardment was lifted the Turks poured a hail of fire into the approaching boats that caused heavy casualties. The survivors were unable to move forward from the beach. Even the use of the collier *River Clyde* as a rudimentary landing ship was inadequate to overcome the effects of the Turkish fire. Although protected on their journey to the beach, the embarked troops were cut down as they attempted to exit through doors that had been cut in the ship's hull. After the initial landing attempts failed, the remainder of the men on board the collier were trapped until nightfall. Darkness afforded them the opportunity to get ashore, and the British were eventually able to establish a firm foothold on the beach.

At this point, Liman von Sanders still had no real cause for concern. He had never envisioned stopping the invaders at the water's edge. His plan all along had been to force the enemy to commit itself and then to decide the issue by large-scale counterattacks. As soon as he decided that the Helles landings constituted the main British attack, Liman von Sanders ordered the counterattacks on which he counted so strongly. A shortage of artillery and the firepower of the naval ships arrayed against them forced the Turks to make their attacks at night. On several occasions, they came close to success; each time, however, daybreak and the resulting exposure to naval gunfire forced them to withdraw.

To reduce the effectiveness of British naval gunfire, Liman von Sanders ordered his troops to dig in as close as possible to the British positions. With less than ten meters separating the two enemies in some cases, the British could not fire on the Turkish positions without endangering their own troops. By early May, a stalemate resulted that was not unlike the situation along the western front in France and Belgium. Even with the support of naval gunfire, the British could not generate the prodigious amount of preparation fire that was considered, at that time, to be the key to breaking such a stalemate.

In July 1915, Liman von Sanders began receiving intelligence reports that the British were about to attempt another landing, but the reports gave no firm indication of the location. He discounted the possibility of a landing on the Asian side of the straits because he believed that the earlier French landing there had failed. For reasons that are less clear, he also discounted a possible landing in Saros Bay. Ironically, these two locations were posed as being the most likely landing sites in a message from the German General Staff on 22 July.[16] Faced again with deciding how to meet an amphibious threat, Liman von Sanders stayed with his earlier decision to conduct a mobile defense.

His first indication of the renewed British effort came on the morning of 7 August with reports of attacks out of the ANZAC beachhead and landings to the north around Suvla Bay. In spite of warnings, the British had once again caught the Turks completely by surprise. During the preceding week, the British had secretly reinforced the ANZAC beachhead. During the night of 6–7 August, they landed a two-division corps at Suvla Bay without opposition. The ANZAC troops attacking out of their beachhead at Ari Burnu faced terrible terrain obstacles and fierce Turkish resistance, but they made some significant gains. At Suvla Bay, Lt. Gen. Sir Frederick Stopford, IX Corps commander, was able to land almost twenty thousand men unscathed. Fortunately for the Turks, Stopford chose to dig in near the beach, wait for more artillery, and prepare for a "proper" advance rather than rapidly moving inland to seize the high ground that commanded the beaches and the adjoining plain. General Hamilton was dismayed by this lack of aggressiveness but refused to order Stopford to attack without further delay.

General Stopford's two divisions initially faced nothing more than several Turkish battalions commanded by a German major. The Turks reacted sluggishly; by nightfall on 8 August, the critical high ground remained unoccupied by either side. To correct the situation, Liman von Sanders fired the responsible Turkish commander and replaced him with Colonel Kemal, whose 19th Division was still busy containing the ANZACs in their beachhead. Dog-tired from having been awake for two days, Kemal nevertheless rode to Suvla and ordered the forces arriving from Bulair to take the critical ridge line without further delay. The British had finally begun to move, but the Turks reached the ridge first and forced the British to retreat after a sharp predawn fight. Superior generalship had once again allowed the Turks to contain a landing. In the words of a German officer who was at Gallipoli, "The goddess of victory held the door to success wide open to Stopford, but he would not enter."[17]

British failure to take advantage of this "door" ultimately resulted in a stalemate at what became a combined Suvla-ANZAC beachhead. Unable to break the stalemate, the Turks generally remained content simply to prevent the British from expanding their hold on the peninsula. Denied a victory, the British did manage to end the campaign with an amphibious success. After first thinning out their forces, they withdrew more than eighty thousand men remaining on the peninsula in two separate operations in December 1915 and January 1916. The British made the with-

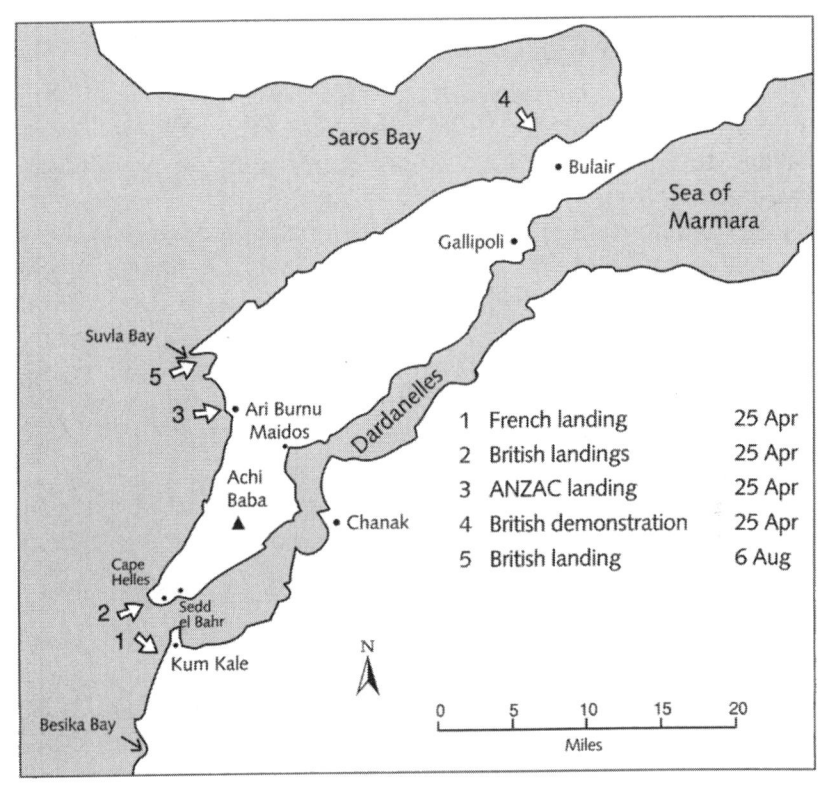

1	French landing	25 Apr
2	British landings	25 Apr
3	ANZAC landing	25 Apr
4	British demonstration	25 Apr
5	British landing	6 Aug

Gallipoli, 1915

drawals at night without losing a single man. Liman von Sanders paid them the compliment of calling the withdrawals "very skillful."[18] He was less complimentary, however, about the contributions of the Turkish and German navies.

In his memoirs, the marshal expressed his annoyance with the attention given in Germany to the exploits of the German submarines during the campaign and generally denigrates the navy's contribution.[19] The navy, in fact, played little or no role in the initial defense against any of the landings at Gallipoli. The waters off the beaches were not mined; submarines were not in the area at the time of the April landings, and they did not contest the August landing. Nor did the Turkish navy sail out to engage the invasion fleet on 25 April. The combined Anglo-French fleet almost certainly would have defeated a Turkish sortie, but the resulting battle might well have irreparably disrupted the landings in the process. During the course of the campaign, however, the Turkish and German navies did carry out several actions that offer glimpses of what might have been.

The Turks had strikingly demonstrated the effectiveness of mines during the 18 March attempt to force the straits. In contrast, the absence of mines off the invasion beaches gave the British a tremendous advantage. Even a token mining effort would have hindered the attackers significantly, giving Liman von Sanders additional time in which to implement his mobile defense. A similar effect might have been achieved by light naval forces, such as torpedo boats. On the night of 12–13 May, well after the British had established themselves ashore, the Turkish torpedo boat *Muavenet-i Millet* sank the British battleship *Goliath* near the mouth of the straits. This action not only reduced the size of the British fleet but raised the morale of the Turkish soldiers ashore, who had suffered from the fleet's guns without being able to strike back.

German submarines were to have an even greater impact. On 25 May 1915, the U-21 arrived off Cape Helles at the end of an arduous journey from Wilhelmshaven, Germany. Wasting no time, her captain, Lt. Otto Hersing, attacked and sank the British battleship *Triumph* that same afternoon. Two days later, Hersing repeated his exploit by sinking the old battleship *Majestic*. The effect on Turkish morale was electrifying. The material benefits were even greater. Fearing more attacks, the Royal Navy withdrew all but the smallest of its ships to the safety of Mudros harbor on Lemnos, where they could be protected by torpedo nets. In the words of one disillusioned British observer, "I saw them in full flight, transports and battleships, . . . which gave the effect of a number of dogs running away with their tails between their legs. The sense of abandonment was acute."[20]

For the defenders, the British withdrawal meant instant relief from the rain of naval gunfire that had tormented them. Only after the arrival in July of cruisers and monitors with added protection against torpedo attack did the Royal Navy fully return to the support of the forces ashore. Although more German submarines eventually reached the Aegean, greater vigilance by the Royal Navy prevented the Germans from duplicating their earlier successes off the Gallipoli beaches. U-boats eventually sank no fewer than eighteen transports sailing between Egypt and the Dardanelles, but these attacks were too late and too limited to affect significantly the British efforts ashore.[21] Nevertheless, these limited successes illustrate the potential harm that submarines could have caused off Gallipoli at the time of the initial landings.

Another form of warfare, air support of ground and naval forces, made its appearance at Gallipoli. Both sides employed aircraft in a variety of roles. The British made aviation history by deploying a seaplane carrier, the converted tramp steamer *Ark Royal*, with the invasion fleet. Seaplanes remained in use during the campaign, but they were augmented before the first landings by land-based naval aircraft operating from the island of Tenedos off the Gallipoli coast. During the course of the campaign, these aircraft were used for reconnaissance, spotting of artillery and naval gunfire, aerial photography, bombing attacks on Turkish positions, and a variety of miscellaneous tasks. One unsuccessful bombing attack was made on a submerged German submarine, and two Turkish ships were sunk by aerial-delivered torpedoes, the first such sinkings in history. The Turks also used aircraft and made at least one unsuccessful air attack against the *Ark Royal*. Clearly, airplanes would become a major factor in future amphibious operations, but whether they would be more valuable for the defense or offense was uncertain at that time.

Observations

By denying the British their goals of opening the Turkish Straits and driving Turkey out of the war, the Turks achieved an impressive strategic victory at Gallipoli. Operationally, Liman von Sanders was able to achieve this victory by waging what Dupuy and Dupuy call "a brilliant elastic defense."[22] Unfortunately for students of amphibious warfare, this strategic victory at Gallipoli has obscured Liman von Sanders's failure to find an adequate defense against the amphibious assault. During the course of the campaign, the defenders were unable to destroy the amphibious force at sea, stop the landings at the water's edge, or throw the invaders back into the sea after they were ashore. Because the ratio of troops in the landing force to those available for the defense does not support the conclusion that the defenders were simply overwhelmed numerically, other reasons for the failure must be found. The greatest organizational weakness of the Turkish defense was the lack of an overall commander on the scene. Recognizing this weakness, the Turkish General Staff admitted after the war that the Turks should have had one supreme commander in charge of both land and sea defenses.[23]

The Turks never tried a naval defense, which is perhaps understandable, given the disparities in size and capabilities between the opposing navies. Nevertheless, the results of several naval actions show what might have been possible. Submarines, torpedo boats, and mines all achieved individual successes during the campaign. Had those forces been employed as part of a well-planned naval defense fully coordinated with the ground efforts, the results might well have been spectacular.

Lord Horatio Kitchener, British field marshal and war secretary, had said at the start of the campaign that he had two concerns, submarines and gas warfare.[24] The former threat materialized; the latter did not. Chemical warfare was not a consideration by either side at the time of the first landings at Gallipoli because the Germans had made their first gas attacks on the western front only three days earlier. Fearing the introduction of gas warfare at Gallipoli, the British eventually issued gas masks to the troops. The Turks never employed gas at Gallipoli, but the Germans were introducing chemical warfare troops into the theater when the campaign ended.[25] Once the opposing forces had been trained to deal with chemical warfare, it never had a decisive effect on the great battles in Europe. What the effect would have been of a gas attack launched by the Turks against the British force landing at Suvla is uncertain, but the threat of chemical warfare has remained a consideration for amphibious planners ever since.

Turkish attempts to conduct a defense at the water's edge failed at Gallipoli. The British and Australians are quick to point to the valor and determination of the landing force as a factor. That those qualities were exhibited is beyond question. Given similar qualities displayed by the Turkish defenders, however, other reasons must be found to explain why they were unable to prevent the attackers from getting ashore. The basic answer is that Liman von Sanders intended the defense at the water's edge to delay, rather than to defeat, the invader. In most cases, the defenders achieved that aim.

In attempting to implement his plans, Liman von Sanders was constantly frustrated by the effects of British naval gunfire. He states:

> [T]he artillery effect of the hostile battleships constituted a support of extraordinary power for the landing army. No heavy land artillery can so easily change position and direct its fire on the enemy's flank and rear as was possible to the guns of the ships.[26]

In comparison, General Hamilton offers a more ambivalent view of the subject. Writing in his diary on 25 April 1915, for example, he says, "The shots from our naval guns, smashing as their impact appears, might as well be confetti for all the effect they have upon the Turkish trenches."[27]

Although Liman von Sanders had based his defense around a mobile concept, he was no more successful in throwing the invaders back into the sea with counterattacks than he had been in preventing them from getting ashore in the first place. Three factors influenced this failure. The first was deception. Allied demonstrations at Besika and Saros Bays and the subsidiary landing at Kum Kale masked the location of the main landings long enough for the Allies to get a foothold ashore at Anzac Cove and the Helles beaches. The second factor was the superior mobility of naval forces. Even after the site of the main landings became obvious, the attackers could move forces faster by sea than the defenders could move on shore. The third factor was naval gunfire. As Liman von Sanders came to appreciate, naval gunfire gave his opponents the means to defeat the counterattacks on which his mobile defense ultimately depended.

Gallipoli cost each side more than 250,000 casualties. Because the Allies gained nothing for this great price, the operation must be regarded as a disaster. Ironically, the scope of the disaster caused the British to investigate thoroughly the reasons for their failure. These investigations and later studies by the British and Americans became the starting point for the development of modern amphibious doctrine. The victors, on the other hand, made no similar effort to learn and document the techniques of successfully defending against a landing.

Preparations for Invasion:
Great Britain, 1940

[W]e shall fight on the seas and oceans, we shall fight with growing confidence and growing strength in the air, . . . we shall fight on the beaches, we shall fight on the landing grounds, . . . we shall never surrender, . . .
Winston S. Churchill, 4 June 1940

Because the British Isles are so close to the European continent, they frequently have been subject to invasion. From the Spanish Armada of 1588 to the present, all attempted invasions have been unsuccessful, but the attempts have given the British a great deal of experience in dealing with the prospect of invasion. Perhaps it is understandable, therefore, that in the period between the two world wars, the British relied more on their traditional approach to home defense than on methods derived from an analysis of the campaign at Gallipoli.

Although the Gallipoli campaign was the subject of extensive study, the lessons learned were those of the attackers and even these lessons were skewed. In spite of the numerous amphibious successes at Gallipoli, the British concluded that such operations were of limited use, at best, and "folly," in the words of British Adm. Roger J. B. Keyes, when attempted in daylight against a defended beach.[1] An enemy that disagreed with this assessment and wished to invade Britain would have to contend first with the Royal Navy.

Over the years, the Royal Navy developed a three-tiered concept of defense against invasion. The first tier consisted of preemptive attacks against forces of the enemy before it could mount an invasion or a blockade of its embarkation ports. In Nelson's words, ". . . the enemy's ports are our first line of defence."[2]

The second line of defense was the battle fleet, which would intercept any invasion force before it could reach British shores. At best, the fleet would destroy the enemy at sea. At worst, the fleet would engage the enemy's warships and force the troop transports either to turn back or to proceed without protection. If they chose the latter course, they would face the Royal Navy's third line of defense, a flotilla of light craft of various types. Any invaders who managed to slip through this three-tiered defense and land on British soil would be dealt with by the British Army.

In 1908, the Committee of Imperial Defence noted that, although the Royal Navy's command of the seas was the ultimate guarantor of Britain's security, an impermeable cordon around the British Isles could not be assumed. An invasion force might be small enough to slip through undetected. The army, therefore, must be big enough to require an invader to come with a force so large that it could not fail to be detected by the Royal Navy. This policy was successful during World War I.

By the start of World War II, however, a new factor had been added: air power. Although its importance as a factor in modern war had been accepted by that time, its impact on an invasion of Great Britain remained in dispute. Some proponents of air power held that modern aircraft would allow an enemy to bomb Britain into submission, which would make a seaborne invasion unnecessary. Others anticipated a defensive role for the Royal Air Force (RAF) to make invasion impossible. Before the invention of the airplane, an invader could reach Britain only by sea. By the start of World War II, alternatives existed in the form of invasion by parachute, glider, and air-landed forces. Given the number of troops required to ensure success, however, an all-airborne invasion was not a feasible option. This did not bother most proponents of air power because they envisioned a different type of airborne assault, a strategic bombing campaign that would obviate the need for invasion.

While the threat of bombing was being played up by advocates of strategic bombing, others held that the airplane would strengthen the defense. British military theorist B. H. Liddell Hart, in summarizing the view of air power as a defense against invasion in 1939, notes that the vulnerability of troop transports and landing craft to air attack had made one of the most difficult of military operations "much more difficult, indeed almost impossible."[3]

The degree of uncertainty about whether the offensive or defensive aspect of air power would prevail can be seen in the maneuvering of Marshal Hugh Trenchard when he was chief of the air staff. Although considered one of the fathers of strategic bombing, Trenchard was not ready to rule out completely a defensive role for the RAF. In 1921, he unsuccessfully attempted replacement of the Royal Navy by the RAF as the service most directly responsible for the defense of Britain against invasion, whether by air or sea.[4]

With the start of war in 1939, these varied theoretical concerns suddenly became urgent defense considerations. In hindsight, the British clearly exaggerated the threat of invasion in 1940. This exaggeration must be put in perspective, however, by reviewing two conditions that existed in mid-1940. First, much conventional wisdom concerning invasion had been turned on its head by events earlier in the war. Both German and British thinking, for example, held that a seaborne invasion could succeed only if the invader maintained control of the sea, at least locally. In spite of this conventional view, the Germans had successfully invaded Norway by sea without first challenging the Royal Navy for control of the sea. Similarly, the successful British troop evacuation from the French port of Dunkirk in the face of heavy opposition by the Luftwaffe (German air force) called into question the ability of the RAF to prevent a German invasion.[5]

Second, these basic uncertainties were exacerbated by the fear and expectation that Adolph Hitler was harboring yet another secret weapon or technique to be unleashed during an invasion of Britain. The invasion of Norway had included the use of paratroopers and a fifth column of Norwegian collaborators. The attack through the Low Countries had added the employment of glider-borne assault troops to deal with fortifications previously thought to be impregnable. The speed and ferocity of the blitzkrieg across France still had Allied leaders in a state of shock. Many wondered what new surprises were coming.

The Situation in Great Britain

Faced with the possibility of defending against a sea blockade and aerial bombing campaign in addition to an invasion, the British had to estimate Germany's capability to carry out a cross-channel landing. Within Britain's intelligence community, estimates of Germany's capability in this regard changed drastically between the mid-1930s and the early part of World War II. In January 1937, the Joint Planning Sub-Committee of the Chiefs of Staff Committee concluded a report on the subject of invasion by saying that it considered a large-scale seaborne attack "very improbable," but, "If it were attempted we are confident that our naval and air forces would defeat it without the help of our land forces."[6] The report concluded that the threat of any large-scale airborne attack was also negligible. In November 1939, the chiefs of staff credited the Germans with the capability of a landing in Britain with an initial force of twenty thousand men but stated that such a capability did not constitute a serious enough threat to British security to warrant interfering with the training of the Field Force or delaying its dispatch overseas. The report also estimated that the Germans had four thousand parachutists and six thousand other troops trained for air-landing operations.[7]

Following the fall of France and the escape of the British army from Dunkirk, British estimates of German capabilities changed significantly. In spite of the creation of an aerial reconnaissance system that produced much detailed information about German invasion preparations, British intelligence made many errors in estimating German capabilities. Two months after the German glider assault on the Belgian fortress of Eben Emael, for example, the Joint Intelligence Sub-Committee remained unconvinced that the Germans had employed gliders in that operation.[8] British naval planning of the period was based on the assumption that the Germans would employ the battleship *Bismarck* and the battle cruisers *Gneisenau* and *Scharnhorst* to support an invasion. In fact, however, the *Bismarck* was not yet operational, and the two battle cruisers were out of action with damage incurred in action off Norway.[9]

As the likelihood of invasion increased during the summer of 1940, British intelligence estimates became more pessimistic with regard to German capabilities. Immediately before the invasion of the Low Countries in May 1940, British military intelligence concluded that Germany could employ up to twenty divisions for an invasion of the British Isles without affecting the security of other fronts.[10] In November, the figures had risen to twenty seaborne divisions and two to four airborne divisions.[11] By August 1941, the figures were at twenty-three seaborne divisions for the invasion, eleven more divisions to be used in diversions, and the possibility of as many as eight airborne divisions with fifty-five thousand troops.[12] Contributing to the gloomy atmosphere was the First Sea Lord's opinion that as many as one hundred thousand German troops could reach Britain without being intercepted by the Royal Navy.

Ironically, the British had been preparing to defend against an invasion longer than the Germans had been planning to conduct one. Although Adm. Erich Raeder, commander in chief of the German navy, had asked his staff to undertake a feasibility study of an invasion of Britain as early as November 1939, he made the request on his own initiative and it did not involve the other services. The unexpectedly quick fall of France in the summer of 1940 had left Hitler and the Oberkommando der Wehrmacht (OKW), the high command of the armed forces, unprepared for further operations. Hitler had hoped for a negotiated settlement with the British; only after efforts along those lines were rebuffed did planning for an invasion commence. Fuehrer Directive No. 16, issued on 16 July 1940, ordered the three services to commence planning for an invasion and laid out specific tasks and requirements.[13]

The invasion, code-named Seelöwe (Sea Lion), was to be conducted jointly by the army, navy, and air force, but Hitler did not designate an overall commander or create a planning staff. As a result, disagreements among the services could be resolved only by the OKW or Hitler himself. This problem was aggravated both by a lack of doctrine for amphibious operations and an absence of practical experience in this type of warfare. A serious disagreement quickly arose concerning the geographical dispersion of the landing zones. The army insisted on a wide invasion front with several simultaneous landings. The navy, on the other hand, saw no chance of success unless the landings were conducted on a narrow front and supported by a correspondingly narrow sea corridor from the continental embarkation ports to the landing beaches.[14]

Throughout the rest of the summer, service staffs worked to resolve such conflicts and reconcile the army's operational desires with naval transportation and support realities. The final plan envisioned two landings to be conducted by the Ninth and Sixteenth Armies on Britain's south coast between Bexhill and Worthing. The first wave, spread over ten days, would consist of nine infantry and mountain divisions. Based on German embarkation tables and the amount of shipping available, the Germans estimated that, theoretically, they could land 138,000 men in the first two days of the operation.[15] In addition to the seaborne units, one airborne division and one air-landed division were included in the plan. Initial plans for parachutists to land near Brighton and Dover were replaced with one for a single airborne landing near Folkestone. To divert the attention of the defenders from the actual landings, the German navy planned a diversion code-named Herbstreise (Autumn Voyage). This operation envisioned a number of warships and cruise liners simulating an invasion force moving from Norway toward Scotland.

To counter an invasion, British Home Forces, in November 1940, estimated that it would need eight second-class divisions for beach defense, to be backed up by a field army of four armored and sixteen infantry divisions plus a number of separate brigades. Additionally, more than one hundred unbrigaded battalions were required for the defense of airfields and other important points.[16]

Following Dunkirk, army forces in Britain fell short of this requirement, both in numbers and quality. By the end of the summer, Home Forces could field twenty-nine divisions, but most were short of vital equipment.[17] Of seven hundred tanks taken to France, for example, only twenty-five had returned. Further, the replacement of tanks, artillery pieces, and antitank guns was hampered by the priority given to Britain's aircraft industry. Fortunately for the British, German intelligence consistently overestimated British strength. During the second half of 1940, German estimates showed between thirty-four and thirty-nine British divisions available for defense.[18]

In an effort to compensate for the lack of regular army forces, the British government, in May 1940, authorized the creation of an unpaid volunteer force known initially as Local Defence Volunteers (LDV) and later as the Home Guard. Response was overwhelming; by the end of May, three hundred thousand men had enrolled.[19] Military effectiveness of the volunteers was questionable, but they provided forces to man roadblocks and local defenses, which government leaders hoped would delay an enemy until the army could arrive.

During the critical period of late summer 1940, the composition of the Royal Navy's Home Fleet varied, but it normally included four or five battleships and battle cruisers, an aircraft carrier, dozens of cruisers and destroyers, and as many as one thousand armed patrol vessels of various types.[20] The RAF was also well prepared to meet an invasion. During the battle for France, when most available army forces had been deployed to the continent, the RAF had carefully husbanded its forces in Britain against an anticipated invasion or aerial attack on the United Kingdom. As a result, by July 1940, forty-eight squadrons of single-engine fighters were available that could put as many as six hundred planes into the air simultaneously, if necessary.[21]

Offsetting the capabilities of the Royal Navy and RAF to a degree was the lack of a single overall commander to control the forces of all three services in their efforts to defeat an invasion. The command system in place had forces from each service controlled through separate chains of command with no overall coordinating authority short of the Chiefs of Staff Committee. In May 1940, the chiefs of staff had established the office of Home Defence Executive to coordinate the defensive efforts of the three services, but Gen. Alan Brooke, who later became commander in chief of Home Forces, regarded the lack of a true joint commander to be the greatest weakness of Britain's defensive organization.[22]

On 26 May, the chief of the air staff recommended the creation of a "super commander-in-chief" capable of making decisions rapidly enough to deal with an enemy "whose strategy is marked by the utmost speed of decision and ruthlessness in action."[23] The chiefs of staff considered this proposal, but, in July, they rejected it on the grounds that the size and complexity of the forces involved made command by a single individual impracticable. They also noted that experience had shown that joint operations could be controlled adequately by close cooperation.[24]

Two important geographic factors bearing on British defense plans were the English Channel and the potential landing beaches. Naval planners on both sides generally appreciated the degree to which the channel presented a formidable obstacle to a seaborne invasion. In addition to the distances involved, most sailors were familiar with the treacherous sea conditions of the channel and the susceptibility of the region to unpredictable storms. Naval considerations, therefore, tended to indicate a crossing in the vicinity of Dover, where the channel was at its narrowest.

German Army planners, on the other hand, showed less concern about the channel as an obstacle. In spite of having been warned by Hitler not to regard the operation as simply a river crossing, most army planners appear to have operated on that basis. On 3 July 1940, for example, Col. Gen. Franz Halder, chief of staff of the army, characterized the concept for Sea Lion as being similar to a large-scale river crossing.[25] With respect to terrain features, the army focused on landing beaches. The two most promising areas were East Anglia north of the Thames Estuary and the coastline of Kent and Sussex southeast of Dover. The former required a longer sea transit but offered good ground for an armored attack on London after a beachhead was gained. The latter offered the best sea approach, but the coastline had significant military drawbacks. Long sections were backed by cliffs, and egress from otherwise satisfactory beaches was hindered by a canal and large marshes. In making their plans, both attackers and defenders arrived at the same potential landing beaches and the same operational tradeoffs to be resolved. On 8 September 1940, General Brooke noted in his diary: "Everything pointing to Kent and East Anglia as the two main threatened points."[26]

In addition to deciding where to concentrate their defenses against the anticipated German invasion, British planners also faced the question of timing. Given the weakened condition of the British army after its return from Dunkirk, many British leaders feared that the Germans would launch an immediate attack. Gen. Sir Hastings Ismay, Churchill's personal chief of staff, held a different opinion. In his view, the need for the Germans to regroup after their rapid victory in France and the preparations required for a major landing would give the British a respite of at least several months.[27] After the war, Col. Gen. Kurt Student, commander of Germany's airborne forces, told Liddell Hart that an airborne assault on key British cities immediately after Dunkirk might have shocked an already demoralized British public into capitulation.[28]

Based on the analysis of intelligence about the staging of German invasion forces and the moon and tide conditions, the British estimated 8–10 September to be the most likely dates for a German landing.[29] The British came remarkably close to the date selected by the Germans. In August, the German naval staff had announced that 21 September was the earliest that naval preparations could be completed. Eventually, the 24th was designated S-Day, the date of the projected landing in Britain.[30]

The British Plan

As the British confronted the possibility of invasion during the summer of 1940, military planners faced an obstacle that seems unbelievable in a nation that had been threatened so many times in the past. They had no doctrine for defending against an amphibious landing. *Field Service Regulations* in effect between the two world wars did not discuss the subject. This lack of doctrine meant that commanders had to develop their defense plans from scratch.

In setting out the basis for a plan, Prime Minister Winston Churchill relied on a traditional approach that engaged an invader as often and as far forward as possible. In a 5 August minute (memorandum) titled "Defence Against Invasion," Churchill describes his proposed lines of defenses. The first line would be the enemy's ports, which were to be reconnoitered and attacked; the second line, vigilant naval patrols to detect and destroy an invasion force at sea; and the third line, air and naval attacks on the invasion force at the point of landing while the landing was taking place. The army's role was also a traditional one of forcing the enemy to come in such large numbers that the invasion could not escape detection by the navy and air force.[31] If the enemy succeeded in getting ashore, Churchill's plan called for a defense at the beachhead to buy time for mobile reserves to mount decisive counterattacks.

The Royal Navy regarded its role to be the classic one. An Admiralty appreciation (estimate) of the time notes that the navy could attack a German expedition before departure, during passage, and at its point of arrival.[32] Because attacking German invasion forces at their embarkation ports and at sea required timely information that might not be available, the navy decided to plan its primary defensive effort in the vicinity of the invasion beaches.

The RAF also envisioned an offensively oriented, layered defense not unlike that of the navy. Bomber Command's role paralleled that of the navy. It would attack enemy ships and troops first at their embarkation ports, next at sea while in transit, and, finally, in the beachhead itself. Fighter Command would deal with the Luftwaffe, particularly the dive bombers supporting the invading ground forces.[33]

Army plans, unlike those of the other services, took effect only upon arrival of the German forces at the invasion beaches. The basic decision facing army planners was whether to prevent the invaders from landing or to destroy them by counterattacks after they had gotten ashore. Answering that difficult question fell to Gen. Edmund Ironside, commander in chief of Home Forces. His immediate problem was to prepare his inadequately trained and equipped army for the invasion that he feared was imminent. He rejected the idea of relying primarily on a mobile defense for three primary reasons: (1) the wide dispersal of possible landing places to be defended; (2) his lack of confidence in his troops to do anything other than hold fixed positions; and (3) his fear that if the Germans were allowed to land tanks, they could not be stopped.

On 27 June 1940, after consideration of these factors, Ironside presented a plan to the chiefs of staff that might be called a mixed defense concept.[34] The three main elements of his plan were a fixed defensive "crust" along the coast; lines of antitank obstacles, called "stop lines," between London and the likely landing beaches; and mobile reserves to attack the enemy either on the beaches or elsewhere.

To support a defense at the water's edge, the British constructed a variety of obstacles and fortifications, with the primary function of preventing the enemy from landing. If that failed, however, they were expected to delay the enemy until the mobile reserves could arrive and carry out a counterattack. The obstacles offshore included naval mines, antiboat booms, belts of builder's scaffolding erected in shallow water, tetrahedrons made of pipe, and steel rails embedded into the beach in staggered rows to sink landing craft. Above the high water mark, the obstacles continued: barbed wire, antitank ditches, concrete antitank obstacles called "pimples," and as much as three hundred miles of more builder's scaffolding. By June 1940, fifty thousand antitank mines had been issued to the troops along the beaches and orders placed for two hundred thousand more.[35] Where possible, the British flooded low areas behind the beaches to restrict the movement of vehicles and the landing of paratroops. To cover these obstacles by gunfire, the British constructed a large number of fortified positions along the coast.[36]

In addition to conventional obstacles and fortifications, the British launched another program—unprecedented since medieval times—to use flame warfare as a defensive weapon. On 9 July 1940, the British government created the Department of Petroleum Warfare to explore the ways of employing fire as a weapon. The first result was the static flame trap. With this device, consisting of perforated pipes fed by gravity from nearby fuel tanks, a designated location would be showered with fuel that could be ignited from a nearby observation post.[37] About two hundred flame traps were installed to block exits from likely landing beaches and other places where vehicular traffic would be channeled. Other fire weapons included the flame fougassé, a forty-gallon drum filled with a petroleum mixture and a propelling charge; vertical flamethrowers for defense against low-flying planes; oil-filled antitank ditches; and underwater fougassés to prevent seaplane landings.

By far, the most spectacular development was the flame barrage, a scheme designed to set the sea on fire off beaches likely to be invaded. Piping was set up so that oil could be pumped onto the surface of the water, where it was ignited either by flares or sodium pellets. Tested successfully on 24 August 1940, the flame barrage literally made the sea boil. Realizing that such testing could not be hidden from the public, and probably the Germans, the British exploited the experiments with a propaganda campaign emphasizing the fearsome potential of the new flame weapons.

While the British were constructing a defense at the water's edge, they were also debating whether that approach was really the best defense against a German invasion. General Ironside, with mixed feelings about his concept, noted in his diary, after criticizing the Maginot Line (defensive fortifications built by the French prior to the war for protection of their eastern border): "We are now engaged in putting up minor Maginot lines along the coast."[38] Ironside also believed that the chiefs of staff were giving him conflicting guidance. They had indicated that they were not satisfied that the plan emphasized the need to resist a landing with all means available during the highly vulnerable period when the enemy would be disembarking on the beaches.[39] At the same time, they criticized the plan for leaning too much in favor of a defense at the water's edge. Churchill himself had come to believe that the battle would be decided by mobile counterattacks. Accordingly, on 21 July 1940, he replaced General Ironside with General Brooke, who more closely shared Churchill's views about the way to defend against the impending invasion.

Recognizing that he could not be strong everywhere, Brooke reduced the inherited three-tiered defense to a two-tiered one by eliminating the stop lines created by his predecessor. Brooke did not object to such static positions only in principle; his experience in France had convinced him that massive roadblocks scattered throughout the country would cripple the mobility of his own counterattack forces more than they would impede a German invader. As a consequence, the new Home Forces commander stopped construction of such obstacles and removed as many of the existing ones as possible.[40] Under Brooke's plan, the focus of the defense would be counterattacks by infantry and armored divisions of the field army.

The British had also developed a plan for using chemical warfare against an invasion. Called Plan Y after the code name for mustard gas, this plan called for contaminating the beaches with chemical bombs delivered by air over a three-day period. The purpose was not to stop troops from landing but to impede the follow-on unloading of supplies and equipment by forcing the troops to work in gas masks and protective suits.[41] The British also had available other chemical weapons, including aerial spray tanks and artillery shells. Attempting to determine today whether the British would have initiated gas warfare in response to an invasion is difficult. Policy at the time was to use chemical warfare only in retaliation, but Churchill states, in reference to an invasion, "They would have used terror, and we were prepared to go to all lengths."[42]

The Invasion That Never Came

In early July 1940, the Germans began the aerial assault on Great Britain that has become known as the Battle of Britain. On 20 August, Vice Adm. Bertram Ramsay, commander of naval forces at Dover, wondered whether Hitler started the air campaign in order to gain air superiority for an invasion or simply to destroy the country and demoralize its citizens. Ramsay leaned toward the invasion thesis, but the debate goes on even today.[43] Air Marshal Hugh Dowding, commander in chief of Fighter Command, agreed with Ramsay and stated that the mission of his fighters was a defensive one to stop the possibility of invasion.[44]

Regardless of whether the Germans intended to invade or bomb the British into submission, the Luftwaffe had to achieve at least local air superiority over southern England. The heaviest aerial combat of the battle, which occurred from mid-August through the latter part of September, was characterized by a shifting of German objectives. By winning the Battle of Britain, the RAF denied the Germans an indispensable prerequisite to invasion, that of air superiority.

While Fighter Command engaged in its life-and-death struggle in the skies over England and the channel, the other parts of Britain's military were not idle. Bomber Command attacked airfields and embarkation ports in France and destroyed more than 10 percent of the invasion shipping assembled by the Germans.[45] To supplement the bombing campaign, the Royal Navy carried out a series of naval gunfire bombardments of French invasion ports and the German batteries at Cap Gris-Nez on the French coast near Calais. Realizing they would probably not be able to support a landing with heavy naval gunfire ships, the Germans had constructed several large naval batteries at Cap Gris-Nez. Mounted in steel turrets and massive concrete casemates, the guns—some with bores as large as sixteen inches—could fire across the channel on potential landing beaches.

By the end of June 1940, the British had created a defense that could have met all criteria of Soviet Admiral Gorshkov's ideal defense against invasion through engagement of the invasion force at every step—from embarking to moving inland from the beaches (see chapter 1). Meanwhile, the army waited. As September arrived, both sides realized that only a limited period remained before winter conditions in the channel would preclude any landings. On 4 September, Hitler announced that if the British were wondering why nothing had happened, they should rest assured that the Germans were coming. In spite of his boast, Hitler delayed Operation Sea Lion several times and indefinitely postponed it on 12 October 1940.[46] The British continued serious anti-invasion preparations through 1941, but the threat had passed.

Observations

In anticipation of a German landing, the British developed a balanced defense. Without sea control, the Germans probably would not have been able to get an invasion force to the beaches. Even if they had, they almost certainly would not have been able to keep the troops supplied. Had an invasion force reached the beaches, lack of naval gunfire support and specialized landing craft and equipment would have made gaining a sustainable beachhead extremely difficult. The only part of the British defense that the Germans were trained and equipped to deal with was

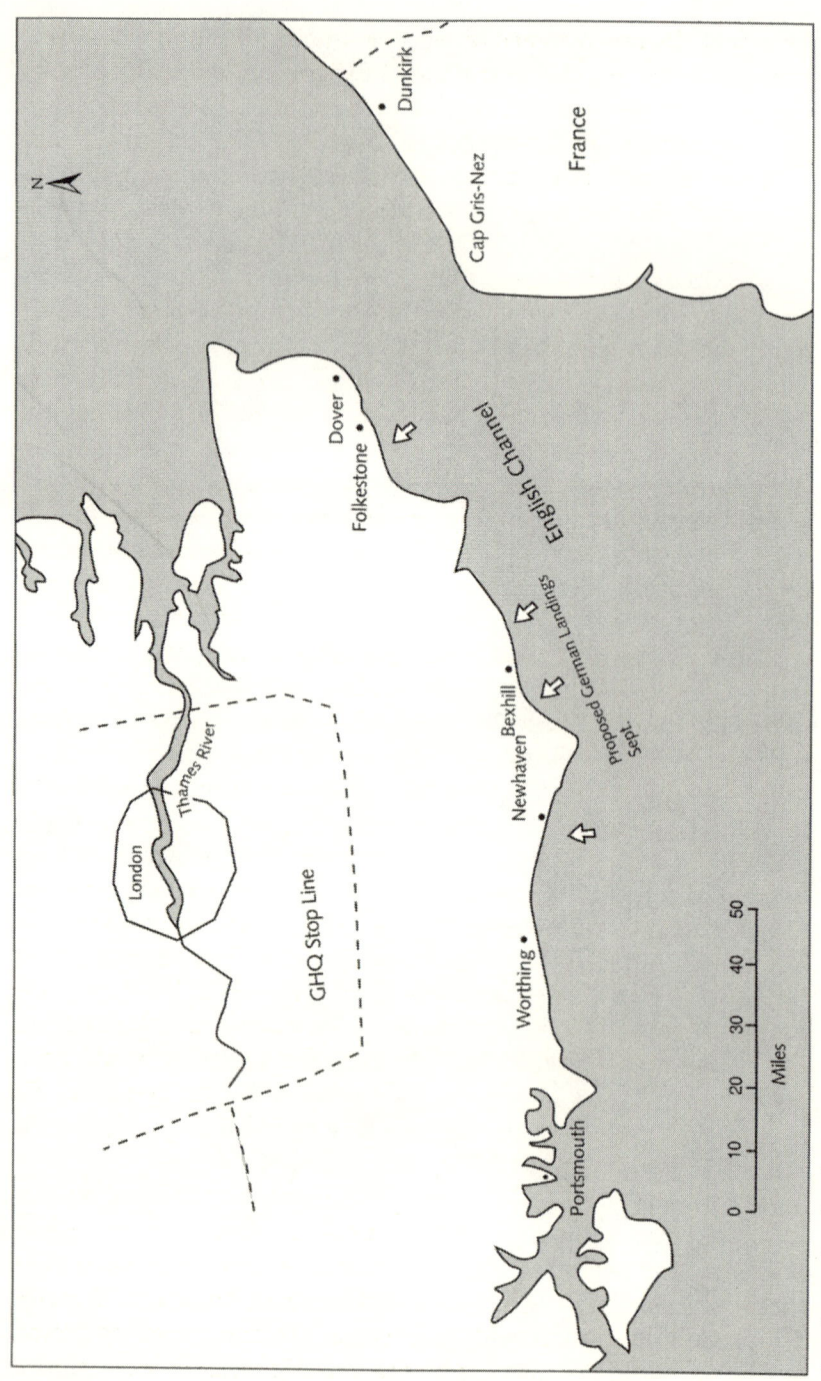

Southeast England, 1940

the mobile defense instituted by General Brooke. The Germans, in fact, received word of the change from a defense at the water's edge to a mobile defense with a sense of relief. On 23 August 1940, Field Marshal Gerd von Rundstedt, commander of Army Group A, wrote that if they could gain a beachhead and break out of it with mobile forces, "our superiority in this form of operation will show itself clearly."[47]

In preparing for Operation Sea Lion, the British approached unity of command but stopped short of actually achieving it. Their command structure reflected a long history of combined operations conducted by cooperation between the services rather than through unity of command. The Germans, on the other hand, had no such tradition to fall back on when they failed to create a single operational commander with the power to resolve the many contentious issues that arose among the services. In this respect, command arrangements favored the British.

Had the Germans executed Operation Sea Lion as planned—an unlikely assumption at best—they would have landed the assault elements of nine divisions by sea, plus air-delivered forces, during the first two days of the invasion. Given that only one or two divisions would have defended the beaches initially, the resulting force ratio would have favored the Germans. The British, however, had perhaps another ten divisions capable of moving rapidly to the beachhead. With German reinforcement capability limited, the resulting battle could have been close. In any case, had the German invasion succeeded, it would not have been the result of overwhelming German forces.

At the end of the campaign in France in 1940, both sides found themselves unready for an invasion of Britain. The Germans were unprepared to conduct an amphibious operation, and the British were not ready to defend against one. As ill-prepared as the Germans might have been, their chances for success were greatest right after Dunkirk when the British were in a state of shock and at their weakest with respect to material preparedness. The British realized that any delay would work to their advantage. As General Ironside noted on 17 June regarding the German failure to act, "They will be very stupid if they delay much longer."[48]

Sea control has been the classic prerequisite to conducting an amphibious operation. By the time of Operation Sea Lion, the airplane had become a weapon powerful enough to raise the question of whether air superiority could make up for a lack of sea control. Air-power advocates on both sides believed it could, but because the Germans never achieved air superiority, the premise was never tested. Vice Adm. Kurt Assmann, the official German naval historian, probably assessed the situation correctly in 1958 when he wrote:

> Had the German Air Force defeated the Royal Air Force as decisively as it had defeated the French Air Force a few months earlier, I am sure Hitler would have given the order for the invasion to be launched—and the invasion would in all probability have been smashed.[49]

Admiral Assmann's thesis was never tested. As the German situation on the eastern front worsened, Hitler's postponement of Operation Sea Lion became permanent. When the Germans and British eventually faced one another across a landing beach, their roles were reversed.

4

German Mobile Defense:
Sicily and Salerno, 1943

It must be the objective of the fight for the coast to throw the enemy back into the sea or to prevent him from gaining freedom of operation after he has landed. A more or less considerable loss of territory is of minor importance.
Field Marshal Albert Kesselring

Hitler's decision to postpone Operation Sea Lion, although he did not realize it at the time, marked a fundamental shift in Germany's focus on amphibious warfare. In capturing Norway, the German armed forces had used naval means that fell short of true amphibious operations. Sea Lion would have been Germany's World War II initiation into the art of landing against a defended shore. As it turned out, the Germans were never again in a position to attempt a large-scale amphibious operation. Their concern with landings would become one of defense, but this did not manifest itself immediately.

When Hitler postponed the invasion of Britain, he did so in order to concentrate German military efforts on the invasion of the Soviet Union, which took place in June 1941. Before that happened, however, the Italians invaded Albania and set off a chain of events that led to German forces being committed to combat in both the Balkans and North Africa. The need to supply forces fighting in North Africa expanded the war into a naval conflict between the Royal Navy and the Italian Navy, which was supported by land-based aircraft from the Italian and German air forces.

With the exception of some British commando raids and Germany's seaborne operations during its primarily airborne invasion of Crete, the conflict in the Mediterranean did not become an amphibious war until the Allied landings in North Africa on 8 November 1942. For the previous two years, British Commonwealth forces had battled Italian and

German armies back and forth across the North African desert during a campaign in which both sides had suffered spectacular reverses. After the battle of El Alamein, Egypt, in October 1942, the British Eighth Army had begun an offensive that drove back the Germans and Italians across North Africa and into Tunisia. On 8 November, the Allies conducted a series of landings at Casablanca in Morocco and Oran and Algiers in Algeria to form the second jaw of a vice that eventually squeezed the Axis forces into a pocket in Tunisia. Unable to escape, they surrendered in May 1943. Almost a quarter million German and Italian soldiers were taken into captivity.

The loss of North Africa posed a serious question for Axis leaders: What would the Allies do next? Operating from a base in North Africa, the Allies had many choices that ranged from Greece and the Balkans to southern France. Axis leaders believed the logical choice to be one of three large islands off the Italian peninsula: Corsica, Sardinia, or Sicily. Italy's Marshal Pietro Badoglio and Germany's Luftwaffe Field Marshal Wolfram Freiherr von Richthofen reasoned that the capture of Sardinian airfields would place the Allies in the best position to attack Italy itself.[1] The Italian Supermarina (naval headquarters) agreed on Sardinia because the Allies would have difficulty in sweeping minefields between North Africa and Sicily.[2] Hitler believed that the Allies would land on Sardinia or the Greek peninsula of Peloponnesos.[3] His assessment was influenced by documents recovered by the Spanish from the body of a British military courier that had washed ashore in Spain after an airplane crash in the Atlantic. In fact, the body and the documents had been set adrift from a British submarine as part of an elaborate deception scheme called Operation Mincemeat.[4]

Italian Premier Benito Mussolini, on the other hand, held the opinion that, although Sicily was the most threatened of the islands, the Allies probably would land in southern France or the Balkans.[5] His opinion on Sicily was based on the fact that occupation of the island would open shipping routes through the Mediterranean to the Allies. By that reasoning, Mussolini had correctly anticipated the decision made by the Allies at Casablanca in January 1943. The Allies were unable to agree on an overall strategy, but they accepted both that a cross-channel invasion of France was not possible in 1943 and that the offensive momentum gained in North Africa must be continued. They decided to attack Sicily by summer.

The Situation on Sicily

Increasingly unpopular because of Italian losses abroad, Mussolini realized that a successful Allied invasion of Italy would cause his dictatorship to fall. He ordered that Sicily be held at any cost. A serious question remained whether the Italian armed forces were capable of carrying out the Duce's order. The Italian Sixth Army, commanded by Generale d' Armata Alfredo Guzzoni, was responsible for the defense of the island. Before the arrival of German reinforcements in June, the Sixth Army consisted of two corps headquarters, five static coastal divisions, four mobile divisions, two coastal brigades, and other miscellaneous units for a total of two hundred thousand men.[6] Of the mobile divisions, only the Livorno Division had the equipment, personnel, and training needed to pose a serious threat to an enemy landing.

The Italian navy also had forces based in Sicily. The seaward approaches to the naval bases at Syracuse and Augusta were protected by coastal defense guns manned by sailors. On the land side, however, the fortress was only lightly defended by local troops. Although the Italian navy had begun the war with a modern fleet, it had never lived up to its potential. By early 1943, its most powerful remaining ships had been taken to La Spezia in northern Italy for protection from Allied air strikes. To reach Sicily in the event of invasion would mean a twenty-four hour run with limited air cover. The only naval units operating from Sicily were a small number of fast-attack craft.

Because he was looking for an acceptable way of getting Italy out of the war, Mussolini did not want large-scale German forces in Italy. Faced with the threat of an Allied invasion, however, he accepted two German divisions for the defense of Sicily. The first to arrive was the Divizion Sizilien, which was eventually redesignated the 15th Panzer Grenadier Division. After several months of training in Sicily, the division had become familiar with the area and could be expected to give a good account of itself against an invasion. The second German division was one that could have been conceived only in the byzantine world of Hitler's Third Reich. The Hermann Goering Panzer Parachute Division had no parachute capability whatsoever. The title was an honorary one apparently bestowed to increase the prestige of this mechanized infantry division composed of Luftwaffe ground personnel commanded by air force Maj. Gen. Paul Conrath. Although the division was well equipped and included one company of the new Tiger heavy tanks, Conrath had little experience in ground combat.

The presence of these two German divisions in Sicily posed an organizational problem for the commander in chief of German forces in Italy, Field Marshal Albert Kesselring. Starting his career as an army officer, Kesselring had switched to the new German air force in 1935. During the early part of World War II, he established a reputation for personal bravery while leading air forces in several theaters. In December 1941, Hitler appointed Kesselring supreme commander, south. Initially, the title had little significance, but, in October 1942, Hitler gave Kesselring command of all German forces in the Mediterranean except the combined German-Italian Panzer Army fighting in North Africa.[7] Although the German navy had little in the Mediterranean for Kesselring to command, the Luftwaffe still had almost a thousand aircraft scattered around the central Mediterranean in mid-1943.[8] As a result of Allied bombing, only fifty German and seventy-nine Italian planes remained operational on Sicily by D-day.[9]

Unfortunately for Kesselring, the need to accommodate his Italian allies negated much of the advantage that his joint command authority might otherwise have given him. Coalition politics demanded that General Guzzoni command all army forces on Sicily, German as well as Italian. To maintain some control of German units, Kesselring appointed Lt. Gen. Fridolin von Senger und Etterlin, a veteran of the eastern front, as liaison officer to General Guzzoni. General von Senger und Etterlin was responsible for coordinating the employment of German forces on Sicily, an assignment that gave Kesselring an inside view of the situation there.

Thanks to Ultra—highly classified decryptions of intercepted Axis radio messages—Allied intelligence had an extremely accurate picture of the enemy situation on Sicily. When General Eisenhower, supreme allied commander in the Mediterranean, became aware that two German divisions had been added to the Sixth Army's order of battle, he expressed concern that their presence might upset Allied invasion plans. This comment evoked a response from Prime Minister Churchill that if two German divisions could alter the course of the invasion, the ability of the Allies to win the war was questionable.[10]

Although their reconnaissance aircraft had detected the buildup of Allied troops, equipment, and ships in North Africa, the Axis commanders had few details about the makeup of the force being marshalled for the coming invasion. In fact, the Allied force consisted of the British Eighth Army under Gen. Bernard Montgomery and the U.S. Seventh Army under Lt. Gen. George S. Patton. The Eighth Army would land four divisions and one brigade over the beaches and another brigade by glider. The Seventh Army would land four divisions across the beaches and one regiment by parachute.

The physical nature of Sicily posed several problems for the defenders. The first was its size. The island of approximately ten thousand square miles (the size of the state of Vermont) has almost five hundred miles of coastline. From the coast inland, the ground rises sharply to broken terrain. Roads were few and of poor quality, a factor that limited the mobility of both attackers and defenders. With respect to timing, Field Marshal Kesselring estimated that Sicily's defenders had until the middle of July to prepare for the coming attack.[11] He was astounded that the Allies had not swiftly followed up their victory in Tunisia when Sicily was unprepared for a landing and was thankful for every day that his enemy gave him to get ready.[12]

The Axis Plan

In many ways, the question of how to defend Sicily was a forecast of the controversy that would take place among German leaders during the planning for their defense of Normandy. Lacking a doctrine for defending against a landing, German and Italian leaders were forced to develop their plans from scratch. Naval leaders from both countries agreed that the available Axis naval forces were not capable of playing decisive roles in the defense. Adm. Karl Doenitz, organizer of Germany's earlier U-boat victories and commander in chief of the entire German navy since January 1943, went so far as to state that the best use of submarines would be as cargo transports to keep Sicily supplied.[13] In addition, the small number of available Axis aircraft limited the Luftwaffe's ability to deal with an enemy landing. All services agreed that the outcome of the invasion would be determined by ground forces.

The German leaders believed strongly that the most vulnerable moment of a landing occurred while the troops were still in the landing craft as they attempted to get ashore.[14] This view would dictate a defense at the water's edge. German fortification experts who had worked on the Atlantic Wall in France visited Sicily to advise the Italians, but time and shortages of construction materials precluded any major efforts to fortify the coast significantly. The large number of available landing sites, the limited number of Italian coastal divisions, and the poor quality of Italian troops all reduced the possibility that the Italians would be able to stop a landing before the Allies could establish a beachhead. Planners also disagreed on the placement of coastal defense guns.[15] Naval officers wanted the guns placed on the coast where they could fire best at enemy ships. Army officers, on the other hand, wanted the batteries inland where they would be out of effective range of naval guns and capable of firing on the landing force after it was ashore.

Planning a mobile defense also presented problems. Rapid response was crucial. Placing the counterattack forces too close to the beaches, however, exposed them to enemy naval gunfire and increased the risk that the landing would catch them out of position. The answer to the latter problem was to concentrate mobile forces farther back from the coast where they could respond to the largest number of threatened beaches. Unfortunately, that approach also lengthened response time, placed a premium on correctly timing the movement of forces, and posed an additional danger caused by the Sicilian terrain. Because the ground rose sharply behind the beaches, the Germans feared that tanks attacking down the slopes toward the beaches would present particularly lucrative targets for naval guns.

After weighing all of these factors, General Guzzoni settled on an overall plan that essentially reflected a mobile defense concept. The coastal divisions, aided by counterattacks from Italian mobile divisions, would delay the landings as long as possible. Given the small number of gun emplacements, minefields, and anti-landing obstacles that existed, however, little was expected from these efforts. General Guzzoni did hope that this phase of the defense would give him time to determine the location of the main Allied landing. Once he made that determination, he would counterattack the beachhead with the two heavy German divisions. Although he considered southeastern Sicily to be critical to his defense, he assigned the inexperienced Hermann Goering Division to that sector. He then ordered the 15th Panzer Grenadier Division to western Sicily to guard against the possibility of a landing there. Fearing that indecision, poor communications, or the fog of war might somehow delay action against a landing, Field Marshal Kesselring ordered the two German division commanders to launch a counterattack as soon as they ascertained the enemy's objective, whether or not they received orders from Sixth Army headquarters.[16]

The Battle for the Gela Beachhead

Shortly before midnight on 9 July, General Guzzoni placed the Sixth Army on full alert.[17] The immediate cause for this action was a report

German Panzer Mark IV tanks. During the Allied landings in Sicily and Italy in 1943–44, the Germans used a mobile defense concept based on counterattacks by tanks such as these.
(U.S. Army photo, No. SC 191848-6)

that Allied convoys of varying size were approaching Sicily. The extensive aerial and naval bombardment of the nearby island of Pantelleria, followed by its surrender on 11 June, had already convinced most of Sicily's defenders that their turn was coming soon. Shortly after midnight, Sixth Army headquarters began receiving reports of Allied airborne landings on Sicily. Italian estimates of the strength of the landings ranged from four to ten enemy airborne divisions, with 20,000 to 120,000 soldiers.[18] In fact, the airborne spearhead consisted of slightly more than 5,000 parachutists and glider troops from the U.S. 82d Airborne and the British 1st Airborne Divisions. Bad weather and inexperienced pilots caused most of the planes to miss their drop zones. Some transports returned to North Africa without dropping their troops, many gliders crashed into the sea, and most of the paratroopers landed in isolated groups far from their designated objectives. Disastrous in most respects, the dispersion of the Allied airborne forces did confuse the defenders as to the location of the main landings.

At 0145 on 10 July, General Guzzoni alerted his two corps commanders to expect landings along the southeastern coast and in the vicinity of Gela and Agrigento.[19] His prediction was proved correct an hour later when British units began landing across beaches on the Gulf of Noto and the Pachino Peninsula and American forces were coming ashore on the west near the towns of Scoglitti, Gela, and Licata. Resistance on the beaches varied greatly. In a few cases, the Italian coastal divisions put up a credible defense, but opposition against the invaders was generally light. Heavy seas and the confusion that frequently attends a night landing caused some Allied units to land on the wrong beaches and lose unit integrity. The sooner that General Guzzoni could counterattack, the greater the chances were that his forces could drive the invaders back into the sea. As with the airborne landings, however, the wide dispersion of the invasion beaches made determining the location of the main landings difficult.

Of the various locations threatened by the Allied landings, Syracuse was the most important. The port was fortified from the sea, however, and protected from the rear by the proximity of the Napoli Division and the separate German unit, Kampfguppe Schmalz. Therefore, General Guzzoni decided to launch his counterattacks at the American beaches around Gela and assigned the mission to the Herman Goering Division. Its commander, General Conrath, planned a two-pronged attack, each prong the axis for a tank-infantry battle group. Unknown to the Germans, as they were preparing to attack, Italian Mobile Group E from XVI Corps launched its own attack against Gela with light tanks. One arm of the attack was turned back by American infantry supported by naval gunfire, but another fought its way into the town. The Italian tank force was met by U.S. rangers who repelled the attack after a sharp fight.

Meanwhile, the attack by the two battle groups of the Herman Goering Division had bogged down. After a late start, the Germans found themselves facing both exceptionally bad terrain for armored warfare and fierce resistance from scattered American units supported by an apparently endless supply of naval gunfire. Inexperienced in tank-infantry coordination, a number of the German units faltered. General Conrath relieved some officers and threatened others with court-martial, but even those drastic actions were not enough to get the stalled attack moving. An attack to the west by the Livorno Division fared no better. By nightfall on D-day, the Allies had an increasingly solid hold on the beachhead, and time was running out for the defenders.

A defender attempting to defeat an invasion with a mobile defense is, in effect, conducting a race with the attacker to build up combat power at the site of the landing. Both are starting from scratch. The amphibious attacker has a detailed plan for the buildup ashore, however, and is counting on the superior mobility of naval forces to win the race. The longer the landing is allowed to proceed unmolested, the greater the chance that the amphibious attacker will prevail. As the Germans were to learn at Sicily, Allied developments in amphibious equipment—notably, the landing ship, tank (LST) and pontoon causeways—allowed the early landing of armored vehicles. This, in turn, permitted the invaders to meet all but the most rapid of counterattacks with tanks of their own.

Early on D-day, the Luftwaffe, conducting its own form of counterattack against the beachhead, had sunk a destroyer and a minesweeper and shot down several Allied planes spotting for naval gunfire ships. Although the air attack had no direct impact on the outcome of the battle, it made Allied antiaircraft gunners jumpy. The next night, additional Allied airborne units attempted to jump into the beachhead as reinforcements. Although efforts had been made to ensure that Allied gunners were aware of the coming drop, another attack by German aircraft immediately before the paratroopers were scheduled to arrive reinforced the effects of the previous morning's air raid. When the transports carrying the paratroops arrived over the beachhead, many of them were shot down by American gunners.

Faced with an expanding Allied beachhead, General Guzzoni and his German allies fully appreciated the need for haste. On 11 July (D + 1), the Hermann Goering Division resumed its attack against Gela. The Americans used naval gunfire, particularly from the 6-inch guns of the cruiser *Boise,* with good effect against the German attacks. Many sources credit naval gunfire with being the decisive factor in saving the beachhead. Lt. Gen. Omar N. Bradley, commander of the U.S. Army II Corps, notes in his memoirs, for example, that without naval gunfire the 1st Division "might have been thrown back into the sea."[20] In fact, credit for stopping the Germans can be shared broadly. By 1100, German tanks had advanced to a point two thousand yards from the main landing beaches and so close to the troops defending the beachhead that the Americans could no longer call in naval gunfire. Artillery pieces were landed in DUKWs (amphibious trucks) and driven to positions where gunners could fire directly on the advancing Germans. In the final analysis, American soldiers dug in and stopped the Germans with infantry weapons, antitank guns, and artillery fire.

Although the Americans had neither the intention nor plans to withdraw from the landing beaches, the Germans believed differently after they intercepted a message indicating, or so they thought, that the Americans were preparing an evacuation of the beaches. No Allied records of such a message have been found, however, and the source of this confusion remains a mystery. The German perception of an American defeat was reinforced when General Conrath reported to Sixth Army headquarters that his division's attack had forced the Americans to reembark.[21]

The Allies had given no indication of landing in western Sicily, but General Guzzoni could not disregard that possibility. Until he could be sure that no more landings were planned, he felt required to prepare for that contingency. By noon on D-day, however, he decided that the Allies had committed themselves and ordered the 15th Panzer Grenadier Division to return from western Sicily. Disagreeing with General Guzzoni's assessment, Field Marshal Kesselring countermanded the order. He eventually relented, but the resulting delay precluded any chance of an immediate counterattack against an Allied beachhead.

As the Allied buildup across Sicily's beaches continued, the Axis leaders were forced to decide whether to reinforce the island's defenders. By 13 July, Kesselring had decided that the opportunity to defeat the Allied landing was lost but that adequate forces might be able to hold a defensive line across the island. On 14 July, General of Panzer Troops Hans Valentin Hube arrived in Sicily with the XIV Panzer Corps headquarters to take command of the two German divisions already on Sicily plus the 1st Parachute and 29th Panzer Grenadier Divisions, elements of which were beginning to arrive on the island.

General Hube, a veteran of World War I who had lost an arm at Verdun, had established the reputation on the eastern front of being a hard-fighting leader who was not afraid to speak his mind to Hitler. For more than a month, General Hube carried out a defense and then a delaying action toward the port of Messina. As a result, the Allies were not able to secure Sicily until 17 August. The resulting delay allowed the Germans to escape with most of their heavy equipment across the Straits of Messina to the toe of the Italian boot.

The Axis Situation Between Sicily and Salerno

Following the loss of Sicily, Field Marshal Kesselring again faced the question of what his enemy would do next. Although he had decided that control of the sea and air allowed his enemy to land almost any-

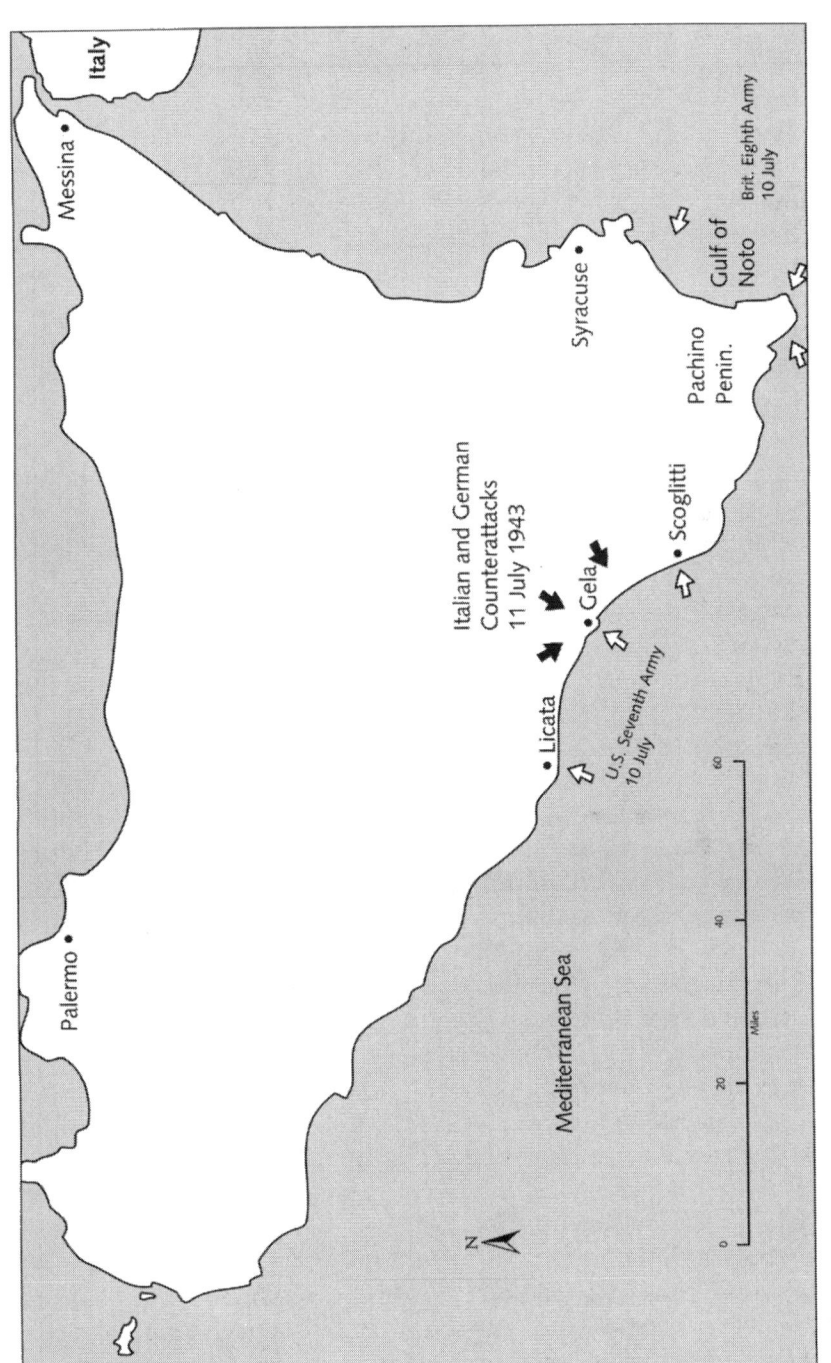

Sicily, 1943

where, he deduced two limitations: the weather and the need for Allied landings to be supported by land-based aircraft.[22] Although attributing the defeat at Sicily largely to poor performance by the Italians and inadequate numbers of German divisions, Kesselring reached several somewhat contradictory conclusions about defending against future landings. He continued to believe that a landing was most vulnerable while the enemy troops were still in their landing craft but concluded that the Allies' aircraft and naval gunfire would overpower a defense at the water's edge, regardless of how strong that defense might be.[23] The answer was a defense in depth, but one that allowed the defender's mobile reserves to counterattack the beachhead immediately after the start of the landing.

To oversee the defense of Italy, the Germans reorganized their command structure. Hitler, a master at playing off his subordinates one against another, split the responsibility for the defense of the peninsula. He assigned northern Italy to Army Group B under Field Marshal Erwin Rommel, who was now recovered from the illness that had forced him to relinquish command in Tunisia before the German surrender there. Hitler left Field Marshal Kesselring in command of southern Italy and gave him the Tenth Army headquarters to control the two German corps fighting in the south. General of Panzer Troops Heinrich von Vietinghoff, a combat-tested veteran, arrived in Italy from the eastern front to assume command of the Tenth Army.

After the withdrawal of his forces from Sicily, Kesselring had 8 German divisions in Italy located from Rome south. Rommel's Army Group B had 8 1/2 divisions in northern Italy, but Hitler had so far refused to release any of them to Kesselring for the defense of the south. The Italian Seventh Army added another 3 mobile and 6 coastal divisions.[24] Thanks particularly to Ultra, Allied planners had formed a reasonably accurate picture of Axis capabilities. For example, they were able to identify the 3 German divisions in the Naples-Salerno area and track their movements.[25]

German air forces under Kesselring's command still presented a significant aerial threat and were about to write a new chapter on defending against a landing. As early as 1938, the Germans had begun developing radio-controlled aerial bombs and missiles.[26] By 1943, they had two types of these weapons in operation. One was a radio-controlled 1400-kilogram bomb, designated PC 1400X but commonly called Fritz-X. The second weapon, the Henschel Hs 293A, was a true guided missile with a rocket motor to propel it in flight. In July and August, special German squadrons employed limited numbers of both types of weapons, but Allied fleet units generally remained unaware of them.[27]

In planning the defense of Italy, Kesselring began to anticipate possible locations for an Allied landing. Although he claims to have understood his enemy's reliance on land-based fighter support,[28] his distribution of forces indicates something less than full confidence in that understanding. The range of Allied fighters would have prevented them from supporting a landing north of Salerno, but two of the German divisions in the area were located north of there around Naples.

In spite of being within fighter range of Allied fields in Sicily, Salerno still posed some serious problems for an invader. Even if the Allies could secure a beachhead there, they would have to cross the mountains between the beaches and the real invasion target of Naples, twenty-five miles to the north. Behind the invasion beaches was a large open plain. The rivers crossing the plain limited the ability of the defenders to conduct rapid counterattacks with tanks but also posed problems for the attackers. The Sele River, which runs into the Bay of Salerno, split the landing area into northern and southern beaches. When U.S. Gen. George S. Patton learned of the Fifth Army's intention to land on both sides of the river, he predicted that the Germans would counterattack down the river to split the Allied beachhead.[29]

The German Plan for Salerno

When Patton was making his prediction on 1 September, the Germans had no detailed plan for the defense of Salerno. The German high command had ordered the Tenth Army to oppose strongly any landings in the vicinity of Naples but to conduct delaying actions in response to landings nearer the foot of the peninsula. General von Vietinghoff had reached an agreement with his Italian counterpart regarding antilanding operations under which the Italians would defend the coast, thereby freeing German divisions to conduct mobile operations, including counterattacks against a beachhead.

The mobile unit for Salerno was the 16th Panzer Division, which deployed four combat teams, each consisting of an infantry battalion supported by tanks and artillery. Three were located two to three miles from the beach to conduct rapid counterattacks, and the fourth was farther to the rear in division reserve.[30] Additional infantry platoons occupied hastily constructed positions along the beaches between Salerno and Agropoli. The Italian 222d Coastal Division manned six coastal batteries, constructed barbed wire obstacles, and laid land mines along Salerno's beaches. The Italians also laid an extensive field of naval mines in the bay. In carrying out his overall plans, Field Marshal Kesselring was aided by the delay between the escape of German forces from Sicily on 17 August and British Field Marshal Bernard Montgomery's amphibious attack across the Straits of Messina on 3 September. Knowing he would have been unable to resist an earlier British landing, Kesselring regarded the respite as a gift from the Allies.

Planning for the defense at Salerno became more urgent when German aerial reconnaissance detected Allied convoys headed northeast from Palermo on 7 September. Kesselring still considered Rome to be a possible target, however, so no specific action was taken with regard to Salerno. On 8 September, von Vietinghoff placed the XIV Panzer Corps on highest alert but made no move to concentrate his forces at Salerno. His problems were greatly compounded on the evening of 8 September when he received word of the Italian armistice. The news caught most Italian military leaders by surprise. General von Vietinghoff's Italian counterpart initially thought that the announcement was an Allied propaganda ploy. Reaction by Italian units varied greatly. Some voluntarily turned over their weapons and equipment to their erstwhile allies. The commanding general of the 222d Coastal Division at Salerno refused to allow his unit to be disarmed and was shot by the Germans as a result. German soldiers were in the process of taking over former Italian defensive positions at Salerno when the first Allied units began landing there at 0310 on 9 September.

The Battle for the Salerno Beachhead

The U.S. Fifth Army caught the Germans by surprise before they were fully prepared to meet an invasion. The 16th Panzer Division only recently had been reconstituted and was untested in combat. The Tenth Army was getting organized and experiencing communications problems. To make matters worse, General Hube, the XIV Panzer Corps commander who had performed so brilliantly in Sicily, was on leave. At about 0800 on 9 September, General von Vietinghoff decided that Salerno was, in fact, the main landing and ordered the XIV Panzer Corps to concentrate there and drive the Allies into the sea.

Although the Tenth Army commander had acted quickly and decisively, communications problems and indecision on the part of some subordinates conspired to prevent the concentration of forces that he had sought. As a result, the best that the 16th Panzer Division could accomplish on D-day was to conduct a number of uncoordinated counterattacks with small groups of infantry and tanks. All of these attacks were beaten back by a combination of infantry antitank tactics and naval gunfire. By the end of the day, the British X Corps north of the Sele River and the U.S. VI Corps to the south had established shallow beachheads that were relatively secure but subject to frequent shelling by German artillery.

General von Vietinghoff was beginning to discover the difficulties of conducting a mobile defense. He had two divisions immediately north of Salerno, but he was reluctant to bring them to the beachhead for fear that the Allies could make another landing at Naples. He had also ordered the 26th Panzer Division and the 29th Panzer Grenadier Division to move to Salerno from the south, but fuel shortages delayed their arrival by two days.

The German commander planned a coordinated attack against the beachhead on 14 September but advanced the date one day when he detected a split between the two Allied corps. Shortly after noon on 13 September, elements of the 16th Panzer Division and the 29th Panzer Grenadier Division attacked down the Sele River corridor, as General Patton had predicted earlier. Initially, this attack was perceived by the Americans as a stiffening of German resistance to U.S. advances, but, by the end of the day, the Fifth Army faced a situation that bordered on crisis. Gen. Mark W. Clark, Fifth Army commander, made arrangements to evacuate his headquarters by PT boat on ten minutes' notice, and his staff started working on plans for a full-scale evacuation of the beaches.[31] In his memoirs, General Clark admitted that, for a while, he thought the Germans actually would drive the Fifth Army back into the sea.[32]

By the end of the day, German forces had fought their way so close to the American beaches that General von Vietinghoff sensed that victory was within his grasp. The Tenth Army war diary for that day carries the entry, "The battle for Salerno appears to be over."[33]

While the Tenth Army was conducting its counterattack against the Allied beachhead, German attempts at a naval defense were also having an impact on the landing. In spite of Allied minesweeping, the German minefield had forced the Allies to launch their landing craft as far as twelve miles out from the beaches and also had restricted the ability of naval gunfire ships to support the troops ashore. On the afternoon of D-day, the monitor HMS *Abercrombie,* whose 15-inch guns were the largest in the invasion fleet, struck a mine and had to leave the area for repairs.

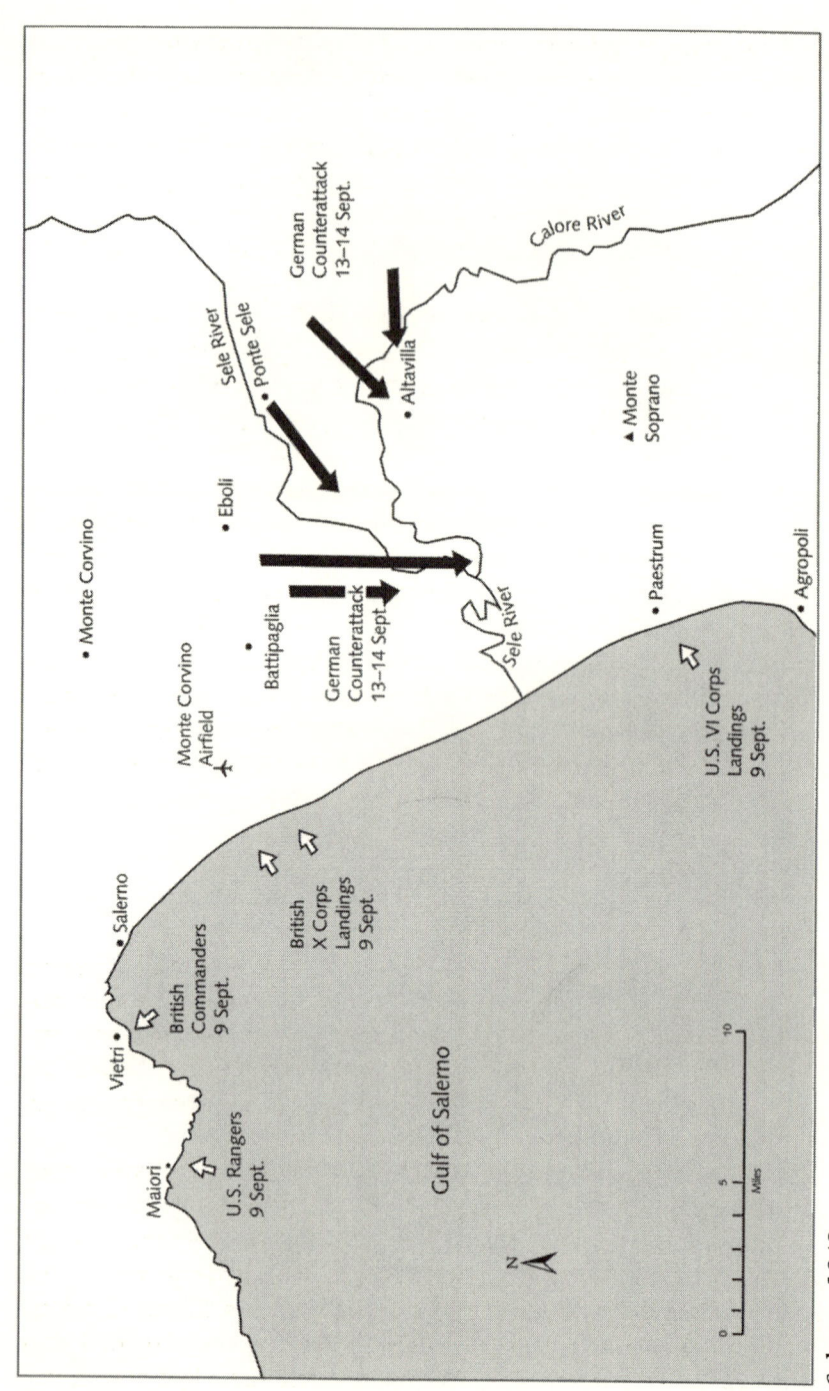

Salerno, 1943

Using the new guided weapons, the Luftwaffe was able to inflict even greater damage on the invasion fleet than had been caused by the mines. German orders called for attacks on transports, landing craft, and merchant ships, but, as naval gunfire began to take a toll on the German ground forces, the Luftwaffe shifted its priority to warships providing naval gunfire support.[34] On 11 September German planes attacked the U.S. cruisers *Philadelphia* and *Savannah* with guided bombs.[35] They narrowly missed the *Philadelphia,* but hit the *Savannah* with a Fritz-X that pierced a forward turret, exploded in a lower handling room, and tore a large hole in the ship's bottom. Attacks on 13 and 16 September damaged the light cruiser HMS *Uganda* and the battleship HMS *Warspite,* respectively. None of the damaged ships sank, but all were forced to leave the invasion area for repairs.

In spite of the combined German air-land efforts against the beachhead, the beleaguered Allies continued to hold. Although Clark had additional divisions available in Sicily and North Africa, he feared that they could not reach Salerno by ship fast enough to save the situation. As a result, he called on the 82d Airborne Division to reinforce the beachhead by air drop. Meanwhile, the British Eighth Army was slowly closing on Salerno from the south. Faced with the eventual arrival of Montgomery and the resulting necessity of repositioning his forces for further delaying operations up the Italian peninsula, von Vietinghoff abandoned his efforts to destroy the Salerno beachhead. He began to withdraw his forces on 17 September.

The Situation After Salerno

Based on the experiences of Sicily and Salerno, Field Marshal Kesselring refined his concept of a mobile defense against a landing. The new concept called for positioning units to fire on the landing force as it approached the coast, bringing tactical reserves to bear on the landing within six hours, and having the advanced elements of strategic reserves reach the beachhead within twenty-four hours.[36]

The Allies gave Kesselring a chance to test his concept when they landed two divisions at Anzio on 22 January 1944 in an effort to maneuver around strong German defensive positions farther south. Caught by surprise, the German commander reacted without panic and, by the end of the day, had massed approximately twenty thousand troops around the beachhead.[37] He was unable, however, to build up his forces fast enough to allow for a decisive counterattack that might have driven

USS Savannah, *following bomb hit at Salerno, 1943. During the Allied landing there, the Germans used radio-controlled bombs against Allied ships. A bomb struck a turret on the* Savannah, *exploded in an ammunition handling room, and put the ship out of action.*
(U.S. Navy photo, No. 54357)

the landing back into the sea. As a result, the landing that had been conceived as a bold stroke to restore momentum to the Allied offensive became a stalemate in its own right. After four months of battle that tested the endurance of troops on both sides, the stalemate was broken by the approach of the remainder of the Fifth Army that had finally broken through the German defenses to the south.

Observations

Because the Germans had weak naval forces in the Mediterranean and the Allies had neutralized the Italian navy by June 1943, the Italian invasions essentially pitted Allied air-naval-ground forces against Axis air-ground forces. Allied air forces had achieved a degree of air superiority over each of the beachheads before the respective D-days, but Allied control of the air was by no means absolute, as it was in some cases in the Pacific. One important lesson was that a landing against an enemy still contesting control of the air over the beachhead could be successful.

In carrying out his defenses at Sicily, Salerno, and Anzio, Field Marshal Kesselring had two advantages that have not been enjoyed by most defenders. First, he had unified command over all German forces used in the defense. Unfortunately for the Germans, this unity of command was limited by alliance politics with the Italians and a general lack of German naval forces for Kesselring to command. The Germans created a second advantage by their choice of tactics. Rather than resisting the Allied landings at all costs, they chose to withdraw and save their forces to fight again. As a result, German commanders and units were able to gain experience in defending against amphibious operations, learn from their past mistakes, and apply these lessons in defending against later landings.

To some degree, this experience made up for a serious defect: lack of doctrine for defending against a landing. With many of the same commanders participating in the defenses of Sicily, Salerno, and Anzio, the Germans were spared relearning the same lessons over and over again. The Allies, on the other hand, had the dual advantage of a continuum of commanders and units at the three landings and an established doctrine for conducting an amphibious operation. In Italy, as Kesselring later noted, both sides were learning lessons that they would apply later during the invasion of France.[38]

Delay continued to work to the advantage of the defenders. German commanders expressed both surprise and relief at the respites they were given by the Allies between the end of the fighting in Tunisia and the landing in Sicily and between the end of the fighting there and the landing of Montgomery's Eighth Army in Italy proper.

As might be expected from army officers—particularly those with cavalry backgrounds and a great deal of experience with armored warfare—the Germans chose a mobile concept to defend against the Allied landings in Italy. The success of this style of defense depended on counterattacking the enemy beachhead early after the landing and with enough force to destroy the invaders before they could establish a secure beachhead. This, in turn, rested on three factors: (1) correctly positioning the mobile forces before the landing, (2) making an early decision to employ them, and (3) having the ability to get the forces to the vicinity of the landing in spite of enemy efforts to interdict them. The long coastlines of Sicily and Italy offered so many possible landing sites that correctly positioning mobile defensive forces required both good luck and good professional judgment. Because of the number of potential landing places and the mobility of amphibious forces at sea, the defenders probably would not commit their reserves until they had made an absolute determination that a landing was not simply a feint. In addition, Allied air and naval gunfire made movement of German mobile reserves to counterattack positions extremely slow and hazardous.

Naval gunfire was also used to disrupt counterattacks against the beachheads. To say that it was the decisive factor in stopping those attacks would be unfair to the soldiers who faced their German opponents on the ground. At the same time, leaders on both sides were quick to acknowledge the important role of naval gunfire in defeating Axis attempts to employ a mobile defense concept against Allied landings during the Italian campaign.

While relying largely on a mobile defense concept in Italy, the Germans did not entirely disdain a naval defense. Their methods—mines, submarines, motor torpedo boats, and air attacks—proved to be more annoying than decisive. Had these elements of a naval defense been employed in a more coordinated manner, however, they might have delayed the landings enough to have made the armored counterattacks ashore more effective. These pinprick attacks also raise a question of what might have happened if heavy naval forces had been available to the Axis defenders. Italian Adm. Franco Maugeri speculated that had the Italian navy not surrendered, but boldly sailed its battleships and cruisers into Salerno Bay at the start of the landing there, the result would have been an Allied disaster on a greater scale than Gallipoli.[39] As improbable as this scenario might seem, it does point out how poorly the Axis leaders employed naval forces in an anti-landing role when those forces were still available in significant numbers.

German Defense at the Water's Edge:
Normandy, 1944

Everything must be directed towards destroying the enemy landing force while it is still on the water, or at the latest during the landing itself.
Field Marshal Erwin Rommel

The German preparations for the anticipated Allied invasion of France at Normandy constitute perhaps the classic case study of defense against an amphibious assault. The Germans had several years to prepare for the coming invasion, and the proponents of competing defensive concepts expressed their arguments with particular clarity. Many of the high-ranking participants in the defense either survived to write about their experiences or left papers that explain the reasons for important German decisions.[1]

Although the Germans built powerful gun positions along the English Channel to support Operation Sea Lion, they began to appreciate the need to defend the coast of occupied Europe by what came to be called the Atlantic Wall. This line of coastal defenses eventually ran from above the Arctic Circle in Norway to southern France. On 14 December 1941, Field Marshal Wilhelm Keitel, chief of staff of Germany's OKW, signed a directive on coastal defense that ordered, in Hitler's name, the creation of a "new Westwall" that could repel even the strongest Allied landing while requiring the smallest possible number of permanently assigned defensive troops.[2] This document listed the top three priorities for construction, in order, as Norway, the Franco-Belgian coast, and Brittany-Normandy.

The reasons given for Norway's priority were the geographic and weather conditions that made employment of mobile forces difficult. Not mentioned, but probably relevant, were the British commando raids on Norway early in the war. Although the raids had little direct impact on the war, they infuriated Hitler and helped to ensure that more than three hundred thousand German troops would be tied down in Norway, even though they were desperately needed elsewhere.

On 19 August 1942, the British launched the biggest of their amphibious raids against the French port of Dieppe. Although a withdrawal was planned from the start, the Dieppe raid was carried out to achieve a range of broad objectives aimed at preparing the Allies for the eventual return to the continent. Among these objectives were exploring the problems associated with capturing a port; testing Allied capability to land large forces, including tanks; and discovering the weaknesses of German defenses. Although the operation was disastrous for the Canadian division that made up most of the landing force, British planners learned valuable lessons from the raid, particularly that capturing a port by frontal assault was impractical. Other means would have to be found to support invasion forces after a landing until the port could be captured from the rear. Using evidence from the same operation, the Germans reached a somewhat different conclusion that the Allies would be forced to seize a major port at the start of an invasion. The later experience at Salerno, where the Allies made such an effort to capture Naples, reinforced the view formed by the Germans after Dieppe about the importance of denying the Allies early access to a port.[3]

As a result of this thinking, Hitler declared the most important European ports to be fortresses and ordered that they be held at any cost. A disproportionate amount of the German fortification effort, therefore, was devoted to protecting these fortresses, as opposed to defending the coasts between them against a landing. As many as two hundred thousand troops were also tied down guarding the fortified ports. Naval guns and heavy artillery pieces were collected throughout occupied Europe and placed along the Atlantic Wall. Engineers from Organization Todt, a quasi-military construction corps, supervised a herculean effort to mount these guns. By D-Day, the Atlantic Wall contained thousands of permanent emplacements and weapons ranging in size from 16-inch naval rifles to machine guns.[4]

In spite of German propaganda claims to the contrary, the Atlantic Wall had significant weaknesses that worried Hitler. To correct the problems, he moved Field Marshal Rommel from northern Italy in November 1943 and ordered him to carry out an inspection of the Atlantic Wall.

Casemate, part of the Atlantic Wall, Normandy. Large-caliber coastal defense guns were mounted in massive, reinforced-concrete casemates as part of the Germans' anti-landing defense.
(U.S. Coast Guard photo)

The Situation at Normandy

Rommel began his inspection in Denmark on the last day of November and was soon forced to consider the purpose of the defenses he was inspecting. No one seriously thought the wall would deter the Allies from eventually attempting a landing, but Hitler believed that, if he could defeat the invasion when it came, the impact might actually reverse the course of the war in the west.[5] After his inspection, Rommel concluded that the defenses, as they were then, would not be capable of stopping the Allies. Part of the problem was that no coherent plan of defense existed. In the four years leading up to D-Day, for example, Organization Todt had used more than ten million cubic meters of concrete in building the fortifications, but many of the positions were poorly sited and some had to be destroyed.[6] As General Senger und Etterlin had pointed out earlier in Italy, the navy and army could not agree on where to locate coastal batteries or even how to construct them. Clearly, the Germans needed a comprehensive plan.

A critical question was where to concentrate the defenses on the thousands of miles of occupied coast. At one time or another, German leaders, including Hitler, predicted that the landing would occur at almost every possible site between Norway and southern France, and many made several predictions. Hitler initially believed that the invasion would occur in France at the Pas-de-Calais, but, in April 1944, he began to express the view that Normandy was also a likely location.[7]

By 1944, the Germans were forced to make most of their decisions about defense in an intelligence vacuum. All of their spy networks in Britain had been turned by Allied intelligence, and Allied air defense severely limited the ability of the Luftwaffe to carry out aerial reconnaissance or photography over the British Isles. To develop their defensive plans, the Germans had to rely on intuition and an understanding of Allied amphibious techniques. Based on their analysis of earlier landings, they were confident that the Allies would land somewhere within fighter range of airfields in Britain.[8] Using this rule, they decided that the two most likely sites were the Pas-de-Calais and the beaches of Normandy. The former represented the narrowest point of the channel, a factor considered critical by the Germans in 1940 when they had planned Operation Sea Lion. A landing at the Pas-de-Calais also afforded the Allies the most direct approach into the heart of Germany. Normandy, on the other hand, offered rapid access to major ports, also considered a critical factor by the Germans.

Both Normandy and the Pas-de-Calais fell within the area controlled by Field Marshal Gerd von Rundstedt, commander in chief, west. Hitler had called von Rundstedt out of retirement at the start of the war, fired him in 1941 from his command on the eastern front and forced him to retire again, and reinstated him in 1942 to command the defense of the west. As invasion became more likely, the OKW placed two army groups under von Rundstedt's command. At von Rundstedt's suggestion, Hitler had given Rommel a command assignment in addition to his duties as inspector of the Atlantic Wall. As commander of Army Group B, Rommel was responsible to von Rundstedt for the coast from the Loire River in France to the Dutch border with Germany. Both of the most likely landing sites fell in Rommel's area. The Fifteenth Army, under Col. Gen. Hans von Salmuth, was responsible to Rommel for the sector north of the Orne River that included the Pas-de-Calais. The Seventh Army, under Col. Gen. Friedrich Dollmann, had responsibility for the southern sector, which included Normandy. South of the Seventh Army, Col. Gen. Johannes Blaskowitz's

Army Group G was responsible for defending France's Biscay and Mediterranean coasts.

By June 1944, the Germans had fifty-eight divisions in the west. Ten of these were panzer or panzer grenadier divisions. The remainder were infantry divisions of one type or another, including some made up of Luftwaffe ground personnel. In April, the army had revised its system of classifying divisions.[9] Infantry divisions were rated as field divisions when they were capable of participating in mobile operations, limited employment divisions when they were somewhat less capable, or static divisions when they were capable only of defending a fixed position. Of the infantry divisions in the west, fourteen were field and the remainder limited employment divisions. That none of the divisions at Normandy were of the least capable class did not mean that the Germans there had no problems. Many of the defenders were former Soviet soldiers who had volunteered for service in the German Army after their capture on the eastern front. The origin of these troops not only raised questions about their reliability in the coming invasion but caused a variety of administrative problems as well. The 276th Division, for example, had soldiers from more than twenty-five Soviet ethnic groups and was forced to issue paybooks in eight languages.[10]

Intelligence agents, aerial photography, beach reconnaissance, and Ultra intercepts gave Allied planners an almost perfect picture of the Atlantic Wall and the troops manning it. One of the Allies' best sources was Gen. Hiroshi Ōshima, the Japanese ambassador to Berlin. Although the Germans appeared to have little interest in Japanese anti-landing expertise, the reverse was not true. Between 24 October and 1 November 1943, General Ōshima visited the Atlantic Wall and held discussions with Field Marshal von Rundstedt and his chief of staff, Lt. Gen. Guenther Blumentritt. General Ōshima's subsequent messages to Tokyo, intercepted and decrypted by the Allies, gave them a comprehensive picture of the German defenses.[11]

In laying out guidelines for defending against the invasion, Fuehrer Directive 40 of 23 March 1942 stated that specific commanders, including von Rundstedt, would have, "command authority over tactical headquarters of the services, the German civil authorities as well as units and organizations outside of the armed forces that are within their respective areas."[12] This policy, however, was never put into effect. Field Marshal von Rundstedt commanded only army forces and not even all of them within his command area. Each service had its own distinct chain of command. Adm. Theodor Krancke, commander of Navy Group

West, reported directly to the naval high command, and Field Marshal Hugo Sperrle, commander of the Luftwaffe's Third Air Fleet, reported to the high command of the air force.[13]

Although unified command would have improved von Rundstedt's ability to coordinate his defense, it would not have greatly increased German combat power. On 31 May 1944, the Third Air Fleet had only 891 aircraft, of which 497 were operational.[14] German naval forces capable of responding to a landing in the Normandy area consisted of a small number of destroyers, torpedo boats, and fast-attack craft in addition to Group Landwirt, seventeen submarines assigned to an anti-invasion role.[15] As a last-ditch effort, the German navy also created a force of Kleinkampfverbände (KdK), or small battle units. Following the lead of the Italians, the German navy developed a variety of midget submarines, manned torpedoes, and explosive motorboats, some of which were employed unsuccessfully at Anzio. According to Vice Adm. Helmuth Heye, who commanded the KdK, "The tactical aim was to attack the enemy with a great number of various types of small fighting units at the very moment of his landing."[16]

Because Allied counterintelligence efforts had largely blinded the Germans, they were susceptible to a massive Allied operation of deception put into play to deflect German attention from Normandy. A major part of the effort was the creation of an imaginary First U.S. Army Group (FUSAG) staged in England. Its location indicated that it would be employed in a landing at the Pas-de-Calais. Because this concept matched their perceptions about the Allied invasion plan, the Germans believed in the existence of FUSAG and continued to do so long after the Allies had landed in Normandy. Counting this imaginary Allied force, German intelligence estimated at the end of May that the Allies had seventy-nine divisions staged in Britain for the invasion when, in reality, they had about fifty-two.[17]

The remaining issue for the Germans was the date of the Allied landing. They agreed that it would happen in 1944; the consensus was sometime in May. Based on their understanding of Allied amphibious doctrine, the Germans thought that their enemies would land at high tide on a date when that occurred several hours before daylight. This consideration and the weather further restricted possible invasion dates. One thing was certain. Rommel did not have much time to prepare for the coming landing. As he told his aide, "I have only one real enemy now, and that is time."[18]

The German Plan for Normandy

One of the more serious problems facing Rommel was the lack of doctrine for the defense against a landing. Various headquarters had issued instructions about anti-landing defense, but no single comprehensive doctrine seems to have been issued. On 12 December 1943, the OKW issued a directive titled "Preparations for the Imminent Large-Scale Battles in the West." Based on a study of earlier Allied landings, this document lays out a relatively accurate description of how the Allies conducted a landing, with comments on Allied intelligence, landing techniques, airborne operations, tactical flexibility, and supporting arms. The directive credits supporting arms, particularly air support, as the source of Allied superiority. The directive then lists the consequences of Allied landing tactics on German defensive measures. After discussing construction, location, and camouflage of fighting positions; the use of tanks; and other aspects of the defense, it notes, "According to the experience made in Italy, the best way of eliminating an enemy breakthrough is by means of an *immediate counterattack* [emphasis in the original]."[19]

Rommel's personal studies of the Italian landings, on the other hand, pointed him toward a defense at the water's edge. He agreed that any breakthrough should be met with an immediate counterattack but discounted the possibility of moving armored forces, other than those stationed immediately behind the invasion beaches. Rommel apparently had not studied the experiences of the Japanese (who were in the process of abandoning the defense at the water's edge at the time of Normandy). Adm. Friedrich Ruge, who advised Rommel on naval matters, did not remember even hearing the name Tarawa at the time.[20]

In attempting to implement his defensive concept, Rommel ran into opposition from his immediate superior, Field Marshal von Rundstedt, who supported a classic mobile approach using massed armored forces to counterattack a beachhead once the Allies had firmly committed themselves. He received support for this view from Col. Gen. Heinz Guderian, inspector general of panzer troops at the time, and General of Panzer Troops Freiherr Leo Geyr von Schweppenburg. The latter was the commander of Panzer Group West, an organization responsible for the training of panzer forces in the west but with no actual command authority.

Geyr von Schweppenburg believed that Rommel's concept doomed the panzers, the most powerful force in the defender's arsenal, to piecemeal commitment and the possibility of being pinned down behind the beaches by Allied supporting arms. His answer was to concentrate the panzer units far back from the coast, perhaps as far as Paris, and launch them en masse against an Allied landing.[21] While not disagreeing in theory, Rommel argued that Geyr von Schweppenburg's concept was based on his battle experience on the eastern front where the Germans had air superiority. Rommel's experience in North Africa, on the other hand, told him that Allied air power would prevent the Germans from moving centrally located panzer forces to the site of a landing fast enough to have a decisive impact.

In the midst of these competing ideas, the OKW reached a compromise. Rommel and Blaskowitz each received control of three panzer divisions. The remaining three panzer divisions and a panzer grenadier division became von Rundstedt's reserve under Geyr von Schweppenburg. Von Rundstedt could not commit this powerful reserve, however, without permission from the OKW.

In spite of Rommel's failure to win full support for his concept, he launched a determined effort to construct a defense at the water's edge. He envisioned a coastal belt about five or six miles wide to give some depth to the defense. His ability to man such a defensive belt was limited by the number of available infantry divisions. German troop allocations continued to reflect the view that the Pas-de-Calais was the most threatened area. The Fifteenth and Seventh Armies had approximately the same number of divisions, but the former's divisions held an average front of fifty miles, whereas the latter's had to cover more than two hundred miles.[22] A German rule of thumb at the time held that six miles was the longest defensive frontage that a division could handle.[23]

Largely to rectify this serious weakness, Rommel conceived an unprecedented barrier plan to disrupt and delay the Allied landing. The plan relied heavily on a combination of mines and obstacles. To deny Allied glider forces the use of potential landing zones in the rear of the coastal belt, Rommel's troops erected upright poles topped with captured shells activated by trip wires strung between the poles. Because of their appearance, these obstacles became known as "Rommel's asparagus." Rommel also intended to turn the coastal zone into an immense minefield with as many as 200 million mines. When he began his effort, almost 2 million land mines were already in place, and his troops laid another 4.5 million before D-Day.[24]

In addition to these landward defenses, Rommel planned other surprises for his enemy. Prevented by insufficient troops from extending his

Defense at the water's edge, Normandy. The Germans placed thousands of antiboat obstacles and millions of land mines.
(U.S. Navy photo, No. 45714)

defense to the rear, Rommel planned to gain some depth with successive offshore obstacle belts. Antiboat obstacles would affect the landing force at what most experts agreed was its most vulnerable point. Rommel designed four successive belts of obstacles to extend seaward from the high-water mark.[25] Logs were embedded in the sand below the high-water mark to impale landing craft. When tests of these particular obstacles against captured Allied landing craft proved unsatisfactory, many of the logs were topped with mines. The Germans also adapted captured Belgian and Czech antitank obstacles for use against landing craft.

Hitler wanted to employ flamethrowers in a defensive role and bury barrels of fuel on the beaches, thereby forcing an invader to "wade through fire."[26] Flamethrowers were tested against landing craft, and some were eventually installed but not to the extent envisioned by Hitler. German engineers constructed a variety of antitank walls, ditches, and individual obstacles. Other specialized weapons included torpedo tubes, torpedoes that could be launched from a beach, and miniature remote-controlled tanks filled with explosives.

The German navy also had an important role in defeating a landing.

German remote-controlled Goliath demolition vehicles. Shown here in American hands at Utah Beach, Normandy, these miniature "tanks" were among many specialized defensive weapons used unsuccessfully against landings.
(U.S. Navy photo, No. 252746)

The navy had developed both an anti-invasion coastal mine, known as the KMA, and a pressure-activated naval mine called the "Oyster." The latter posed a serious threat because the Allies had no capability to sweep pressure mines. Mine warfare is a two-edged sword that must be wielded carefully by a defender. Once laid, mines have a limited life, and minefields must be reseeded periodically to maintain their effectiveness. German mines had a mechanism that deactivated the firing device no later than eighty days after laying.[27] Minefields that would stop an Allied invasion force would also interfere with the Germans' ability to use vital coastal shipping routes. Accordingly, the navy decided to delay the laying of most naval mines until an invasion was imminent. Rommel disagreed, but he had no authority to overrule a naval decision.

The navy also planned to use the small craft available along the coast to attack any invasion force and to lay Blitz-Sperren (lightning minefields) to block the landing beaches. An incident on 28 April at Slapton Sands, England, during which German fast-attack craft attacked Allied amphibious forces conducting a training exercise for Normandy, showed the potential of this form of naval defense. In a matter of minutes, the German boats sank two LSTs with torpedoes and damaged another; the attack caused more casualties than the Americans were to suffer at Utah Beach on D-Day.[28] The Germans also planned to use conventional submarines, as well as newly developed one-man types, against the landing.

The Battle for the Normandy Beachhead

Although the Germans knew an invasion was coming, they could not keep their forces on full alert indefinitely. As a result, they evaluated the situation daily and issued an invasion assessment ranging from very probable to improbable. Weather played a major role in making these assessments. Unfortunately for the Germans, the weather in Europe comes from the west. Earlier in the war, the Germans had received weather reports from submarines in the Atlantic and clandestine weather stations on Greenland and other islands in the North Atlantic. Allied actions had reduced the ability of the Germans to use these sources, which placed the Germans at a disadvantage regarding weather predictions. Because weather along the coast on 5 June was considered by the Germans to be too severe for a landing, the Seventh Army relaxed its alert status. The army commander had previously scheduled an anti-landing war game to be held at Rennes the next day for his subordinate commanders. Rommel had left his headquarters on 4 June for southern Germany to visit his wife on her birthday and to confer with Hitler.

During 1943, German counterintelligence had broken a French resistance net and discovered how the Allies intended to notify French partisans of the start of the invasion.[29] At 2115 on 5 June, a German radio monitoring unit picked up the second half of the alert message indicating that D-Day was imminent. After receiving this message, the Fifteenth Army went on alert. The message was passed first to Rommel's headquarters and then to von Rundstedt's. Considering both the bad weather that made a landing unlikely and an earlier false alarm, von Rundstedt's staff decided not to alert the Seventh Army at Normandy. On 5 June, Allied minesweepers had begun their work within sight of the French coast, but the Germans apparently disregarded this indicator of the coming invasion as well.

The bad weather that kept German reconnaissance aircraft grounded and patrol boats in port prevented the Germans from discovering that the Allied fleet had sailed on 5 June. Based on predictions of a three-day break in the weather, General Eisenhower had made his fateful decision to launch Operation Overlord. The first indications received by the Germans of the invasion were reports of Allied airborne operations that began about 0200 on 6 June. The British were landing east of the Orne River, and American paratroopers were dropping along the flooded areas inland from the stretch of coastline now known as Utah Beach. German commanders were alerted, but, initially, no one was certain that these operations were part of the awaited invasion.

Any doubt was dispelled by the arrival of an armada of more than five thousand ships and landing craft off the beaches, from les Dunes-de-Varreville in the west to Ouistreham in the east, and the start of a naval bombardment shortly before 0600. After a bombardment of less than an hour, troops from the U.S. 4th Infantry Division began landing across Utah Beach, the westernmost of the Allied beaches at Normandy. Concurrently, the U.S. 1st Infantry Division began landing about twelve miles to the east across Omaha Beach. After an hour's delay, British and Canadian forces commenced landing across Sword, Gold, and Juno Beaches, still farther to the east. Each landing force had its own set of problems, but, at Omaha Beach, the Germans came closest to realizing the potential of Rommel's concept of a defense at the water's edge.

The bad weather that allowed the Germans to be caught by surprise also did them one favor. The U.S. Eighth Air Force had planned a massive aerial bombardment of Omaha Beach shortly before H-hour, but cloud cover forced the bombers to rely on instruments to locate the target. Fearful of hitting their own forces, the bombers delayed their drop several seconds as a safety factor. As a result, thirteen thousand bombs were relatively harmless as they fell inland, rather than on the German defenders. The naval gunfire preparation was largely unaffected by the weather, but it was limited by a short bombardment time deliberately chosen to avoid giving the Germans time to react. The naval gunfire suppressed the fire of German coastal batteries but actually destroyed less than 14 percent of the German positions.[30]

The lack of prelanding fire support put a premium on the early landing of tanks to deal with the German bunkers and gun positions. To accomplish this, the British had developed a version of the Sherman tank that could float with the aid of an inflatable canvas screen mounted on the hull. Propellers moved it through the water, and it had treads for land travel. Because of this propulsion system, it was known as the dual drive

(DD) tank. Remembering the problems with obstacles at Dieppe and aware of the German preparations at Normandy, the British had developed the tank and a wide range of other specialized armored vehicles, including engineer vehicles, flame tanks, mat layers, and mine clearance vehicles, for the invasion.[31]

At Omaha Beach, the DD tanks were a disaster. Launched as far off the coast as six thousand yards, twenty-seven out of thirty-two swamped before reaching the beach. Deprived of the tanks for fire support and lacking the specialized engineer vehicles of the British, the Americans had to attack the German bunkers with infantry weapons and destroy the mines and obstacles by hand until tanks and bulldozers could be landed. The obstacles posed a particular problem. Within two hours, the rising tide covered the obstacles and prevented the engineers from destroying them. Enemy fire, obstacles, and general confusion on the beach caused the landing craft to back up at sea. Casualties mounted, and the beach became increasingly congested as assault units were unable to dislodge the defenders from the draws leading off the beaches.

Unfortunately for the Americans at Omaha Beach, they suffered from one of the few Allied intelligence failures. Allied planners had initially located the German 352d Division, one of the fully capable field divisions, near Saint-Lô in reserve. In March, the division had moved one of its regiments into defensive positions on the cliffs overlooking Omaha Beach. The move was eventually detected by Allied intelligence but not in time to warn the assault divisions before they landed. In spite of this unexpected resistance, some soldiers, aided greatly by naval gunfire, began to move forward. During the morning, the Americans' progress was almost imperceptible to the German defenders and they reported that they had stopped the landing. They had not, although they came the closest of any beach defenses to accomplishing this goal. American casualties at Omaha on D-Day were about two thousand, the highest number on any of the Allied beaches. General Bradley admitted later that a unit less experienced than the 1st Infantry Division might well have been thrown back into the sea by the Germans.[32]

When the Allies landed at Normandy, two of the three panzer divisions directly under Rommel's command were located in the Fifteenth Army's area and therefore unavailable for an immediate response. Only the 21st Panzer Division was in the invasion area, with elements on both sides of the Orne River around Caen and its artillery along the beaches. At 0500 on D-Day, Rommel's headquarters released the division for a counterattack against the British airborne landings east of the Orne.

Around noon, the division was ordered to cross the river in order to attack the British forces that had landed at Sword Beach. British glider troops had seized the now-famous Pegasus Bridge near Bénouville, which forced the German division to move back to Caen in order to cross the river. Because of the resulting delay, the division's counterattack, the only significant one to take place on D-Day, did not begin until 1600.

Although the British held along the beaches, one battalion of the 21st Panzer Division broke through to the coast and threatened to split the British beachhead. The British reaction forced the lone battalion to pull back (a few stragglers held out in a Luftwaffe communications bunker until 17 June). Before dark, the commander of the 21st Panzer Division called off his attack and began to establish a defense against the Allied advance. By the end of D-Day, the Allies had failed to reach their initial objectives but had landed by sea more than 130,000 men from six divisions.

Shortly after receiving word of the Allied airborne landings, Field Marshal von Rundstedt ordered the 12th SS Panzer Division to move to Caen and the Panzer Lehr Division to stand by for such a move. Following these orders, von Rundstedt requested approval for the moves from the OKW, which had kept a string on the armored reserve in the west. The OKW did not approve von Rundstedt's request and directed him to hold any further movement of the two divisions until Hitler approved personally; that approval came about 1600 on D-Day. In the meantime, the weather had cleared and Allied fighters were ranging over the battlefield. Lacking air cover of their own, the panzers were forced to wait until dark to continue their move toward the beaches. The plan was to conduct a two-division coordinated counterattack under the command of the I SS Panzer Corps on 8 June. This attack was postponed and eventually canceled as the Germans became overwhelmed with defensive problems.

To the west, Rommel was trying to prevent the Americans from capturing the port of Cherbourg and, to the east, trying to stop the British from taking Caen and breaking out of the beachhead toward Paris. Although von Rundstedt was planning even bigger counterattacks, the OKW ordered him on 29 June to cancel them and concentrate on containing the beachhead. Before D-Day, Rommel had confided to an old friend that if he could not drive the Allies back into the sea within four days, an invasion would succeed.[33] In retrospect, Rommel was correct, but the Germans were hardly ready to concede defeat at the time.

The Germans still had significant armored forces in the west that remained uncommitted to the battle at Normandy. Two circumstances

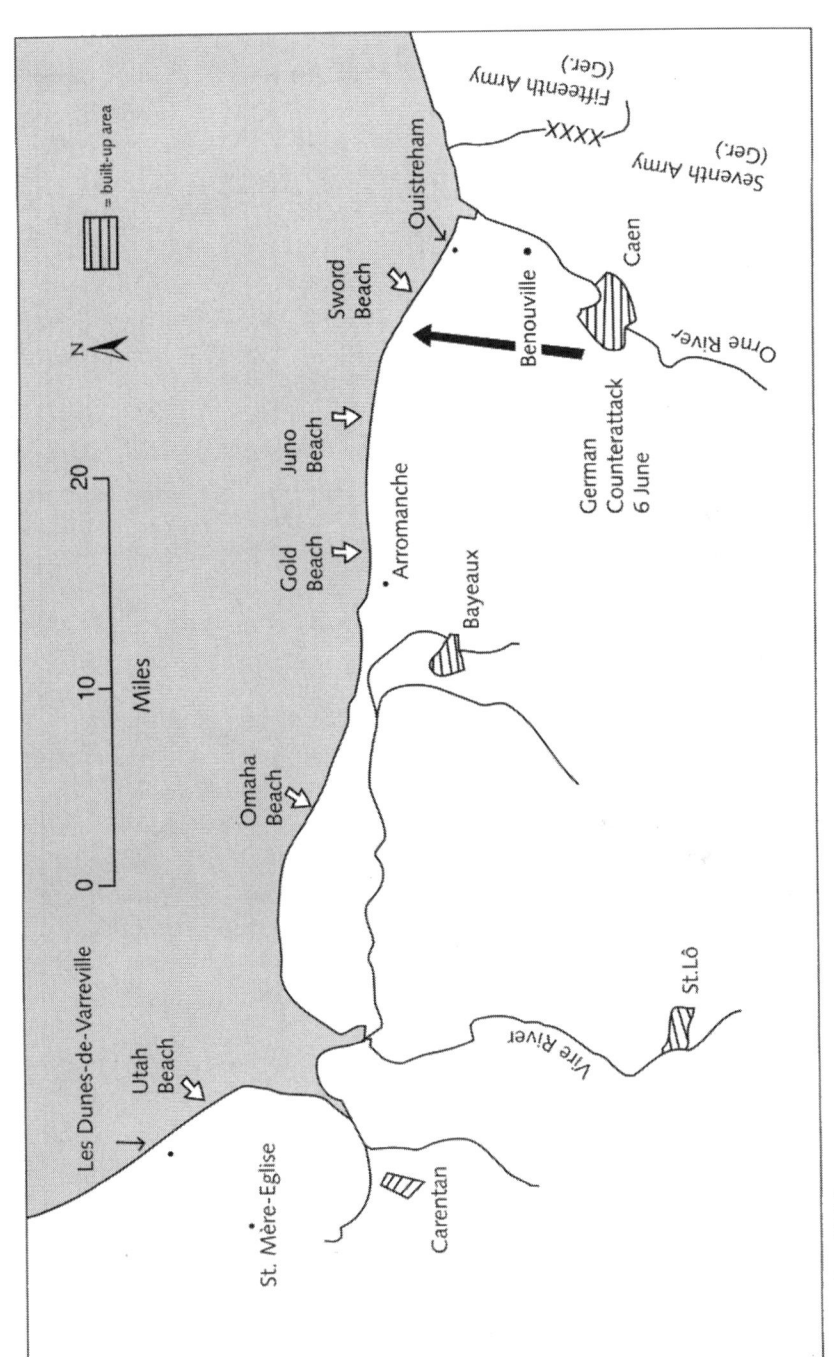

Normandy, 1944

militated against these forces being used decisively to defeat the Allied landing. The first was Hitler's belief that the Normandy landing was simply a supporting attack for a main landing that was still to come at the Pas-de-Calais. This belief was kept alive by the German overestimation of forces remaining in Great Britain and the active Allied deception efforts. As a result, the German dictator would not allow Rommel to shift forces from the Fifteenth Army area until July. The second circumstance was the difficulty experienced by the Germans in moving widely dispersed panzer forces for a counterattack in the face of Allied air superiority. One armored battle group, for example, took more than ten days to move 120 miles from Brittany to the battle area.

Independent of Rommel's efforts ashore, the German navy conducted a limited-scale naval defense against the Allied invasion fleet. Early on D-Day, torpedo boats sortied from Le Havre. Their torpedoes missed the battleships *Warspite* and *Ramillies* but sank the Norwegian destroyer *Svenner*. Unfortunately for the Germans, Allied air superiority hampered movement at sea as badly as it did ashore. Later, night attacks against Allied units, which were usually warned by Ultra intercepts, generally proved unsuccessful.

The Germans had somewhat better luck with their mines. In spite of a sweep operation that involved more than three hundred Allied minesweepers, the small number of mines the Germans had laid before the invasion sank several ships on D-Day and hampered the landing. During the following weeks, the Germans continued to lay mines, including four hundred of the new Oyster mines, by aircraft. Although this type of pressure mine remained unsweepable, examination of one salvaged by the Allies revealed that they would not be triggered by ships sailing at extremely slow speeds. In spite of a variety of Allied countermeasures, German mines sank or damaged forty-three Allied vessels during the operation.[34]

Aggressive antisubmarine efforts by the Allies neutralized the German plans to use submarines against the landing. By 30 June, only four of the twenty-five U-boats ordered to operate against invasion shipping in the English Channel had reached the target area. Of the thousands of Allied ships sailing through the area, German submarines managed to sink only six.[35] The Germans also attempted to employ a variety of midget submarines, manned torpedoes, and explosive motorboats from the KdK at Normandy. Because these units were not fully ready when the invasion started, they had no impact on the D-Day landings. In July and August, however, they had some limited successes. Their most spectacular victory occurred on the night of 7-8 July when a manned torpedo badly damaged the Free Polish Navy cruiser *Dragon*. Beyond repair, the *Dragon* was scuttled to become part of the breakwater at an artificial harbor built by the Allies off the invasion beaches.[36]

Luftwaffe efforts at a naval defense also failed. Allied air patrols generally kept German aircraft away from the invasion area, which made conventional attacks difficult, but the Luftwaffe tried to employ the guided bombs that had been successful at Salerno. Although most attempts were unsuccessful, the Germans did manage to sink one destroyer with these weapons.[37] In the meantime, Hitler had become so concerned about the effect of naval gunfire on the battle for Normandy that he made the Allied battleships a top priority target to be attacked by all possible weapons. On 29 June, he went so far as to declare that the sinking of six or eight battleships would have "the greatest strategic consequences."[38]

Desperate fighting by the defenders, coupled with the sluggish performance of some Allied units, allowed the Germans to contain the beachhead until late July when the Americans broke out at Saint-Lô. Shortly thereafter, the Allies landed successfully in southern France. Neither there nor at the Scheldt estuary in the Netherlands, where the Allies conducted several landings in October and November, were the Germans able to find a solution to the problems of anti-landing defense that had eluded them at Normandy.

Observations

Of all the varied reasons given for the German defeat at Normandy, the one most cited by German participants is the fragmented German chain of command. In spite of Hitler's guidance that the defense should be in the hands of one man, no unified command system existed short of Hitler himself. This virtually ensured a lack of coordination among the services both in preparing the defense and in fighting the battle. The requirement for Hitler to make or approve all important decisions concerning the employment of armored reserves resulted in inevitable delays and doomed to failure any ideas of a mobile defense. Unlike von Rundstedt, General Eisenhower, the Allied supreme commander, exercised command over all the services involved in the landing. His ability to make air, ground, and naval operational decisions without consulting higher authorities gave him an immeasurable advantage over his German opponents.

The Normandy operation illustrates the difficulty of evaluating Admiral Gorshkov's thesis that most landings simply overwhelmed the defender by weight of numbers. Before the landing, the Allies had about fifty-two divisions available in the United Kingdom for the invasion, compared with fifty-eight German divisions available to von Rundstedt for the defense. The amphibious landing pitted three Allied corps with five assault divisions against a single German corps with two divisions along the actual invasion beaches that were backed up by a reserve panzer division relatively close to the coast. Through surprise, the attackers achieved numerical superiority over the defenders but hardly to an overwhelming degree. Although enemy resistance and bad weather caused Allied reinforcement of the beachhead to fall behind schedule, the Allies nevertheless built up their combat power by sea faster than the Germans could by land.

Incredibly, the Germans grossly underestimated the range of Allied naval guns. General Geyr von Schweppenburg, for example, claims that the navy informed him that the naval guns could reach no farther than ten to twenty kilometers inland.[39] Consequently, the Germans were surprised to find themselves under naval gunfire much farther inland. The German situation might have been much worse had Allied planners taken the advice of Maj. Gen. Charles H. Corlett. Gen. George Marshall, U.S. Army chief of staff, had transferred Corlett from the Pacific, where he had commanded the 7th Infantry Division, to Eisenhower's staff in order to give the Allied leader the benefit of his amphibious experience in the Pacific. After reviewing the plans for Normandy, Corlett made several recommendations, including the use of more pre-H-hour naval gunfire.[40] Although the limited availability of gunfire ships and the decision to give up preparation fire in favor of gaining surprise largely prevented Corlett's recommendation from being accepted, there was also a feeling among American planners that Pacific experience had little relevance in the European theater.

One pleasant surprise for the Allies was the lack of gas attacks by the German defenders. Theoretically, chemical warfare would seem to have been an ideal weapon for the Germans, particularly as part of a defense at the water's edge. Defending troops would be both warned and protected, particularly those in concrete emplacements that could be made gasproof. Aware of this threat, the Allies had required assault troops in earlier landings to carry gas masks and, in some cases, wear impregnated clothing. At Normandy, Allied opinion differed. British troops left their chemical warfare equipment behind and landed without gas masks.[41]

American commanders, on the other hand, worried about the effect of a chemical attack on troops landing in open boats or fighting their way across the beaches. General Bradley commented that even light usage of a persistent gas by the Germans on Omaha Beach could have cost his troops their foothold there.[42] When he made that statement, he was thinking in terms of mustard gas. Had he known more about German chemical capability, he would have been even more worried.

Unknown to Allied intelligence, the Germans had developed two nerve gases, tabun and sarin. By D-Day, they had produced enough tabun to use it tactically.[43] Lt. Gen. Herman Ochsner, commander of German chemical troops, concluded that the use of gas against a landing "seemed to hold out good prospects of success, and no technical difficulties were expected."[44] In spite of those prospects, the Germans had no plans to use gas at Normandy.

The reasons for the German failure to use chemical warfare have been the subject of much speculation. The many horrors perpetrated by the Third Reich rule out humanitarian reasons. Explanations range from a personal reluctance on the part of Hitler, who had been gassed in World War I, to fear of Allied retaliation. Retaliation could have affected a variety of targets ranging from German cities to the draft horses on which the German Army relied, even at that late stage of the war. The decision by the Germans not to employ gas at Normandy appears to have been based largely on factors other than whether its use might have defeated the landing.

Beginning with the earliest commando raids, the Germans struggled to find a successful defense against the amphibious assault. The panzer orientation of the German army instinctively drew most of its leaders toward a mobile defense concept. In spite of the consistent failure of the mobile defense in the Italian landings, many Germans believed the fault was not in the concept but, rather, in the execution. In their views, the key to success was a quick decision and early movement of armored forces to the beachhead. Rommel agreed in theory, but he realized that the German command system and Allied air power probably would prevent a mobile concept from being successfully executed. Rommel's answer to these problems, a defense at the water's edge, was doomed by other factors, including the sheer length of coastline to be defended, a successful Allied deception effort, and the combined amphibious power of the Allied armed forces.

6

The Americans Try Their Hand:
Wake and Midway, 1941–1942

Before venturing the defense of atolls as advanced bases, full consideration should be given to the many difficulties of their defense.
Tentative Manual for Landing Operations, 1934

When the United States entered World War II in December 1941, following Japan's naval attack on Pearl Harbor, Hawaii, the German threat of invading Britain had largely passed and the British were preparing to shift from a defensive perspective regarding amphibious warfare to an offensive one. Before the Americans were able to conduct amphibious operations in the Pacific, they too had to go through a period of carrying out defensive operations.

Although the U.S. Army was responsible for American coastal defense and the protection of major overseas bases, the defense of advanced naval bases presented a different problem. The U.S. Marine Corps was a natural choice to seize and defend such bases; following the Spanish-American War, advanced base operations became an increasingly important mission for the Marines.[1] In 1901, the secretary of the navy directed the Marine Corps to create an expeditionary force, later named the Advanced Base Force, for the defense of advanced naval bases.

Between the two world wars, the seizure of advanced bases began to take priority over their defense. In 1923, the Advanced Base Force was renamed the Marine Corps Expeditionary Forces, and work on amphibious operations intensified. A Marine force for the seizure and defense of advanced naval bases was made an integral part of the U.S. Fleet in 1933. One proposed name for it was Fleet Base Defense Force, but the final choice was Fleet Marine Force, a name that would become synonymous with amphibious landings in the Pacific during World War II. In 1939, the Marine Corps began forming defense battalions for the protection of advanced bases; by the time of the attack on Pearl Harbor, seven were in existence.[2]

In addition to creating special defensive forces, the Marine Corps also developed a doctrine for the defense of advanced naval bases. The process began in earnest with the appointment of Brig. Gen. James C. Breckinridge as commandant of Marine Corps Schools at Quantico, Virginia, in 1932. General Breckinridge was determined to make the curriculum of Marine Corps Schools conform to the special missions of the Marine Corps, which included both the seizure and the defense of advanced naval bases. He started his program during the school year 1932–33 with a detailed study of the amphibious operations at Gallipoli during World War I. The following year, classes were suspended so that the staff and students could begin work on the Marine Corps' *Tentative Manual for Landing Operations*.

Issued in 1934, the *Tentative Manual for Landing Operations* contained doctrine for both amphibious landings and anti-landing defense. A 1935 revision removed the defensive doctrine, which was issued separately in 1936 as the *Tentative Manual for Defense of Advanced Bases*. For amphibious landings, a 1938 revision, titled *Fleet Training Publication No. 167, Landing Operations Doctrine, U.S. Navy,* was published; as amended in 1941, 1942, and 1943, it guided U.S. amphibious operations during World War II. For defensive operations, the 1936 doctrine remained in force until 1943, when the navy issued the *Base Defense Manual*. At the beginning of World War II, the Marine Corps was in the unique position of having a true doctrine for anti-landing operations.

Although United States military planners had considered the possibility of war against Japan since the late 1890s, deteriorating U.S.–Japanese relations between the two world wars placed an increased importance on the Marine Corps' capability to both seize and defend advanced naval bases. American planners explored ways of relieving an anticipated Japanese siege of the Philippines. The Japanese, on the other hand, sought a way of defeating the numerically superior American fleet as it headed west. Their answer was a strategy of "interception-attrition operations" that would use aircraft, submarines, and light surface forces to whittle down the U.S. fleet to the point where it could be defeated in a decisive fleet-versus-fleet battle.

Island bases played an important role in the strategies of both the United States and Japan. For Japan, air and naval bases on the Caroline,

Palau, and Marshall Islands would block U.S. access to the Philippines and the Japanese homeland. For the Americans, Pearl Harbor in the Hawaiian Islands would provide the only major fleet base between the Philippines and the U.S. West Coast. The United States had rejected Guam as a possible site for a major base because the harbor at Apra was inadequate and the island's location exposed it to early attack by the Japanese. Other U.S. possessions, including Midway, Johnston, Palmyra, and Wake Islands, that ranged to the west from Hawaii could act as a defensive screen for the fleet base at Pearl Harbor. Wake, in particular, also could provide a potential springboard for future offensive actions. An airfield on Wake, for example, would place U.S. bombers within range of the Japanese-held Marshalls. Such considerations were somewhat academic, however, because Japan, Britain, and the United States had agreed in 1922 to prohibit both the fortification of the Pacific islands and their development as naval bases. The Hawaiian Islands were excepted from the treaty, but Wake and Midway were not.

Treaty considerations did not prevent the U.S. Navy from planning for the use of the outlying islands in case of war. In 1934, for example, the navy surveyed the lagoon at Wake to determine its suitability for use as a seaplane base. The following year, the director of the navy's War Plans Division wrote to the chief of naval operations regarding Wake and Midway: "Either is suitable for use as an auxiliary seaplane base, or a limited base for submarines and light forces provided channel and anchorage improvements are made."[3]

To provide improvements that otherwise would be prohibited by the 1922 treaty, the navy encouraged Pan American Airways to develop the two atolls as bases for their trans-Pacific Clipper flying boats. Pan American started that process in 1935. A 1939 Marine Corps study concluded that the defense of Wake depended on an ability to repel Japanese carrier- and land-based air attacks and that Wake would fall because the navy would not risk the fleet in the island's defense.[4] One positive step was taken in 1941, however, when a supplemental congressional appropriations act allowed the navy to begin construction of an air base on Wake.[5]

Development of an advanced base on Wake raised the question of base defense. The mission was an obvious one for a Marine defense battalion; on 23 June 1941, the chief of naval operations directed that elements of the 1st Defense Battalion be established on Wake "as soon as possible."[6] Initial elements of the battalion arrived on 19 August 1941. When Maj. James P. S. Devereux arrived on 15 October, he assumed command of the battalion and, temporarily, of Wake Island itself. He was relieved as island commander on 28 November by Comdr. W. S. Cunningham, a naval aviator. With the arrival in December of twelve PBY flying boats and twelve F4F-3 Wildcat fighters from Marine Fighting Squadron 211 (VMF-211), the stage was set for Wake's eventual trial by fire.

The Situation at Wake Island

As war clouds gathered over the Pacific, Commander Cunningham's mission took on two aspects. In a narrow sense, he was to hold Wake against an anticipated Japanese assault. In a larger sense, Wake was to play a role that fascinated both U.S. and Japanese naval leaders throughout World War II. Both navies adhered to the concept that a battle between the two fleets could possibly decide the outcome of the war. A possibility of precipitating such a battle would be to hold out an isolated island outpost as bait. In April 1941, Adm. Husband E. Kimmel, commander in chief of the U.S. Pacific Fleet (CinCPac) noted to the chief of naval operations (CNO) that Wake could play just such a role.[7]

In the period immediately before the war started, U.S. naval leaders had a reasonably accurate assessment of Japanese capabilities and intentions regarding Wake Island. In October 1941, Admiral Kimmel estimated that any Japanese force that moved to seize Wake would include four cruisers, six destroyers, and one carrier with forty-eight planes and one thousand troops.[8] His estimate approximated the three cruisers and six destroyers used by the Japanese in their first attempt to seize Wake two months later, but Kimmel overestimated by twice the number of landing troops and was incorrect regarding the carrier. In the first attempt, the Japanese relied only on land-based aircraft from the Marshalls. All elements of the naval task force assigned to seize Wake—landing force, ships to transport and support it, and aircraft from the 24th Air Flotilla in the Marshalls—were commanded by Rear Adm. Shigeyoshi Inouye, commander of the Japanese Fourth Fleet.[9]

To defend against the attack, Commander Cunningham had 449 Marines, 74 unarmed naval and Army Air Corps personnel, and 1,200 civilian construction workers. Of the Marines, 61 belonged to VMF-211 and flew or serviced its twelve F4F-3 Wildcat fighters. The task of physically defending the island against a landing fell to the 15 officers and 373 men of the 1st Defense Battalion under Major Devereaux. As Marine detachment commander, Devereaux nominally commanded VMF-211 as well. After the war, however, Maj. Paul A. Putnam, VMF-211's commanding officer, revealed that he had received secret orders from Vice

Adm. William F. Halsey that placed the squadron under the admiral's personal control and subject to sudden recall.[10] Devereaux was under the command of Cunningham, the island commander, whose chain of command went back to CinCPac.[11]

Personnel shortages limited Devereaux to manning only six of his twelve 3-inch antiaircraft guns and half of his heavy machine guns. All six 5-inch seacoast guns were manned, but the Marines had a limited amount of conventional fire-control equipment and no radar.[12] In their plans, the Japanese had estimated that the Americans had fifteen fighter planes, 1,000 troops, and 600 laborers on Wake.[13]

Two geographic aspects of Wake affected its defense. The first was its location 2,000 miles west of Hawaii. Also, Wake was more than 1,000 miles from other U.S bases at Guam to the west and Midway to the east, but it was well within range of Japanese bombers from the Marshalls, 660 miles to the south. The second geographic aspect involved the characteristics of coral atolls. In developing defensive doctrine, the Marine Corps had specifically identified a number of these characteristics, including the lack of cover and concealment from air attack and naval gunfire, limited area to emplace and disperse antiaircraft and seacoast batteries, a lack of depth for defense, and numerous landing places.[14] The three islands that make up the atoll cover 2,600 acres and have a total coastline of more than 21 miles. The *Tentative Manual for Landing Operations* recognizes better knowledge of the terrain as one of the advantages of a defender. The question facing the defenders of Wake Island was whether their superior knowledge would outweigh the many disadvantages they faced.

The American Plan

In planning the defense of Wake, the American commanders had the advantage of a doctrine for the defense of an island base against an amphibious operation. In most respects, the eventual loss of Wake reflects the inability of the defenders to adhere to the doctrine. The *Tentative Manual* recognizes two types of anti-landing defenses: (1) a mobile defense based on strong counterattacks, which it designates the "active defense," and (2) a defense at the water's edge, which it calls the "decisive defense at the water's edge."[15] The doctrine also clearly recognizes the difficulty of implementing either type of defense on a small atoll. An attacker is considered to be most vulnerable while transferring troops to the landing craft and forming boat waves for the landing. Although it exhorts the defenders to make all efforts to stop the landing at this point, the *Tentative Manual* also recognizes that "the enemy's ships' gun and aerial bombardment will be particularly violent at the water's edge and directly inland," requiring that the defensive position be concealed, hardened, and dispersed for the defenders' protection.[16]

The small size of Wake limited the ability of Major Devereaux to site both his seacoast and antiaircraft batteries. The *Tentative Manual*, for example, recommends 1,000 yards between primary and alternate positions for antiaircraft batteries, a physical impossibility for most batteries on Wake.

The *Tentative Manual*, however, is not entirely unrealistic. Anticipating the conditions that might surround the defense of an advanced base such as Wake, it notes that the defenders would require "the highest order of skill and ingenuity in economizing, organizing, and disposing the forces."[17] In meeting this charge, the Marines found ways to use cement bags and empty ammunition boxes in place of sandbags, site 3-inch antiaircraft guns for dual employment as seacoast guns, improvise sound detectors, and jury-rig a means of using welding oxygen to augment VMF-211's short supply for its pilots. Unfortunately, improvisation could not make up for the lack of both naval and land mines, barbed wire, and other barrier materials recommended by the *Tentative Manual*.

Time and bureaucracy also worked against the defenders. Until the actual Japanese attack, naval planners gave a higher priority to the construction of Wake's airfield than to its defense. Doctrine recognized the need to bury communication wires, for example, to protect them from enemy fire. The Marines were unable to accomplish this with hand tools in Wake's hard coral surface, but they could not get permission from the civilian contractor to use its mechanical ditchdiggers. Neither were the Marines able to use the contractor's personnel to mount the seacoast guns and fortify the positions. The Marines were able to mine the runway with heavy dynamite charges at 150-yard intervals.[18] The *Tentative Manual* discusses both the offensive and defensive aspects of chemical warfare. It notes: "Troops debarking from transports and other surface craft into small boats are an exceedingly vulnerable chemical target."[19] The defenders of Wake had no chemical weapons, but they were equipped with gas masks.

With the exception of the twelve fighters of VMF-211 and the 5-inch seacoast guns, the defenders of Wake Island lacked the forces needed to conduct a naval defense. The small size of Wake also precluded a mobile defense. By elimination, Major Devereaux planned a defense at the water's edge. Compounding his shortage of gun crews was a complete lack of infantry to conduct even local counterattacks. This lack of organic infantry was a particular weakness of the defense battalion organization. By Saturday, 6 December 1941, the 1st Defense Battalion had its guns mounted. The Marines held simulated gun drills, but no firing. Their first chance actually to fire the guns would be against a Japanese landing.

The Defense of Wake Island

Sunday, 7 December 1941, the date Americans remember for the Japanese attack on Pearl Harbor, was a day of rest and quiet on Wake Island. Wake is west of the international date line and twenty-two hours ahead of Hawaii. That 7 December on Wake was still Saturday, 6 December, at Pearl Harbor. Shortly before 0700 on 8 December, the garrison at Wake received word that Pearl Harbor was under attack by Japanese aircraft.

At 1158 that morning, thirty-six twin-engine bombers from the Japanese 24th Air Flotilla at Roi Island in the Marshalls attacked Wake Island. The primary objective of the attack was Wake's airfield and VMF-211. In that respect, the attack was quite successful. Four Marine Wildcats took off to challenge the attackers. They all returned, but one was damaged on landing. Of the eight planes remaining on the ground, seven were destroyed and one damaged. The attack also killed or wounded more than half of the squadron's personnel.[20]

The next two days followed a similar pattern. Taking off from Roi at dawn each day, Japanese bombers appeared over Wake shortly after 1100. The defenders met them first with Wake's three remaining fighters and then with antiaircraft fire. Although the Marines forced the Japanese to pay a price for their successes, they could not stop the attackers. After the first attack on the airfield, the Japanese turned their attention to Major Devereaux's 3-inch and 5-inch batteries. These attacks damaged some of the guns and also forced the Marines to spend valuable time in moving the guns to alternate positions between attacks. The defenders realized that these attacks were preparatory to an invasion but had no idea of when a landing would come.

The suspense ended just before 0300 on 11 December. Marine lookouts reported a number of ships headed toward Wake from the south. Admiral Inouye would have liked to continue softening up his target for a few more days, but the Japanese war plans had a strict timetable that called for Wake to be seized by the 11th. Just before 0700, three Japanese destroyers began a gunfire run close along the shore of Wilkes Island.

The two 5-inch guns of Battery L opened fire and sank the destroyer *Hayate* with three salvoes, thus giving her the distinction of being the first Japanese surface ship sunk by U.S. naval forces during World War II.[21] After this and several similar, but less decisive, duels between the ships and shore batteries, the Japanese broke off the action. The three remaining fighters of Wake's "air force" then attacked the withdrawing ships; the Marines sank the Japanese destroyer *Kisaragi* and damaged several other ships, including the transport *Kongo Maru*.

As early as 9 December, Admiral Kimmel's staff began planning for the relief of Wake. After a number of delays, reinforcements left Pearl Harbor on 15 December—the carrier *Saratoga,* with VMF-221 embarked, and the seaplane tender *Tangier* carrying Marines from the 4th Defense Battalion and fire-control equipment that included radars, ammunition for Wake's guns, barbed wire, and antipersonnel mines. The voyage of this task force, under Rear Adm. Frank Jack Fletcher, was characterized by caution and delays for refueling that, in hindsight, might have been unnecessary.

The Japanese, following their initial defeat, approached the invasion with increased determination. They listed the causes of the failure of the first landing, in order, as vigorous seacoast artillery fire, determined fighter opposition, adverse weather, and insufficient Japanese forces.[22] Unable to influence the weather, the Japanese worked to correct the other problems before trying again. Land-based bombers continued to pound Wake; on 21 December, they were joined by bombers and fighters from the carriers *Soryu* and *Hiryu*. On 22 December, the Japanese attained uncontested air control over Wake by destroying the island's last remaining Wildcat fighter.

Before dawn on the following day, the second Japanese landing on Wake was under way. At 0245, a Marine searchlight revealed landing barges on Wilkes Island and two larger ships beached on Wake Island. Having earlier felt the effect of the Marines' gunnery, Japanese gunfire ships remained out of range of Wake's 5-inch guns. Lacking infantry force, the Marines were unable to halt the Japanese advance on Wake Island itself. On Wilkes Island, however, the defenders had not only held but were in the process of a counterattack when they received word at 1330 that Major Devereaux had surrendered. Hampered by poor communications, Devereaux was unaware of the situation on Wilkes. Marines attempted to destroy the airfield, but they were unable to start the generators needed to fire the demolition charges.

Meanwhile, Admiral Fletcher's task force, after reaching a point 425

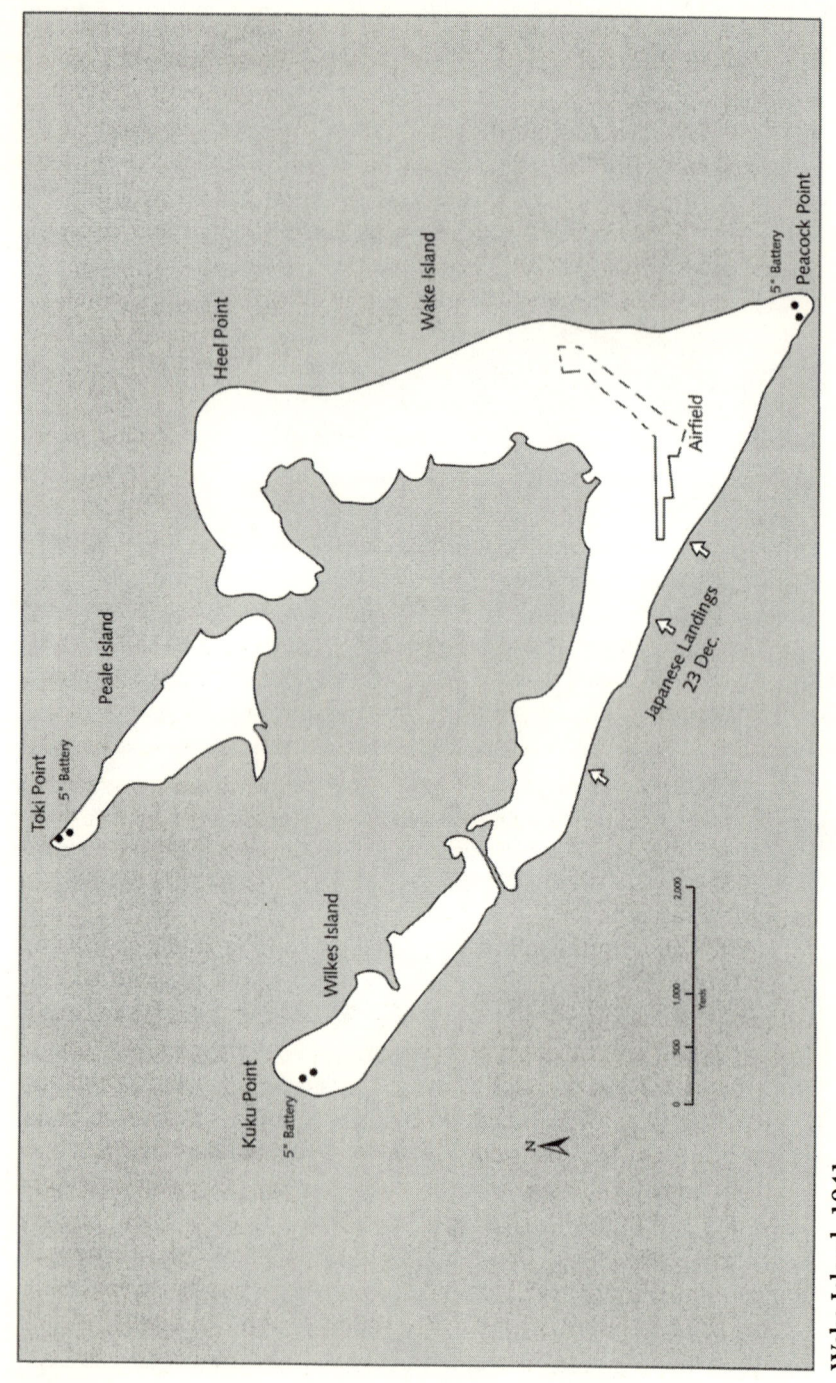

Wake Island, 1941

miles from Wake, was recalled 2.5 hours before the surrender. Without those forces, Wake's defeat was inevitable. Had his landing force not prevailed, the Japanese commander was prepared to beach his destroyers and land their crews to prevent another humiliating defeat.

Wake's defenders, although defeated, could point to several accomplishments. At the cost of 171 casualties, including civilians, the Americans inflicted more than 1,000 casualties on the victors. The heroic defense of Wake also provided a much needed psychological boost for the American public at a very dark time. Finally, although unsuccessful, the defense confirmed the general soundness of the U.S. anti-landing doctrine, an important point for the Marines who were preparing to defend another Pacific outpost at Midway.

The Situation Following the Loss of Wake

Most important, however, the Japanese victory at Wake confirmed the widely held view that an attacker who has gained sea control and air superiority over the defender of a small atoll eventually will be able to land successfully, regardless of any type of defense offered at the beach. The official Marine Corps history of the battle notes that, if the defense force had included a single company of infantry and a platoon of light tanks, it might have repelled the Japanese landing.[23] That might well be true, but without an American naval effort to contest sea control and air superiority, the Japanese would simply have tried again until they succeeded.

Following their success at Wake, the Japanese continued to gain a seemingly unending string of victories in the Pacific. On 15 February 1942, Singapore fell. Earlier in the Malayan campaign, land-based Japanese navy bombers had sunk the British battleship *Prince of Wales* and the battle cruiser *Repulse*. These losses reinforced the views of aviators on both sides that ships were no match for airplanes. One small American success came on 18 April when a group of Army Air Corps B-25 bombers from the carrier *Hornet* bombed Tokyo and several other Japanese cities. The raid, led by Lt. Col. James H. Doolittle, produced negligible military results, but it did have a major psychological impact on the Japanese. Naval leaders were particularly embarrassed by their failure to prevent the attack. This embarrassment appears to have fired an intense desire to lure the U.S. Navy into a major battle, in which the Imperial Japanese Navy could redeem itself.

The first opportunity came on 7–8 May 1942 during the Battle of the Coral Sea. During the action, the first true carrier battle in history, each side sank an enemy carrier. Their losses forced the Japanese to abandon a planned amphibious operation to seize Port Moresby on New Guinea's Papuan Peninsula. Before the battle, a split had developed within the Japanese navy regarding strategic direction. The naval general staff supported an effort to take Fiji and Samoa to cut the sea lines of communication between the United States and Australia. Adm. Isoroku Yamamoto, commander in chief of the Combined Fleet, on the other hand, envisioned an ambitious operation that would begin with the seizure of Midway. He believed that the U.S. Navy would react to such a move, thereby precipitating a major fleet battle. Following a Japanese victory in that battle, the way would be open to seize Hawaii and finish what the Japanese had started at Pearl Harbor.

A compromise combined Yamamoto's Midway operation with a diversionary move into the North Pacific to seize islands in the Aleutian chain. The resulting plan was complicated and would require the U.S. Navy to react in the way anticipated by the Japanese for them to succeed. Unfortunately for the Japanese, American cryptologists had broken the Japanese naval code, known as JN25, and pieced together the outline of the Japanese plan, including the designation of Midway as the main target. Armed with this knowledge, Adm. Chester W. Nimitz, commander in chief, Pacific Ocean Areas, planned to hold Midway by setting a trap for the Japanese invaders.

The Situation at Midway

With the aid of the intercepted Japanese communications, Nimitz's staff estimated that the Japanese naval force at Midway would total thirty-eight to fifty-four ships, including four or five carriers.[24] Although the Midway force of the Combined Fleet had only four carriers, it was much larger overall than the Americans estimated.

Almost one hundred Japanese ships were divided into several major groups, including the main force under Admiral Yamamoto, the First Carrier Striking Force under Vice Adm. Chuichi Nagumo, the Northern (Aleutians) Force under Vice Adm. Moshiro Hosogaya, and the Midway Invasion Force under Vice Adm. Nobutake Kondo. The invasion force was a self-contained task organization with its own naval gunfire ships, supporting aircraft carrier, and minesweepers, in addition to transports.[25] The landing force of about five thousand troops, under the overall command of navy Capt. Minoru Ota, consisted of Ota's 2d Combined Special Naval Landing Force and the army's Ichiki Detachment under

Col. Kiyonao Ichiki.[26] The plan was to land on both of Midway's islands, Sand and Eastern, from the south and use a variety of landing craft and rubber boats, if necessary, to get across Midway's reefs.[27]

U.S. plans for Midway's defense actually began in 1938 when a congressional board identified the atoll as a naval base of strategic importance, second only to Pearl Harbor.[28] In 1939 and 1940, the navy and Marine Corps made a series of surveys; on 14 February 1941, the 3d Defense Battalion arrived on the atoll to construct defenses. Because of the primitive conditions on Midway, the Marine Corps planned to rotate units. The 6th Defense Battalion arrived on 11 September 1941 to relieve the 3d Defense Battalion. Between then and the end of May 1942, the 6th Defense Battalion received a series of reinforcements, including those on the USS *Tangier* that had been intended for the garrison at Wake Island. By the time of the Japanese attack, the 6th Defense Battalion (Reinforced) consisted of a seacoast artillery group of two 3-inch, three 5-inch, and two 7-inch guns; a variety of antiaircraft batteries ranging from 20-mm to 3-inch guns; two provisional companies of infantry, two companies from the 2d Raider Battalion, and a platoon of light tanks.[29] The addition of infantry and tanks to the defense corrected one of the fatal weaknesses of the garrison at Wake Island. Midway's garrison eventually numbered more than three thousand men.[30]

Naval Air Station Midway had been commissioned in August 1941 under the command of Comdr. Cyril T. Simard, an experienced naval aviator who had been handpicked for the job by Admiral Nimitz. Ten days after Pearl Harbor, seventeen SB2U-3 Vindicator dive-bombers from Marine Scout Squadron 231 (VMSB-231) arrived at Midway, after flying from Oahu Island, Hawaii, in what was then the longest massed flight by single-engine planes on record. They had been followed on Christmas Day by fourteen F2A-3 Buffalo fighters from VMF-221. The fighters, originally intended for the defense of Wake, had flown off the *Saratoga*. As a battle off Midway appeared imminent, Commander Simard's Balsa Air Force—so called because of Midway's code name, Balsa—increased with the addition of PBY-5A flying boats from several patrol squadrons and an Army contingent of B-17s and B-26s from Hawaii. A final reinforcement of SBD-2 Dauntless dive-bombers and F4F-3 Wildcat fighters brought Midway's air strength for the coming battle to 121 planes.[31] In accordance with the provisions of the *Tentative Manual*, all of these aircraft were under the command of Cyril Simard, who had been promoted to captain by Admiral Nimitz following a visit to Midway. Unfortunately, no truly integrated plan was developed to coordinate the operation of these disparate groups or coordinate Midway's air force with carrier-borne aircraft that would operate in the area.

The Japanese made a reasonably good estimate of Midway's air strength—two squadrons of flying boats and one each of bombers and fighters—and also noted that the numbers could be doubled in an emergency.[32] They correctly estimated that Midway was strongly defended by a variety of antiaircraft and large-caliber seacoast guns and that the bulk of the defenders were U.S. Marines.

With respect to terrain, Midway's defenders faced the same problems that had plagued the Marines at Wake. Midway's two islands were slightly smaller in size than Wake's three, and the lack of depth posed the same limitations on defensive schemes. Geographically, however, Midway's situation was almost the reverse of Wake's. Whereas Wake had been out of range of U.S. land-based aircraft and within range of Japanese planes, Midway could be reinforced by air from Hawaii. The Japanese, on the other hand, were forced to rely solely on carrier aircraft.

Another important distinction between the two battles related to the time factor. When Wake was attacked, the U.S. Pacific Fleet was still reeling from the results of Pearl Harbor and its commander was understandably cautious about risking his carriers in battle against the Japanese. By the time of Midway, new U.S. naval leadership and American actions in the Coral Sea had produced a more balanced view of both U.S. and Japanese capabilities. The intervening five-and-a-half months had also given Midway's defenders an invaluable respite in which to prepare for a landing, an advantage that had been denied the garrison at Wake. Referring to naval preparations for the upcoming battle, Admiral Nimitz said on 23 May, "Time is everything."[33]

The American Plan

Midway's defenders were precluded from following the target priorities specified in the *Tentative Manual* by Admiral Nimitz's guidance that Midway's air forces were to be used primarily to inflict early damage on the Japanese aircraft carriers. Marine doctrine agreed that the carriers should be the highest priority target when first detected but that emphasis should shift to the transports and landing craft once the landing began.[34] Limited in their ability to stop a landing force at sea, the defenders planned to deal with them ashore. Given the small size of Midway's two islands, Col. Harold D. Shannon, commander of the

6th Defense Battalion, planned an area defense at the water's edge. Unlike Major Devereaux at Wake, however, Shannon had infantry units and tanks with which to make counterattacks should the Japanese succeed in getting forces ashore. Shannon also had been given the time, personnel, and materiel needed to carry out the tenets of the *Tentative Manual*.

In the waters off of possible landing beaches, the Marines laid 380 shallow-water controlled mines that had been improvised from sealed sections of sewer pipe filled with dynamite and wired for electrical detonation.[35] Closer to the beach were underwater obstacles constructed of concrete reinforcing rods. Possible landing beaches were covered with pressure-actuated antitank mines and homemade antipersonnel mines containing 20-penny nails and dynamite that could be detonated electrically or by rifle fire. Colonel Shannon was a veteran of World War I, and the respect that he had gained for barbed wire during that conflict could be seen in his defense at Midway. Barbed-wire obstacles designed to channelize attacking Japanese into the defenders' machine-gun fire were constructed around the perimeter of both islands, and individual gun emplacements were ringed by protective wire. In contrast to Wake, civilian construction crews worked with the Marines in building defenses. As a result, Shannon was able to protect his gun positions, bury his command posts in concrete bunkers, and build enough protective shelters so that every man could sleep underground.

Based on the lesson of Wake, antiaircraft guns at Midway were sited for dual-purpose employment whenever possible. At Midway, both islands had infantry for counterattacks, and the Marines dug revetments in a wooded area on Sand Island for the five light tanks. Radio circuits were paralleled by telephone wire that was buried for protection from enemy shelling. Because the American commanders were concerned about a chemical attack, they issued gas masks and impregnated clothing to all hands and made decontamination materials available. Shannon ordered each position to fight to the last man and gave the troops Molotov cocktails to deal with Japanese tanks. Seacoast and antiaircraft gun crews had practiced against towed targets. All that remained was contact with the enemy.

This occurred at 0925 on 3 June 1942 when a PBY from Midway sighted six large ships seven hundred miles to the southwest. During the epic sea battle on 4 June, Midway's garrison launched a series of air attacks against the Japanese fleet. The island also suffered several attacks by Japanese carrier-based aircraft. Because the decisive Japanese defeat that followed precluded any chance of a successful landing on Midway, the island's defenses were never tested.

Observations

The battles at Wake and Midway illustrate the relationship between amphibious operations and the actions required to achieve sea control and air superiority in the vicinity of a landing. If an attacker is allowed to isolate an island objective by gaining and maintaining sea control and air superiority, the best that a determined defender can hope to achieve is to delay the eventual victory by the attacker. Without sea control and air superiority, the defenders of Wake almost certainly would have been eventually overcome, even with the additional ground forces and equipment that were later available to the garrison at Midway.

At Wake and Midway, the defenders had a doctrine for defense against an amphibious landing. The speed with which the garrison at Wake was overcome reflected, in part, the inability of the Marines there to implement the doctrine. In planning for the defense of Midway, the defenders used the same doctrine, but they had the time and resources needed to implement it.

Although the Battle of Midway was not a naval defense against an amphibious operation, it had the same effect on the planned Japanese landing. After losing their fleet carriers, the Japanese would have been hard-pressed to save their amphibious forces from defeat at sea had they attempted to land on Midway. Colonel Shannon's defensive plan combined a defense at the water's edge with a significant number of naval mines off the beaches. Given the small size of the Japanese minesweeping force, the mines would have presented a significant obstacle. Had the Japanese attempted to land, naval historian Samuel Eliot Morison believes that the Marines would have given them "an even hotter reception" than the Marines were to receive at Tarawa.[36] Morison indicates that, in his opinion, Midway's defenders would have been able to hold the island.

The Japanese themselves attributed their failure to an effective naval defense: "The landing operation against Midway Island in June 1942 failed because the enemy uncovered the plan while the movement was still underway, and launched naval and air attacks against the convoy."[37] In this respect, the *Tentative Manual* is particularly prescient:

> The defense has one marked advantage, at the outset, in that the destruction of the enemy's floating air bases might force the withdrawal of

the landing force without the necessity of defeating that force in a land battle.[38]

Because of the state of American defenses at Wake Island and the lack of a landing at Midway, the ability of fully prepared U.S. forces to defend against a Japanese landing was never tested in those battles. Before such a test could occur, the roles of the two opponents were reversed with respect to amphibious warfare.

Japanese Naval Defense:
The Southwest Pacific Area, 1942–1944

We were prepared to fight to the last man, but we wanted to die gloriously.
Rear Adm. Tomiji Koyanagi, "With Kurita in the Battle of Leyte Gulf"

With their eastward move stopped by the American victory at Midway, the Japanese again turned their attention south. Although one objective was to cut U.S. lines of communication between Hawaii and Australia and New Zealand, Imperial General Headquarters postponed an operation designed to accomplish that aim by seizing New Caledonia, the Fijis, and the Samoan Islands.[1] The combined loss of aircraft in the battles of the Coral Sea and Midway precluded this operation for the time being. Another objective was to consolidate the outer defense perimeter in the South Pacific designed to protect the newly acquired natural resources in the East Indies. Capture of Port Moresby with its airfield was critical to that particular effort, but the Battle of the Coral Sea had thwarted Japanese attempts to achieve that goal by an amphibious assault. On 12 June 1942, the Army Section of Imperial General Headquarters ordered the Seventeenth Army, under Lt. Gen. Seikichi Hyakutake, to seize Port Moresby by an overland attack across the Owen Stanley Mountains that run like a spine down the Papuan Peninsula.[2]

To protect the eastern flank of the New Guinea attack, the Japanese had seized Tulagi in the Solomon Islands for use as a seaplane base. Capt. Shigetoshi Miyazaki, Tulagi's commander, soon recognized the advantages to be gained from a Japanese airfield on nearby Guadalcanal. Planes could bomb American bases in New Caledonia and threaten U.S. sea lanes to Australia and New Zealand. Fighters on Guadalcanal would also protect the important Japanese naval base at Rabaul on New Britain Island 540 miles to the north. The Navy Section of Imperial General

Headquarters approved Captain Miyazaki's idea in early June 1942, and construction troops began arriving on Guadalcanal shortly thereafter. By early August, the field was nearing completion.

Unfortunately for the Japanese, the Americans were also quick to appreciate the importance of the Solomons. The chain of islands represented a two-way street. If the islands provided an avenue of approach for the Japanese to attack U.S. sea lanes, they also provided the Americans an avenue of approach to Rabaul. Gen. Douglas MacArthur, the U.S. theater commander, had initially proposed an invasion of Rabaul, but he encountered resistance from naval officers who considered the target too ambitious to be feasible at the time. The Joint Chiefs of Staff eventually engineered a compromise in the form of a three-phased offensive starting with the seizure of Tulagi and ending with the capture of Rabaul. In June and July 1942, most of the 1st Marine Division was moved to New Zealand, with the expectation that the Marines would spearhead the offensive planned for early 1943. When aerial reconnaissance revealed construction of the airfield on Guadalcanal, the U.S. timetable was advanced drastically and the first landings scheduled for early August 1942.

The Situation at Guadalcanal

The mission of Japanese forces in the region that the Allies (United States, Australia, and New Zealand) called the Southwest Pacific Area (SWPA) was to consolidate the outer defensive perimeter of their newly conquered empire and to counter an anticipated Allied offensive. Although the Japanese had correctly estimated that the Allies would begin their offensive in the southern Solomons, details about American capabilities and intentions were sketchy at best. By early August 1942, the Japanese knew that an American task force with three carriers was approaching the Solomons, but they were unaware of the mission of the enemy force.[3]

The task force in question was an expeditionary force, under the command of then Vice Admiral Fletcher, that included the carriers *Saratoga, Enterprise,* and *Wasp* and an amphibious task force, under Rear Adm. Richmond Kelly Turner, that carried the 1st Marine Division (Reinforced). Although the division was missing one of its three infantry regiments, reinforcements brought its strength to more than 16,000 men. Command structure for the assault was the result of a compromise between Admiral Nimitz and General MacArthur, Nimitz's counterpart in the SWPA.

When planning for the U.S. offensive began, Tulagi and the other initial objectives were located in MacArthur's theater. Guadalcanal did not become an objective until after discovery of the airfield under construction there. Although MacArthur "owned" the objectives, Nimitz controlled the only forces capable of conducting the amphibious landing required to seize the objectives. As a result, the Joint Chiefs of Staff divided the offensive Solomons campaign into three phases: (1) the capture of Guadalcanal, (2) seizure of the other islands in the Solomon group and Japanese positions on New Guinea, and (3) the capture of Rabaul and adjacent bases on New Britain and New Ireland. The boundary between the two theaters was moved slightly to place Guadalcanal in Nimitz's theater. Following seizure of that target, however, Nimitz would turn over to MacArthur adequate amphibious forces to complete the remaining stages of the counteroffensive. Although some American command problems surfaced during the battle for Guadalcanal, the command arrangement provided for unity of command within naval forces and among services.

The Japanese had slightly more than 2,500 men, all of them construction troops, on Guadalcanal. Across Sealark Channel on Tulagi and on the two small connected islands of Gavutu and Tanambogo were fewer than 900 troops from the Yokohama Air Group, a construction unit, and the Kure 3d Special Naval Landing Force (SNLF). The landing force totaled 400 men, the only real combat troops available to meet the coming U.S. landing. The chain of command that linked the defenders of Guadalcanal and Tulagi with Tokyo was a naval one that ran from the Navy Section of the Imperial General Headquarters through the Combined Fleet and the Eighth Fleet.

For administrative purposes, the Imperial Japanese Navy used a system of numbered fleets that could also assume an operational role under a title that best translates to "force." At the start of the war, for example, the Fourth Fleet had been responsible for defense of the newly captured Pacific empire under the operational title of the South Seas Force. As the size of the captured territory expanded, command became unwieldy. To ease this situation, the Japanese high command split the area into Inner South Seas and Outer South Seas Areas on 14 July 1942.[4] Admiral Inouye, Fourth Fleet commander, became the Inner South Seas Force commander and remained responsible for the defense of the former Japanese mandates in the Central Pacific. The southwest Pacific became the Outer South Seas Area, and the navy created the Eighth Fleet to defend it. Vice Adm. Gunichi Mikawa assumed command of the new fleet on 23 July.

Japanese land-based naval aviation came under command of the Eleventh Air Fleet, known operationally as the Base Air Force. Vice Adm. Nishizo Tsukahara exercised command through a number of air flotillas. Naval aircraft at Rabaul and Tulagi belonged to the 25th Air Flotilla, which had the operational title of Fifth Air Attack Force. In case of attack, provisions were made to give Admiral Tsukahara operational control of the Fourth, Eighth, and Sixth (submarine force) Fleets. On 7 August 1942, the day of the American landing, Tsukahara relieved Mikawa as commander of the Outer South Seas Force. To complicate the Japanese command picture further, Tsukahara relinquished his new command shortly thereafter to become commander of the newly established Southeast Area Force, an intermediate level of command between the Combined Fleet and the two South Seas Force commanders.

American intelligence for the Guadalcanal landing had been limited. Estimates of Japanese troop strength ranged from 3,100 to 8,400.[5] Accurate maps of the area were unavailable, and aerial photographs of the landing beaches had failed to reach the 1st Marine Division before D-day. The best the Marines had come up with were hand-drawn sketches made by former residents of the islands that proved to be inaccurate.

Although Tulagi, Tanambogo, and Gavutu are tiny, Guadalcanal is slightly larger than the state of Delaware. The islands in the Solomon group are characterized by great variations in relief and by jungle extending nearly to the water's edge, which results in narrow beaches. Long coastlines and numerous landing beaches usually made defense at the water's edge impractical. At the same time, dense jungle precluded the rapid movement of large forces required by a mobile defense. The remaining option was a naval defense. Had the Japanese completed the airfield on Guadalcanal and made it operational, an American landing would have been immensely more difficult, if not impossible. Any delay in the U.S. attack would have clearly worked to the defender's advantage.

The Japanese Plan

Because the Japanese had not anticipated an American offensive before 1943, defensive plans for the area were very general in nature. The Outer South Seas Force defensive concept envisioned daylight attacks by land-based navy planes as the primary means of defense. Until the airfield at Guadalcanal became operational, the planes would have to come primarily from Rabaul. The plan considered naval surface forces—largely cruisers and destroyers—to be both a secondary means of attack and the bait to lure U.S. naval forces into the range of land-based aircraft. When possible, surface forces would attack at night. Finally, submarines would support both air and surface attacks.

The Struggle for Guadalcanal

On 7 August 1942, U.S. amphibious forces caught the Japanese by surprise at Guadalcanal and Tulagi. On Guadalcanal, the naval construction troops building the airfield quickly fled into the jungle, which allowed the 1st Marine Division to land unopposed. Across the channel at Tulagi, Tanambogo, and Gavutu, members of the Kure 3d SNLF, the Yokohama Air Group, and the 14th Construction Unit conducted a hastily organized defense at the water's edge. Shortly after the Marines landed, the defenders sent a message stating their intention to fight to the last man.[6] By the time the Marines had secured the three islands, 836 Japanese had been killed, 23 had been captured, and about 40 had escaped by swimming to nearby Florida Island.[7]

Although the shore defenses were quickly overcome and the Japanese failed to repulse the landing, the defenders had given their American adversaries a taste of the "fight-to-the-last-man" style of combat that would become the hallmark of Japanese defensive operations in the central Pacific.

As Japanese shore defenses were being quickly overcome, the initial attempts of the Japanese to conduct a naval defense came close to succeeding. On the morning of 7 August, the 25th Air Flotilla at Rabaul diverted an air strike planned against the Allied air base at Milne Bay, New Guinea, to attack U.S. shipping off Guadalcanal. The raid damaged a U.S. destroyer but produced no other significant results. On the following day, the Japanese again tried air strikes. The primary targets were American aircraft carriers, but, failing to find them, the bombers returned to Guadalcanal for an attack on the transports. Alerted, the transports got under way and met the raid with heavy antiaircraft fire. Although one transport was badly damaged and sunk in shallow water, the raid did not halt the unloading of vital supplies for the landing force.

During the air attacks, a Japanese naval force of two cruiser divisions, under Vice Admiral Mikawa, was en route to Guadalcanal to engage the invaders. Aware of the danger posed by U.S. carrier aircraft, Mikawa had carefully planned his approach route to avoid detection. He also timed his arrival at Guadalcanal to allow a surprise night attack on the Allied

Naval defense at Guadalcanal. The Japanese defense included attacks by torpedo bombers on the amphibious ships.
(U.S. Navy photo, No. 12923)

naval forces there, with sufficient time to withdraw out of the range of American aircraft before dawn. During the ensuing battle, called the Battle of Savo Island by Americans, Mikawa's force sank four heavy cruisers but suffered no significant damage itself. After inflicting on the U.S. Navy one of its worst defeats ever, Mikawa was now in a position to destroy the unprotected American transports. Still fearing an air attack and unaware that the American carriers were retreating, however, Mikawa chose to withdraw.

Having failed to destroy the American amphibious force at sea or prevent it from landing, the Japanese reverted to a mobile defense concept ashore that was designed to drive the invaders back into the sea. Because their initial forces on Guadalcanal were not large enough to conduct such a counterattack, the Japanese first had to deliver additional troops to the island. This brought the Japanese army into a previously all-navy operation. Interjection of army forces into the battle for Guadalcanal further complicated the already complex chain of command.

Like the Japanese navy, the army had its own chain of command in the theater that ran from the Army Section of Imperial General Headquarters through Southern Army headquarters at Saigon to the Seventeenth Army under General Hyakutake, who commanded army forces in both New Guinea and the Solomons from his Rabaul headquarters. As Hyakutake was increasingly forced to focus on the defense of Guadalcanal, army headquarters transferred responsibility for New Guinea to the Eighteenth Army and established the 8th Area Army at Rabaul to oversee both the Seventeenth and Eighteenth Armies. Although the nature of the theater required joint operations, the Japanese never achieved unity of command under a common superior in the SWPA. They had to depend on cooperation between the services, but, unfortunately for them, army-navy cooperation was never very good.

As the impact of the American seizure of Guadalcanal sank in, Japanese army and navy leaders agreed on the need to eject the invaders and recover the airfield as quickly as possible. Immediately available for the task was the Ichiki Detachment of 2,000 troops that had been slated earlier to seize Midway Island (see chapter 6). Colonel Ichiki's force was staged in Guam with its shipping. The detachment sailed south and, during the night of 18–19 August, landed 900 men on Guadalcanal southwest of the American perimeter. Although the plan called for the remainder of the detachment to be landed five days later, Ichiki decided to launch his attack on the airfield without waiting for reinforcements. He based his decision partly on an inaccurate estimate of the number of Marines defending their airstrip, which they called Henderson Field in honor of a Marine aviator killed during the Battle of Midway.

Ichiki, an impetuous infantry officer, also based his decision to attack immediately on his contempt for an enemy that he believed to be weak and lacking in martial spirit. Warned by patrols of the impending attack, the Marines prepared by establishing a defensive line along a tidal inlet that they mistakenly called the Tenaru River. Without pausing to conduct an adequate reconnaissance, Ichiki launched a frontal attack on the Marine position at 0200 on 21 August. Slowed by barbed wire obstacles, many of the Japanese attackers died before reaching the Marine positions. After daylight, the Marines counterattacked and killed most of the survivors of the previous night's battle. With no hope of accomplishing his mission, Ichiki burned his regimental colors and committed suicide.

The defeat of Ichiki and his detachment did not end Japanese attempts to recapture Guadalcanal, but it could be said to have marked the end of a Japanese mobile defense against an amphibious operation. Following Ichiki's defeat, the battle for Guadalcanal became a ground battle in the jungle for possession of Henderson Field. The two sides then started a race to build up forces on the island. For the Japanese army, the operation changed from supporting the New Guinea campaign to being the primary focus of the theater. A combination of the operational necessity to control the airfield and the army's wounded pride resulting from its first defeat caused the Japanese to make ever increasing efforts to retake Guadalcanal. Although they had built up their forces on the island to 30,000 men by November 1942, they were not enough to dislodge the 29,000 Americans who had reached Guadalcanal during the same period.[8]

Japanese attempts to reinforce and resupply Guadalcanal resulted in a number of sea battles. Typically, the battles were night surface actions, but carriers on both sides engaged in several day battles. The Japanese tried to use transports and landing barges to reinforce their troops on Guadalcanal, but these craft were too slow to make the round trip down the "Slot" between the Solomon Islands and back before daybreak exposed them to American air attacks. They next employed warships—primarily destroyers and submarines—to resupply Guadalcanal. This effort proved to be inadequate and also diverted the warships from more offensive missions. Facing inevitable defeat, Imperial General Headquarters, on 31 December 1942, decided to evacuate the army from Guadalcanal. During three nights in early February 1943, a total of 10,652 Japanese troops left Guadalcanal with such stealth that the Americans were not aware of their escape.[9]

The Situation from Guadalcanal to Leyte Gulf

The battle for Guadalcanal set a pattern for much of the fighting in the SWPA. The area remained a troublesome, economy-of-force theater for both sides. The U.S. Army's focus was on Europe and the eventual invasion of the continent, and the army sent forces to General MacArthur reluctantly. The Imperial Japanese Army, in a similar position, regarded the war in China as its primary business. Both navies considered the SWPA to be a dangerous place, where ships in restricted waters were constantly exposed to the threat of land-based aircraft. The Americans and Japanese both regarded the central Pacific as the theater most likely to provide the setting for a decisive sea battle between the two fleets.

As it had at Guadalcanal, terrain throughout the SWPA forced the Japanese to rely largely on naval defense. The efforts to conduct such a defense resulted in a chesslike game of maneuver with MacArthur's forces that depended highly on time and space factors; the most important of these was the range of land-based fighter aircraft. Because neither side could rely on the availability of aircraft carriers, both needed airfields to support their operations. The Japanese knew the range of American fighters and could reasonably predict the limits within which the Americans could make their landings. For the Americans, Japanese airfields made logical targets for amphibious operations. The Americans needed sea control and air superiority to conduct their landings. The Japanese, on the other hand, needed sea control both to conduct a naval defense against the American landings and to move ground forces within the theater. As the Allies gained control of the air, they were able to deny the use of the sea to the Japanese during the day.

The Japanese navy was thus forced to operate at night when it was largely protected from American airpower and when its superior night-fighting skills offered an advantage over its opponents. Although the Japanese often prevailed in the night battles, they felt the impact of their losses more than did the Allies. In conducting this naval campaign, the Japanese also appear to have suffered what the British might call a failure of maintenance of the aim. The Allies had several clear objectives. Their initial objective was to seize Rabaul and then move on to the Philippines. As the campaign developed, it became more advantageous to isolate Rabaul rather than seize it, but the overall campaign aims remained intact. The Japanese understood the importance of both Rabaul and the Philippines but were unable to maintain a consistent plan to deal with the Allied advance.

U.S. actions in the central Pacific kept the Japanese in the SWPA off balance at both the strategic and operational levels. The Allies had the forces to support two separate drives toward Japan, MacArthur's in the SWPA and Nimitz's in the central Pacific. The Japanese, on the other hand, relied much more on moving naval forces back and forth between the two theaters. On 1 November 1943, for example, the U.S. 3d Marine Division landed at Cape Torokina on Bougainville in the northern Solomons. In response, the Japanese Combined Fleet ordered air and surface units that had been staged in the central Pacific to move to the Solomons. On 20 November, before the Japanese forces could reach Bougainville, the 2d Marine Division landed on Tarawa in the Gilbert Islands.

In the hope of precipitating a major naval battle in the central Pacific, the Combined Fleet recalled its forces en route to the Solomons. In the process of refuelling at Rabaul, a major part of this force was caught in an American air raid. According to a Japanese officer, the raid was more catastrophic for the Japanese than Pearl Harbor had been for the Americans.[10]

Within the SWPA theater, the Japanese were similarly caught between the two prongs of MacArthur's drive, one along New Guinea's coast and the other up the Solomons through the Bismarck Archipelago to the Admiralties. Most were unopposed or lightly opposed at the beaches, although fierce jungle fighting for airfield objectives often developed after the landings. A typical Japanese naval reaction consisted of air strikes on the beachhead and offshore shipping at daylight on D-day that were followed by night surface attacks as soon as possible. The Japanese navy was never again able to duplicate the success of Savo Island and the resulting opportunity to attack amphibious shipping at a critical moment. Frustrated in their attempts to defeat Allied landings by conventional means, the Japanese looked for new techniques. Two appeared to be promising.

The first was the idea of a counterlanding. The Japanese were not inexperienced in amphibious operations; they had pioneered the development of landing craft and ships during the 1930s. They also had troops trained in amphibious warfare in the theater. Understanding the confusion that reigns early in a landing, the Japanese reasoned that one way to disrupt an amphibious landing would be to counterattack it not from the land but from the sea by a so-called counterlanding.

In response to the American landing at Cape Torokina, the Japanese navy had planned such an operation. Transports from Rabaul would land 1,000 troops to assault the American beachhead, while the escorting cruisers and destroyers attacked U.S. ships nearby. Unfortunately for the Japanese, they were detected some distance from Cape Torokina by U.S. search aircraft. The transports were ordered back to Rabaul at that point. The escorts sailed on and were intercepted by a U.S. Navy force; the resulting action became known as the Battle of Empress Augusta Bay. Before dawn on 7 November 1943, Japanese destroyers did manage to land about 475 soldiers just outside the U.S. beachhead. The counterlanding force caused some damage before the Americans destroyed it after daylight.[11] In the course of the SWPA campaign, the Japanese attempted several counterlandings but were never able to make a significant effect on an American landing.

The Japanese tested a second defensive idea at Biak, a rugged island

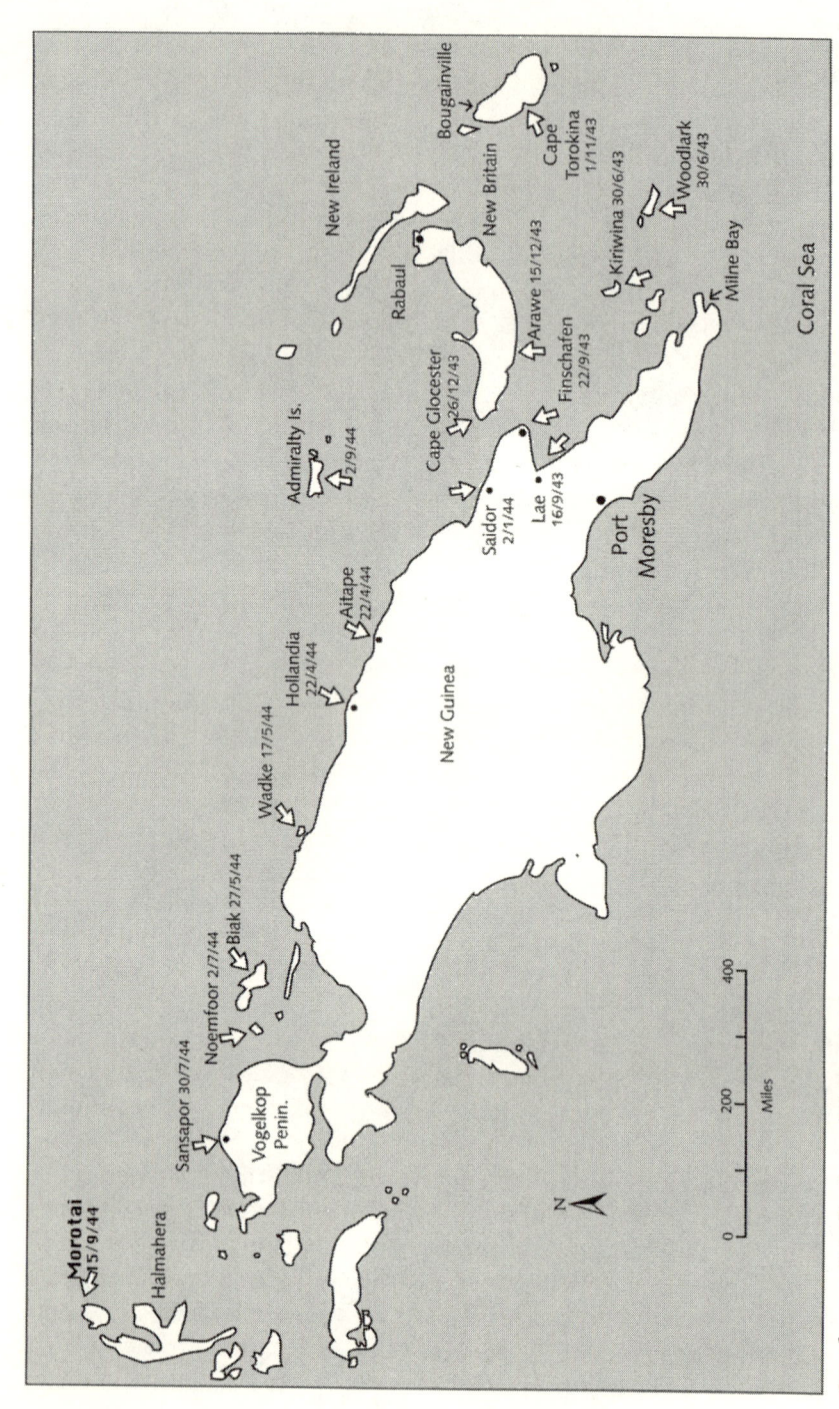

Southwest Pacific Area, 1943–1944

Natural caves, Biak in the southwest Pacific. The Japanese used an extensive network of limestone caves to create a defense in depth in order to delay the American attackers.
(U.S. Army photo, No. SG 239021)

in the mouth of western New Guinea's Geelvink Bay. They had originally envisioned Biak as a major defensive position with several important airfields. Before their plan was fully developed, however, they moved the main defensive line northward and left Biak as an outpost to the main position.

Although the island's defenders still hoped to defeat any landings on the beaches, experience made the Japanese less than confident of their ability to do so. As a result, Col. Nauyuki Kuzume, Biak's commander, created a defense in depth that was designed to deny the Allies the use of the island's airfields as long as possible. Basing his defense on Biak's system of natural limestone caves, Kuzume developed what the Japanese called *dogutsu sakusen* (cave tactics). Natural caves both inland and overlooking some of the potential landing beaches were improved by tunneling and the use of concrete to form artillery casemates, fighting positions, and bombproof bunkers. Defending troops were exhorted to sell themselves dearly and to hold each position to the last man, rather than waste their lives in futile banzai attacks.[12]

Although the Japanese navy had initially given up the hope of using Biak as an air base, it had not abandoned the idea of forcing a decisive sea battle with the U.S. Fleet. By early 1944, the Combined Fleet had developed yet another plan to accomplish that elusive goal—an operation designated A-GO. Japanese planners anticipated that the battle would take place around the Palau Islands but also considered New Guinea and the Marianas as possibilities.[13] Again, however, the Japanese found themselves caught between competing priorities. American carrier raids in the Marianas raised concerns about a landing there. On 27 May 1944, however, two regiments of the U.S. Army's 41st Infantry Division landed on Biak, which forced the Japanese navy to reconsider the impact of losing that island's airfields. As a result, the Japanese navy transferred a large number of aircraft from the central Pacific to the SWPA to attack the invaders.

Additionally, the Japanese began planning a joint operation to reinforce the beleaguered island. Designated Operation KON, the attempted relief developed into three separate operations. All involved warships, transports, and barges to carry the reinforcements. Based on faulty estimates of U.S. strength, including the belief that the Americans had at least one carrier, the relief forces twice turned back upon discovery by U.S. ships or aircraft. For a third attempt, a force was marshalled that included the two most powerful battleships in the world, the *Musashi* and *Yamato*.

On 15 June 1944, before the Japanese could launch their third attempt to relieve Biak, three American divisions landed on Saipan in the Marianas. Repeating the scenario that had played out earlier between Bougainville and Tarawa, the Japanese navy canceled the third KON operation, attempted to return remaining naval aircraft to the central Pacific, and sent the Combined Fleet northward toward the Marianas to execute operation A-GO. The resulting Battle of the Philippine Sea virtually destroyed Japan's naval aviation arm. By failing to focus their aim on saving either Biak or the Marianas, the Japanese ensured that they would lose both. Following a two-month battle for Biak, MacArthur's forces took Noemfoor, seventy miles west of Biak; the Vogelkop Peninsula at the western end of New Guinea; and Morotai Island, between New Guinea and the Philippines, in quick succession. In the Philippines, the Japanese were forced to consider the likelihood of invasion.

The Situation in the Philippines

Because the inner Japanese defense line already had been broken with the loss of the Marianas, the question arose as to the value of trying to hold the Philippines. For the navy, the question was one of oil. Loss of the Philippines would effectively sever the sea lines between Japan and the oil fields of the East Indies. Even if the Combined Fleet could be successfully withdrawn to Japanese home waters, it would be useless without access to fuel. As a result, the navy was willing to gamble loss of the fleet to save the Philippines. Many naval officers also continued to believe that a major naval victory could still turn around the war in the manner of Adm. Heihachirō Togō's victory in the Tsushima Strait, located between Korea and Japan, during the Russo-Japanese War. The army did not have such a singular focus, but many army officers considered the Philippines to be the ideal place to throw off the Allied timetable significantly by conducting a protracted delaying action. The geography of the Philippines also allowed for the employment of land-based aircraft against the American fleet.

Although the Japanese had gained much experience in fighting the Americans, their estimates about a U.S. invasion of the Philippines were not always reliable. In a Southern Army war game conducted in Manila in August, for example, the scenario realistically included an American invasion starting at Leyte with four or five divisions.[14] With respect to estimates of U.S. naval strength, on the other hand, the Japanese made a particularly serious miscalculation. In response to their increasingly desperate situation, they developed four defense plans titled SHO-GO, or victory operations. SHO-1 concerned the Philippines; SHO-2, Formosa; SHO-3, southern and central Japan; and SHO-4, Hokkaido and the Kurile Islands.[15]

In response to U.S. Navy carrier attacks on Formosa in October 1944, the Japanese initiated SHO-2. They launched large-scale air attacks against the U.S. fleet that resulted in the loss of as many as 655 Japanese planes.[16] The ultimate impact on the Japanese was twofold. First, the operation destroyed a large number of aircraft and pilots that otherwise could have reinforced the Philippines. Second, the Japanese made the wildly exaggerated claim of having sunk or damaged 57 enemy warships, including 11 carriers sunk and 8 others damaged.[17] In fact, they had sunk no U.S. ships. Apparently relying on their own exaggerated claim, however, Japanese naval leaders believed that they would execute their SHO-1 plan against greatly reduced U.S. naval forces.

The truth was quite the opposite. The attack force for the Philippines was the U.S. Seventh Fleet under the command of Vice Adm. Thomas C. Kinkaid. For the assault, Admiral Kinkaid had 577 ships, including 6 old battleships, more than 100 other surface combatants, 18 escort carriers, and more than 400 transports and amphibious ships of various types. Kinkaid was supported by Adm. William Halsey's Third Fleet from the central Pacific. With 17 carriers and 6 fast battleships, Halsey's mission was to soften up the target and protect the landing forces from the Japanese fleet. The weakness in American naval plans was not in resources but in the command arrangements. Kinkaid took his orders directly from General MacArthur, but Halsey reported to Admiral Nimitz in Hawaii and operated only in support of General MacArthur. Ground forces for the Philippine assault consisted of the U.S. Sixth Army, under Lt. Gen. Walter Krueger, with six divisions, all but one of which had seen action against the Japanese.[18]

To meet the American attack, the Japanese assembled a large force. It suffered from numerous training deficiencies and materiel shortages, however, and was also encumbered by a complicated command structure that failed to provide the same degree of unified command as did the U.S. system. In August 1944, the Japanese high command elevated the Fourteenth Army to area army status and made its commander, Lt. Gen. Shigenori Kuroda, responsible for the defense of the Philippines. Kuroda's overall force included Lt. Gen. Sosaku Suzuki's Thirty-fifth Army headquarters, nine divisions, and three independent brigades.[19]

In addition to ground forces, the Japanese army had two air divisions, with approximately two hundred planes, in the Philippines.[20] They were part of the Fourth Air Army commanded by Lt. Gen. Kyoji Tominaga. He and Kuroda both reported to Field Marshal Hisaichi Terauchi, commander of the Southern Army. In October 1944, the Japanese had 432,000 men in the Philippines for the defense of the islands.[21]

Although the Japanese navy's air arm had been decimated at the Battle of the Philippine Sea, the navy still possessed a number of powerful ships. Available to Combined Fleet for the defense of the Philippines were seven battleships, including the *Yamato* and *Musashi,* four carriers, and two hybrid battleship-carriers.[22]

General Suzuki estimated that the Americans would attack the Philippines as early as 1 October.[23] In fact, the U.S. plan originally called for an invasion of southern Mindanao on 15 November, with a Leyte landing not scheduled until 20 December.[24] After extensive discussions, which included consideration of bypassing the Philippines in favor of an assault on Formosa, U.S. planners decided to bypass the southern Philippines initially and land at Leyte on 20 October.

The Japanese Plan

Anticipation of an American landing in the Philippines resulted in a discussion among Japanese commanders on anti-landing defense, not unlike the one that had preoccupied German commanders during the period before Normandy. With the exception of the urgency of the situation, the Japanese leaders found few areas of agreement, either between the services or within them. For the August war game in Manila, they had chosen Leyte as the site of the American landing because that location represented the weakest point for the defenders. General Kuroda, however, believed that Luzon afforded the greatest opportunity for an extended land defense, a view shared by Gen. Tomoyuki Yamashita, who took over Kuroda's command of the 14th Area Army shortly before the planned U.S. invasion date.

Japanese army doctrine still directed commanders to annihilate an amphibious attacker at the beach. Based on a lack of success with defense at the water's edge and the favorable experience with cave tactics gained at Biak and the Marianas, however, the army commanders began to hedge their bets. The Army Section of Imperial General Headquarters began work on an anti-landing concept that included an initial main line of resistance far enough inland to limit the effects of prelanding naval gunfire bombardments, construction of defensive positions in depth to delay an enemy advance after landing, and strong reserve forces held back for counterattacks.[25]

Lt. Gen. Shira Makino, commander of the 16th Division, which was responsible for the defense of Leyte, adopted the new concept for this defense. He neither mined the beaches nor erected underwater obstacles. He halted efforts to construct fortified positions along likely invasion beaches and started construction farther inland. With only a single division to defend a large island, Makino was limited in his ability to conduct counterattacks. The Japanese army made plans to reinforce Leyte, but the ability to carry them out depended on its willingness to shift forces from Luzon, where it planned to fight its primary battle, and on the navy's ability to transport the reinforcements to Leyte. The navy's focus, however, was not on transporting troops.

Most of the navy's senior leaders still clung to the hope of a dramatic naval action, even if it resulted in the final destruction of the Combined

Fleet. The plan for SHO-1 reflected just such a view. In short, this complicated plan called for Vice Adm. Jisaburo Ozawa's Mobile Force, consisting of Japan's remaining aircraft carriers, to act as a decoy in drawing Admiral Halsey's Third Fleet from Leyte Gulf and its mission of protecting the invasion forces. With Halsey away, two powerful Japanese battleship forces would approach Leyte Gulf from different directions, break through the remaining U.S. naval defenders, and attack the vulnerable transports off the landing beaches. One remaining question was how to protect the Japanese surface ships from American airpower during their voyage to Leyte Gulf.

Having lost most of their remaining carrier aircraft during the Battle of the Philippine Sea, the Japanese were forced to rely on land-based planes to protect their fleet and attack that of the enemy. Army and navy air forces operated through separate chains of command, with no common superior short of Tokyo; plans for combined use of the air forces had to be based on cooperation—never good between the two services—and on an agreement regarding division of labor. Because most army pilots had no experience with navigation out of sight of land, they were given the mission of attacking enemy transports during the landing. The navy pilots were assigned the primary mission of attacking American carriers. Timing was critical. The Japanese high command considered American amphibious operations to have three distinct phases: (1) air strikes several days before a landing, (2) air and naval gunfire strikes immediately before the landing, and (3) the actual landing of troops.[26] Perhaps a contributing factor in earlier Japanese failures at defense had been attacking enemy aircraft carriers prematurely, with the result that the available Japanese air forces were inadequate to attack the landing itself. If so, the solution was to hold back their forces initially in order to deliver a powerful blow at the right moment.

The complicated Japanese plan developed for the defense of the Philippines required experienced aviators and enough time to prepare the defense. Earlier defeats had already deprived Japan of its best aviators. The U.S. decision to advance MacArthur's timetable for the Leyte landing now deprived the Japanese defenders of the time required for their preparations.

The Battle for the Philippines

On 18 October 1944, the Japanese activated SHO-1, based on an intercepted U.S. message that a landing would be made between Dulag and

San Jose on the east coast of Leyte.[27] Two days later, four divisions from the U.S. Sixth Army began landing across those same beaches. Resistance on the beaches was sporadic, as indicated by American casualties. On A-day (a designation chosen by MacArthur to avoid being overshadowed by D-Day in June at Normandy), total casualties for the Sixth Army were 49 killed, 192 wounded, and 6 missing in action.[28] The light casualties did not reflect a Japanese reluctance to fight but, rather, General Makino's decision not to fight on the beaches where naval gunfire would give the attackers a significant advantage.

Meanwhile, the Japanese navy was setting into motion the operation that would precipitate one of the world's epic sea battles, a series of actions that have been collectively called the Battle of Leyte Gulf. As prescribed by SHO-1, the First Diversionary Attack Force, under Vice Adm. Takeo Kurita, departed its base at Brunei on 21 October and headed for Leyte Gulf via the Sulu Sea and San Bernardino Strait. Kurita's orders directed him to break into the American anchorage on 25 October and destroy the enemy ships there. Two less powerful Japanese forces with similar missions were to enter Leyte Gulf by way of Surigao Strait. On the night of 24–25 October in Surigao Strait, the smaller Japanese units were ambushed and almost totally destroyed by a U.S. task force commanded by Rear Adm. Jesse B. Oldendorf.

Meanwhile, Admiral Kurita's force appeared to be on the verge of striking a major blow against the American beachhead after an inauspicious start; several of his ships had been sunk by U.S. submarines, and the giant battleship *Musashi* had been sunk by U.S. carrier planes. On the morning of 25 October, Kurita's force emerged from San Bernardino Strait to find that Halsey's Third Fleet, which had been operating off the strait, had been lured north by Admiral Ozawa's empty carriers. All that remained between Kurita's attack force and the beachhead was a U.S. task force of sixteen escort carriers and their protecting destroyers and destroyer escorts. Created to provide close air support for amphibious landings, the task force was clearly no match for the heavy guns of Japanese cruisers and battleships. To the amazement of the Americans, the Japanese withdrew after sinking a carrier, two destroyers, and a destroyer escort.

Apologists for Admiral Kurita point to his state of exhaustion from almost complete lack of sleep for three days and the stress of having his flagship sunk out from under him earlier in the battle. The admiral himself rationalized that, even had he continued on, he would have arrived five days after the landing, too late to affect its outcome. While true, this

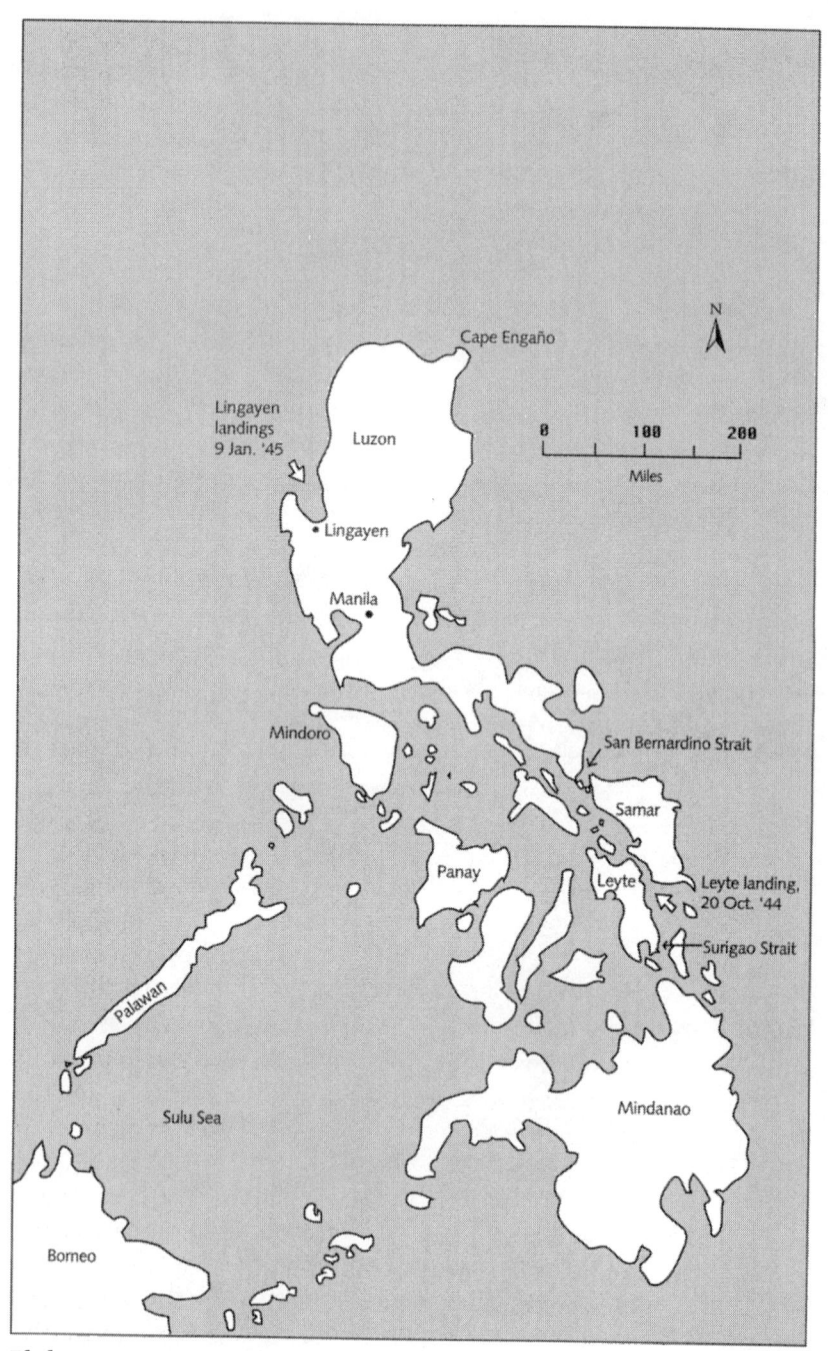

Philippine Islands, 1944–1945

reasoning disregards the fact that his orders called for him to proceed at any cost. Kurita's explanation also fails to account for General Makino's belief that the 16th Division could defeat the U.S. forces on Leyte if the Japanese navy isolated the beachhead and cut off the Americans from their sources of supply.[29] Kurita's orders did have an escape clause, however, that allowed him to temporarily divert his effort in order to attack the main U.S. fleet if the opportunity arose. Kurita might have been hoping for that opportunity. To die fighting battleships and carriers would be to die gloriously; to die attacking empty transports would not.

After the battle, one of Kurita's complaints was that he had not been supported by Japanese aircraft during his perilous journey to Leyte Gulf. The lack of support resulted not from error but from a decision on the part of Japanese air commanders to use available aircraft to attack the U.S. fleet rather than to protect their own.[30] The Japanese aviators began the action with conventional bombing and torpedo attacks, but then introduced a horrific new antiship tactic: the suicide attack.

Suicide had long played a role in Japanese society, usually as a means of atoning for failure or shameful conduct. During the war, Japanese skippers frequently chose to go down with their ships, and soldiers and sailors alike commonly killed themselves and their wounded comrades, rather than be taken prisoner. Pilots of severely damaged planes had chosen to crash into enemy ships instead of trying to escape. During the Biak landing, an army plane had deliberately crashed into an American submarine chaser to sink her. In spite of these precedents, the idea of sending pilots on deliberate suicide missions troubled many Japanese leaders.

Initially, the three senior aviation commanders in the Philippines, Admirals Shigeru Fukudome and Takijirō Onishi and General Tominaga, all resisted suicide tactics. Others, including Rear Adm. Masabumi Arima, commander of the 26th Air Flotilla, believed that Japan's only hope lay in drastic measures. On 15 October, Arima joined an attack launched against the American fleet and announced that he was going to "body-crash" into an American carrier. He actually crashed into the sea, but he became an instant hero to the Japanese public and was given credit for sinking a carrier.[31]

As the seriousness of the Japanese situation became apparent, Admiral Onishi changed his views. The day on which the Americans landed at Leyte Gulf, he created the Divine Wind Special Attack Force consisting of pilots from the 201st Air Group. Although various terms were used to describe the suicide units, the Japanese press began to use the term *kamikaze* and other translations of the characters for "divine wind,"

Kamikaze units, 1944. Disappointed with the results of conventional air attacks, the Imperial Japanese Navy created the first official Divine Wind Special Attack [kamikaze] Force during the battle for the Philippines.
(U.S. Army photo of a captured Japanese print by Ihara Usaburo)

the name given to a storm that had saved Japan from an invasion in 1281. Official kamikaze attacks began on 21 October with an attack against the heavy cruiser HMAS *Australia*, which was badly damaged. The following day off the Leyte beaches, the tug *Sonoma* and *LCI 1065* became the first vessels sunk by the kamikazes.[32]

Suicide attacks against American shipping continued at Leyte and against later Philippine landings, such as the one at Lingayen Gulf, until 10 January 1945, when as many of the remaining Japanese pilots as could flew to Formosa. Those who could not escape joined the army forces to conduct guerrilla warfare against the advancing Americans. During the course of the kamikaze campaign, the Japanese had launched almost two hundred suicide attacks that sank twenty-three Allied ships and damaged eighty-six others.[33]

Although the kamikazes presented an extremely serious problem, they were unable to prevent any of the Philippine landings. The Japanese army was equally unsuccessful in its anti-landing role, although it continued to conduct a land campaign in the Philippines for the remainder of the war.

Observations

General MacArthur, aided by a unified command structure, established one overriding strategic aim—to return to the Philippines—from which he never retreated. Although intermediate objectives, such as the capture of Rabaul, were altered to meet changing circumstances, the ultimate aim remained constant. The Japanese, on the other hand, had no similar maintenance of an aim and found themselves torn between competing strategic, operational, and tactical goals. Reflecting on this problem after Leyte Gulf, Admiral Kurita noted, "We should have chosen the single, definite objective, stuck to it, and pushed on."[34] Although he directed the comment to his defeat at Leyte Gulf, it could sum up the entire Japanese campaign in the southwest Pacific.

General MacArthur attained unity of command at the theater level. Although he did not use a task force system with a single subordinate command of all services involved in a landing, as was done in the central Pacific, MacArthur's close personal involvement generally precluded any serious problems. The major exception occurred at Leyte Gulf with Halsey's Third Fleet, which was not under MacArthur's command. When the fleet was lured away from San Bernardino Strait, it left the way to the beachhead unguarded. In contrast to the American system, the Japanese had no system for unified command short of Imperial General Headquarters in Tokyo. As a result, cooperation between their army and navy ranged from simply poorly coordinated to downright obstructionist. Lack of unity of command was a major obstacle to successful anti-landing defense.

Given the forces available to MacArthur, he can hardly be said to have overwhelmed the Japanese numerically with respect to the theater as a whole. By using the mobility inherent to naval forces, however, he was often able to achieve a more than adequate force ratio at the point of landing. He initially invaded the Philippines, for example, with an army of six divisions. The Japanese had nine divisions plus other forces available for defense. By choosing to land his six divisions at Leyte, MacArthur was able to achieve a force ratio of six to one at the beachhead itself.

Throughout the campaign, conducting the landings as soon as possible, even at the expense of more thorough preparation, worked to the advantage of the attacker. Delay at Guadalcanal would have allowed the Japanese to complete the airfield there, perhaps with disastrous consequences to the Allies. Advancing the timetable for Guadalcanal caused serious problems for the U.S. attackers but allowed them to catch the Japanese defenders by surprise. The controversial American decision to advance the date for the Philippine invasion and to bypass Mindanao in favor of Leyte paid equally great dividends. Adm. Soemu Toyoda, who had commanded the Combined Fleet on its way to Leyte, agreed; he stated that the major reason for failure of the SHO-1 plan was having to execute it before his forces were fully prepared.[35]

Terrain in the theater largely dictated a naval defense against landings. Generally, long coastlines precluded a defense at the water's edge, and jungle terrain inland limited any type of mobile defense. Naval defense, on the other hand, came close to succeeding at both Guadalcanal and Leyte Gulf. Japanese navy leaders never really supported the idea of destroying an enemy amphibious force as long as the possibility of a full-fledged sea battle existed. One of Admiral Kurita's commanders summed up this point of view after Leyte Gulf when he said that sacrificing the Combined Fleet to destroy a bunch of cargo ships would have made Admiral Togo weep in his grave.[36] Although they failed to stop the invasion of the Philippines, the kamikazes appeared to have the potential power to defeat a landing. In less than six months, U.S. amphibious forces would face a naval defense based almost entirely on the suicide tactics pioneered in the Philippines.

Japanese Defense at the Water's Edge:
The Gilberts and Marshalls, 1943–1944

If the enemy starts a landing, knock out the landing boats with mountain gun fire, tank guns and infantry guns, then concentrate all fires on the enemy's landing point and destroy him at the water's edge.
Yokosuka 6th Special Naval Landing Force Battle Dispositions, October 1942

While the Japanese were fighting in the Southwest Pacific Area to hold back MacArthur's advance, a different type of amphibious war was developing in the central Pacific. As 1943 drew to a close, the Americans were about to take a major step in the development of amphibious warfare. Admiral Nimitz was preparing to launch his drive into the central Pacific by deliberately attacking a heavily defended atoll. This assault would be the first test of U.S. amphibious doctrine and technique against this type of target. The Japanese, on the other hand, faced the challenge of turning away such an assault. Surprisingly, the Japanese had not been preparing for this moment as long as the Americans believed.

The Japanese had seized the Marshalls, Marianas, Carolines, and Palaus from Germany in 1914 and occupied them after World War I under a League of Nations mandate. Under the terms of the mandate and also those of a treaty signed with the United States, the Japanese promised not to establish fortifications or bases in the islands that became known collectively as "the mandates." Unfortunately, neither agreement provided for inspection of the mandates and neither contained official definitions of fortifications and bases. A policy of secrecy implemented by the Japanese made many westerners suspicious that the mandates were being turned into military bases. In fact, Japan made no major improvements in the islands until 1934 after it withdrew from the League of Nations.[1]

In 1934, the Japanese began a five-year construction program that concentrated on airfields and seaplane ramps. Although they believed that such developments could be considered economic improvements, rather than bases, they nevertheless concealed the purpose of the projects. No defensive garrisons were sent to the mandates until 1940.[2]

In this period just before the outbreak of war, both the Americans and the Japanese began to focus attention on the British Gilbert Islands to the southeast of the Marshalls. In 1941, President Franklin D. Roosevelt considered asking for lend-lease use of the Gilberts for building air bases. Adm. Harold R. Stark, chief of naval operations at the time, discouraged such a move on the grounds that it might provoke a Japanese preemptive attack.[3] The Japanese, on the other hand, realized that airfields in the Gilberts would threaten their own bases in the Marshalls. Accordingly, in November 1941, the Japanese Combined Fleet issued orders directing the South Seas Force to seize the Gilberts at the start of hostilities. On 9 and 10 December 1941, naval landing forces captured Tarawa and Makin without resistance. The Japanese started construction of a seaplane base on Makin, and a detachment of the unit that captured the island remained there to guard it. All other forces were withdrawn.[4]

During the first year of war against the United States, the Japanese navy's attention was diverted from the Gilberts to the Solomons and New Guinea in the southwest Pacific. Japanese concern grew when the Japanese troops were unable to drive the Americans from Guadalcanal. Ironically, however, one U.S. action conducted to divert Japanese attention from Guadalcanal resulted in reviving Japan's interest in the Gilberts.

On 17 August 1942, ten days after the landing on Guadalcanal, U.S. Marines from the 2d Raider Battalion landed from two submarines on Japanese-occupied Makin atoll. Besides killing most of the garrison on Butaritari Island, the raiders accomplished little of importance. Correctly assessing the purpose of the raid, the Japanese failed to react strategically. The raid did reveal the vulnerability of outlying garrisons to amphibious assault, however, and the Japanese reacted quickly to deal with this weakness. In September 1942, less than a month after the Makin raid, the Yokosuka 6th Special Naval Landing Force arrived in the Gilberts to defend Tarawa and Makin atolls. Shortly after occupation of the islands, the Japanese army brought in a team of experts on fortifications.[5]

The defenders of the Gilberts, of course, were expected to defeat enemy attempts to seize their outposts by amphibious assault, but the mission of these garrisons was more than simply retaining real estate. The disaster at Midway had not deterred the Japanese navy from pursuing its goal of precipitating a decisive naval engagement between the U.S. and Japanese fleets that, possibly, could turn the tide of war in the Pacific. Island outposts in the Gilberts and Marshalls would be the bait to lure the American fleet into battle. Island garrisons were expected to hold out independently for three to seven days, in the opinion of the Combined Fleet staff, until relief could arrive.[6] The time bought by the island defenders would allow the Combined Fleet to deal with its American counterpart.

The Japanese plan might well have worked because American naval leaders in the Pacific held essentially the same view concerning the desirability of a decisive fleet engagement. Vice Adm. Raymond Spruance, who would lead the American assault on the Gilberts, wrote in his "General Instructions to Flag Officers" that if a major part of the Japanese fleet attempted to interfere with the landings in the Gilberts "defeat of the enemy fleet would at once become paramount."[7] From the American view, the assaults on Tarawa and Makin had to be rapid enough to secure the islands before the Japanese fleet could attack the landings, as they had at Guadalcanal.

The Situation in the Gilberts

Although the Japanese had experienced U.S. landings in the Solomons and New Guinea, they knew little in mid-1943 about what to expect in the central Pacific. When U.S. planners began thinking about a central Pacific drive, both available Marine divisions (the 1st and 2d) were in General MacArthur's SWPA. Admiral Nimitz wanted them for the planned attacks on Tarawa and Nauru, but MacArthur also needed them. Under a compromise arrangement, MacArthur released the 2d Marine Division for Tarawa, and the army assigned its 27th Infantry Division to Nimitz for Makin, which had been substituted for Nauru.

Based on lessons learned at Guadalcanal, the U.S. Navy created an amphibious command structure for the Gilberts' operation that was designed to avoid repeating the mistakes of the earlier landing. Overall command of the operation was given to the Central Pacific Force under Admiral Spruance, who controlled all of the forces required to conduct the landings, including land-based aircraft from each service, aircraft carriers, and the Fifth Amphibious Force, which would actually seize the island targets. The Fifth Amphibious Force, under Rear Adm. R. K.

Turner, included Marine Corps and army landing forces and the ships required to land and support them.

The 2d Marine Division was organized in triangular fashion, with three infantry regiments of three infantry battalions each. For amphibious operations, the regiments were formed into combat teams by the addition of troops from the division's artillery and engineer regiments and various combat support and combat service support battalions. Of the division's authorized strength of 19,965 officers and men, 18,088 were available for Operation Galvanic; about 55 percent of them were combat veterans.[8] Because Admiral Turner had held back one regiment as a reserve for either Tarawa or Makin, the 2d Marine Division could count on only two regiments for the assault on Betio Island, the main Japanese position at Tarawa atoll. Unfortunately, this gave the attackers an advantage of only two to one against the defenders, rather than the generally accepted minimum of three to one.

Since the arrival of the Yokosuka 6th SNLF in September 1942, the Japanese had steadily built up the garrison on Betio, which had become the centerpiece of the Gilberts' defense. In December, the 111th Construction Battalion arrived with two of the four 8-inch coastal defense guns that were eventually mounted on the island. From the start of 1943 until the American landing in November, the fortification of Betio continued at a high pitch. By January, the Japanese had the airfield ready for test landings by land-based bombers, and the garrison test-fired one of the 8-inch guns in February. That same month, Rear Adm. Saichiro Tomonari arrived from Saipan to take charge of the newly created 3d Special Base Defense Force. In March, this new organization, which had incorporated the Yokosuka 6th SNLF into its structure, was reinforced by the arrival of the Sasebo 7th SNLF.[9] Although the defense of the Gilberts and other island groups in the Japanese Inner South Seas Area was a navy responsibility, the army was also prepared to contribute forces to the effort. In April 1943, the army established a number of South Seas detachments, with the first detachment planned for the Gilberts. The transport carrying that force was sunk the following month by an American submarine. A replacement detachment was organized but, subsequently, was diverted to Bougainville in July.[10]

When Rear Adm. Keiji Shibasaki assumed command of the Gilberts' defense on 21 July 1943, he inherited an all-navy force from Admiral Tomonari. This was essentially the force that would face the American assaults on Betio. On 20 November 1943, it consisted of approximately 4,600 men.[11] The force was part of a primarily naval structure designed to protect Japan's central Pacific flank while the army dealt with the southwest Pacific and the mainland of Asia. The admiral reported to the commander of the Fourth Fleet, who reported, in turn, to the commander in chief of the Combined Fleet. The Fourth Fleet was not a fleet in the normal sense but a land-based organization created in 1939 to oversee the defense of bases in the central Pacific.

In order to determine what they would be up against in the Gilberts, the Americans mounted an all-out intelligence effort, including interviews of individuals who had lived in the islands. They took aerial photographs from long-range aircraft flying from fields on Funafuti Island in the Ellice group and Canton Island in the Phoenix group, as well as from carrier planes, during the preassault strikes to soften up the defenses in the Gilberts. The submarine *Nautilus* made an eighteen-day reconnaissance of potential landing beaches, during which her crew took two thousand periscope photos.

The Americans had also broken the Japanese naval codes and were reaping a harvest of invaluable information. Because of the obvious value of this intelligence source, great efforts were made to disguise the source of this information. The Americans knew of the four 8-inch guns on Betio from decrypted Japanese radio traffic, for example, but deliberately described them in U.S. documents as 20-cm guns.[12] American planners were told that the caliber of these guns had been estimated from aerial photographs. Intercepted radio traffic was also used to estimate the strength of the Japanese garrison on Betio. Before information about Allied code breaking in World War II was declassified, many accounts of Tarawa claimed that estimates of Japanese strength were based on the number of privies that could be seen on aerial photographs. The final U.S. estimate was between 2,500 and 3,100 troops.[13]

The Japanese had no idea where the Americans would land. In this respect, the vastness of the Pacific Ocean was a disadvantage for the Japanese. They had to establish a network of bases capable of defending their entire outer perimeter, which generally meant airfields no more than three hundred miles from one another. Each airfield had to be defended by ground troops. In the Gilberts and Marshalls, the type of defense was dictated by the nature of the coral atolls that made up the two groups of islands.

On a typical atoll, a lagoon is surrounded by small coral islands and reefs. Tarawa, for example, is a triangle with islands making up two sides and a barrier reef on the third side. Betio Island lies at the western end of the triangle's southern side. Approximately four thousand yards long and six hundred yards wide at the most, Betio is smaller than New York City's Central Park. The highest point in the atoll is only ten feet above sea level. The physical characteristics of Betio severely limited the options available to the island's defenders, and its size precluded a mobile defense. There was no place on Betio to stage mobile counterattack forces out of naval gunfire range while they waited for the enemy to commit its forces to a particular beach. Neither was there room for a defense in depth of the type that the Japanese would conduct later in the war. At Tarawa, the defenders would stop the invasion at the water's edge or not at all. The fringing reefs of coral atolls favor this type of defense. Betio is surrounded by a reef extending out about six hundred yards from the shore on the ocean side. The reef prevents large craft from beaching and, at low water, might even prevent smaller landing craft from reaching the beach. At Tarawa, the reef nearly saved the day for the Japanese defenders.

In addition to the question of where the Americans would start their central Pacific counteroffensive, Admiral Shibasaki also faced the issue of when. The Japanese navy had originally estimated that the Americans could not recover from their defeats at the start of the war before 1943. Guadalcanal had shown the error of that estimate, but U.S. forces had not yet attempted a landing in the central Pacific. In October, the Japanese on Makin captured the three-man crew of an American torpedo bomber shot down on a mission over the Gilberts. Before their capture, the crew members had told the natives to treat them well because the Americans would be coming to capture the islands in December.[14]

The Japanese Plan

In assuming command of the Gilberts' defense, Admiral Shibasaki inherited on Tarawa what is best described as a defense at the water's edge within an overall naval defense. On 25 March, the Navy Section of Imperial General Headquarters had issued a directive giving guidance to the Combined Fleet on dealing with the American counteroffensive in the Pacific. The directive emphasized surprise attacks on American advanced bases but added, "At the same time, measures will be taken to lure the enemy fleet into the open sea and destroy it."[15] The bait, of course, would be the Japanese bases in the Gilberts and Marshalls.

To implement this concept, Adm. Mineichi Koga, who had assumed command of the Combined Fleet after the death of Admiral Yamamoto, issued a series of operational orders on 15 August 1943. Called the "Z" operation, these plans dealt with an anticipated American invasion into

Japanese Defense at the Water's Edge ~ 123

the central Pacific. In September, the Japanese high command redrew its central Pacific defense line to run from the Carolines to the Marianas. Although the Gilberts and Marshalls were outside the new line, Admiral Koga apparently still planned to commit the Combined Fleet to their defense. Operation Order No. 41 reemphasized the concept of destroying the U.S. fleet and gave guidance on the priority of targets.[16] Koga ordered his fleet first to neutralize the American carriers and then to direct the main attack against the transports. He added an escape clause permitting a more general fleet engagement if the opportunity arose.

The remaining orders were aimed at island garrison commanders. Operation Order No. 42 directed them to prepare for any contingency from air raids to full-scale landings. In spite of earlier estimates of relief in a week's time, this order directed each garrison to maintain three months of military supplies in the event that rapid reinforcement would not be possible.[17] Operation Order No. 40 stated: "Each island base will resist independently against the superior enemy until reinforcements arrive, in order to free most of the Fleet's strength for decisive battles."[18]

Anticipating the need to hold Tarawa independently and the necessity of stopping an invader at the water's edge, Admiral Shibasaki's predecessor had issued an order in October 1942 that stated, in part:

> When the enemy is assembling for a landing, wait until the enemy is within effective range, direct your fire on the enemy transport group and destroy it. If the enemy starts a landing, knock out the landing boats with mountain gun fire, tank guns and infantry guns, then concentrate all fires on the enemy's landing point and destroy him at the water's edge.[19]

In implementing this order, the Japanese defenders fortified Betio to a degree unprecedented at the time. The outer limit of the defense was delineated by the 20,000-meter range of the four 8-inch guns. Starting at the seaward edge of Tarawa's fringing reef, the defenders created a layered series of obstacles covered by interlocking bands of fire from weapons ranging from 127-mm dual-purpose guns to small arms. The Japanese had planted antipersonnel and antitank mines on both the reef and the beaches. Anticipating that the Americans would land from the ocean side of the island, Admiral Shibasaki gave those beaches priority for fortification. Fortunately for the Marines, who landed from the lagoon side, mines on the lagoon beaches were not yet armed.[20] After the island was secured, Marines found more than three thousand mines waiting to be laid. To hinder and channelize landing craft, concrete obstacles bristling with iron rails ringed Betio's nine-thousand-yard coastline,

Japanese defense at Tarawa, November 1943. The defense at the water's edge nearly succeeded. It was extremely costly for the U.S. Marine attackers.
(U.S. Marine Corps photo, No. 94875)

where they were supplemented by a double-apron barbed-wire fence designed to hold up disembarked troops.

At the edge of the beach, a coconut log seawall doubled as an antitank obstacle to prevent tracked landing vehicles (LVTs, or amtracs) getting off the beach. Built into this seawall and immediately behind it were gun emplacements constructed of either reinforced concrete or alternating layers of coconut logs and coral sand. After the battle, the Marines discovered to their surprise that these positions had been resistant to all but direct hits from major-caliber naval guns or aircraft bombs. Inland from the beach were many other fortified positions serving as magazines, command posts, personnel shelters, and aid stations. Although these positions were not laid out to provide mutual fire support, they formed the basis of the bunker-by-bunker defense that the Japanese conducted during the fight for Betio. During the battle, the Marines were forced to contend with almost five hundred of these individual positions.

To add flexibility to this impressive defense, Admiral Shibasaki had at his disposal fourteen Type 95 light tanks. Contrary to some accounts, these tanks, with their 37-mm guns, were not dug in as pillboxes. Shibasaki was confident enough in the strength of his defense that he reportedly told his garrison before the battle that a million men could not take Tarawa in a hundred years.[21]

The Battle for Tarawa

Admiral Shibasaki did not have to wait long to have his boast tested. Before that happened, however, events in the southwest Pacific greatly influenced the fate of Tarawa's defenders. On 1 November 1943, the 3d Marine Division landed on Bougainville, which focused Japanese attention on that area. When a Japanese force of cruisers and destroyers, sent from Rabaul to destroy the American landing, was defeated during the resulting Battle of Empress Augusta Bay, the Combined Fleet sent still more ships to renew the effort. Those ships were caught at Rabaul by an American carrier air strike that caused considerable damage. Another strike on 11 November did even more damage; the Japanese lost more than fifty carrier aircraft that had been sent from Truk in the Carolines to help the beleaguered defenders of Rabaul. A significant result of these attacks was Admiral Koga's inability to execute his Operation Plan Z when the invasion of the Gilberts started.

Although the Japanese had anticipated an invasion of the Gilberts as early as September 1943 when U.S. carrier air strikes had hit Marcus Island, the Gilberts, and Nauru, the first real warning of the attack came at about 1700 on 18 November.[22] A Japanese reconnaissance plane spotted a U.S. convoy of three LSTs and one destroyer sailing independently from Canton Island to Makin. Around sunset on the next day, Japanese scout bombers attacked the convoy, without effect, about forty-five miles from its destination. Had the Japanese been more successful, they might have altered the course of the Makin landing. The convoy carried all of the LVTs for the assault there.

At 0441 on 20 November, Betio's defenders fired a red star cluster to alert the garrison that the American attackers had arrived. The 8-inch guns on the southwest end of Betio lacked radar fire control, necessary for accurate firing in the dark, and the gunners had to wait until shortly after first light to open fire. The USS *Maryland* quickly silenced those guns with a direct hit from her 16-inch main batteries, but other guns on the island began to fire at the American transports.

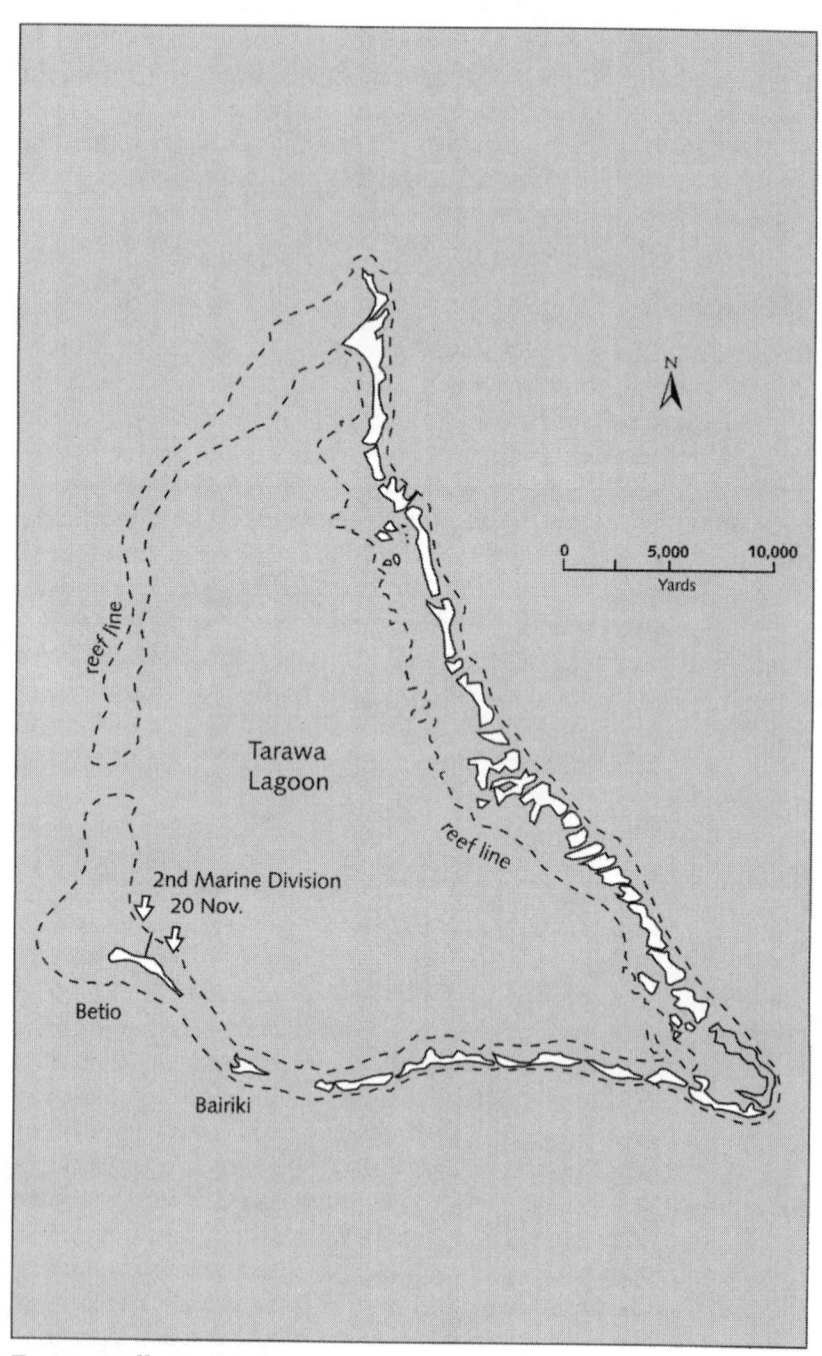

Tarawa Atoll, 1943

At Truk, Admiral Koga received word of the American attack and ordered execution of the Gilberts' portion of Operation Plan Z, called Hei No. 3. The surface-attack part of the plan had been compromised by U.S. carrier attacks, but other forces were put into motion. Land-based and carrier air units were ordered to reinforce the area, and surface units were ordered to transport the army's 1,500-man "Ko" Detachment from Ponape (Caroline Islands) to Kwajalein (Marshall Islands) to prepare for a counterlanding in the Gilberts.

On Betio, the defenders were undergoing the heaviest preassault naval gunfire bombardment to date. During the three hours before the first waves of LVTs touched down, more than 24,000 rounds of naval gunfire, including 1,436 shells from 14- and 16-inch guns on the battleships, slammed into Betio's small area.[23] Following the naval bombardment, carrier planes attacked the island. Fortunately for the defenders, their concrete and coconut log shelters provided them safety from all but direct hits from heavy bombs and naval gunfire. Few lives were lost to the bombardment, but it did cause several major problems for the Japanese.

The ferocity of the bombardment forced the defenders to remain in their shelters while the first American assault waves began their run to the beach. Timing errors on the part of the Americans resulted in a gap between the cease-fire of most naval guns and the arrival of the first LVTs on the beach. The log seawall provided cover for those Marines who reached it, but it also prevented all but a few of the LVTs from carrying their troops inland through the initial belt of defensive positions. The close proximity of the Marines sheltered behind the seawall also precluded calling in naval gunfire or air strikes on the Japanese positions that kept the Marines from moving forward.

Admiral Shibasaki's men were able to recover from the shock of the preassault bombardment in time to pour a withering hail of fire into the follow-on waves of Marines who were forced to wade in from the reef's edge. Lacking adequate information about the amount of water that could be expected to cover Tarawa's reef at the time of the assault, the Americans had rounded up enough LVTs to embark the first three waves. The remainder, in landing craft, were unable to cross the reef.[24]

The naval gunfire and air bombardment had other important effects on the defenders. Damage to fire-control instruments and destruction of much of the island's wire communications network resulted in reduced volume and less accuracy of fire from Tarawa's larger guns than the

Japanese had anticipated. To compound their problems further, Admiral Shibasaki was killed, probably about midday. Early loss of the commander could explain the lack of coordinated counterattacks during the remaining days of Tarawa's defense.

After recovering from the effects of the initial bombardment, Japanese gunners quickly found the ranges of LVTs moving between the reef and beach and of landing craft trying to reach the reef. Four landing craft, medium (LCMs) carrying light tanks were sunk by gunfire before they could reach the reef to unload. Tarawa's shoreline was soon littered with the wreckage of destroyed amtracs. Machine-gun fire prevented all but the most stalwart of the attackers from clambering over the seawall or even attempting to fire over it. The seawall also prevented most of the tanks that reached the beach from getting inland. The tanks that did get through gaps blasted in the seawall faced Japanese tanks and 75-mm guns. By the end of D-day, only two of the Marines' fourteen Sherman tanks were still operational.

Although Betio's defenders had failed to prevent the enemy from getting ashore that day, they had confined the Americans to two tenuous footholds on the beach. One was centered around a long pier that ran out into the lagoon, and the other was on the northwest "beak" of the island. American casualties were heavy, and the Japanese still held three fourths of the island. Opposing forces ashore were approximately equal in size. That evening, Rear Adm. Harry W. Hill, commander of the U.S. Southern Attack Force, and Maj. Gen. Julian C. Smith, 2d Marine Division commander, informed their superiors, "Issue remains in doubt."[25]

In the event that the Japanese failed to stop the landing, their plan called for counterattacks to eject the invaders before they could consolidate their foothold on the beach. The night of D-day would have been the ideal time for such attacks. The answer to why the Japanese failed to do so died with Betio's garrison. General Smith considered the night of D-day to be the critical point of the battle and believed that, by failing to counterattack then, the Japanese lost the chance to defeat the landing.[26]

The remnants of the Japanese defenders, holding on for two more days, forced the Marines to dig them out of their positions bunker by bunker. Most of the surviving Japanese committed suicide rather than allow themselves to be taken prisoner. When organized resistance ended at 1305 on 23 November, all but 146 of the defenders were dead. Only 17 of the survivors were Japanese; the rest were Korean la-

Death over dishonor, Tarawa, November 1943. The Japanese defenders committed suicide rather than surrender, a pattern that continued throughout the central Pacific landings.
(U.S. Marine Corps photo, No. 63466)

borers. The Americans had also paid a terrible price for Betio. The 2d Marine Division suffered 3,407 casualties, 1,115 of whom were killed or missing.[27]

While the Marines were assaulting Tarawa, a 6,470-man regimental combat team from the U.S. Army's 27th Infantry Division was taking Butaritari Island in Makin atoll. Lightly fortified and defended by a 798-man garrison commanded by a lieutenant (junior grade), Makin was a pushover compared with Tarawa. The Americans took four days to secure Makin. They suffered 66 killed and 152 wounded in the fighting ashore. In spite of these relatively light shore casualties, the capture of Makin provides a glimpse of the potential of a naval defense against a landing. At the start of the American invasion, Vice Adm. Takeo Takagi, commander of the Japanese Sixth Fleet, ordered nine submarines to the Gilberts to disrupt the landings. On 24 November, the submarine *I-175* torpedoed the U.S. escort carrier *Liscome Bay* (CVE 56) off Makin.[28] The carrier sank quickly with the loss of 644 lives, including that of the admiral commanding the task group. When those numbers are added to those killed ashore on Makin, the total for the entire operation approached that of Tarawa.

Lessons of the Gilberts Applied to the Marshalls

After the fall of the Gilberts, the Japanese correctly assumed that the Marshalls would be next. Although the Marshalls, in effect, had been written off by the new defensive line, their defenders still had an important role to play. The longer they could delay the Americans, the more time their comrades would have to make the new line impregnable.

As the Japanese prepared for that task, they began to feel the disadvantages of being on the losing side of the island battles. Left in possession of the battlefield at Tarawa, the Americans had exploited it to an unprecedented degree. The Japanese defenses were studied in detail and actually duplicated on the Hawaiian island of Kahoolawe, where they became a training and proving ground for U.S. Navy gunfire ships. Field intelligence teams combed through the rubble for documents. A barracks inspection in Hawaii turned up a Japanese codebook that a sailor had picked up in the Gilberts as a souvenir.[29] Armed with good intelligence and having carefully studied the defenses of the Gilberts, the U.S. Fifth Fleet had a good idea of what to expect in the Marshalls.

The Japanese, on the other hand, were much more in the dark than their opponents. Once again, the immense size of the theater worked to their disadvantage. The Marshalls, with thirty-three atolls, covered more than four hundred thousand square miles. The atolls, arranged in chains, ran generally north to south, with Kwajalein, the largest, approximately in the center. Kwajalein atoll was the administrative center of the Japanese Marshalls. Kwajalein Island, located in the southern part of the atoll, was the military headquarters of the mandate. Roi-Namur (two islands linked by a causeway in the northern part of the atoll) was the site of a major naval air base.

Because of both its location and function, Kwajalein atoll reflected more the atmosphere of a rear headquarters than a frontline outpost. The latter role was reserved for the easternmost atolls, such as Mille, Maloelap, and Wotje, that stood directly between Kwajalein and the advancing Americans. Regarding the question of where the enemy would strike next, a staff officer from the Combined Fleet staff noted after the war, "There were so many possible points of invasion in the Marshalls, that we could not consider any one a strong point and consequently dispersed our strength."[30]

Japanese Defense at the Water's Edge ~ 131

Meanwhile, Admiral Nimitz had decided to take a bold step. Overriding his principal subordinates, all of whom had recommended attacking the eastern atolls first, Nimitz chose Kwajalein as the next target.

The Japanese made little attempt to capitalize on the lessons of the Gilberts campaign. In spite of the introduction of army troops to the islands and the experience gained at Tarawa, the Japanese anti-landing concept for the Marshalls remained identical to the one that had failed in the Gilberts. The defenders were to stop the landing at the water's edge or, failing that, drive the enemy back into the sea by counterattacks.

Although the Japanese had occupied Kwajalein far longer than they had Tarawa, the defenses at Kwajalein, in no way, matched those that the Marines had faced on Betio. The reefs and offshore waters had not been mined, and the defenses remained oriented primarily to the sea side of the atoll, rather than toward the lagoon. No major-caliber coastal defense guns protected the islands, and relatively few smaller-caliber weapons covered the beaches. Some reinforced concrete blockhouses had been constructed, particularly on Roi-Namur, but most gun positions lacked overhead cover. In the words of the V Amphibious Corps engineer, who carefully inspected the defenses after the battle, the Japanese positions on Kwajalein were "surprisingly weak."[31]

Whereas the Japanese defensive concepts remained stagnant, the Americans had introduced numerous innovations in amphibious technique between the Gilberts and Marshalls operations. They included the seizure of nearby islets and emplacement of artillery on them to add to the air and naval gunfire support for the main landings, the employment of underwater demolition teams to reconnoiter the beaches and to destroy mines and obstacles, and the use of rocket craft and armored amphibians (LVT(A)s) mounting 37-mm tank guns in turrets to precede the initial waves of troops. The most vital change was the dramatic increase in naval gunfire used to prepare the invasion beaches and the techniques by which it was employed. At Tarawa the preassault bombardment had lasted for several hours. For the Kwajalein landings, which began on 31 January 1944, the bombardment was increased to several days. Also, the gunfire ships operated close in and concentrated on the deliberate destruction of individual targets on the beach. As a result, the attackers were able to get ashore without the tremendous casualties suffered by the 2d Marine Division at Betio.

After failing to stop the landings at the water's edge, the defenders of Kwajalein and Roi-Namur, as did those at Tarawa, chose to fight to the death, rather than surrender. Although their determination resulted in delaying the inevitable outcome of the landings, the delay was not as lengthy as the Japanese needed.

Meanwhile, more than three hundred miles northwest of Kwajalein, Maj. Gen. Yoshima Nishida, Eniwetok's commander, anticipated an American landing, but he was counting on a respite, during which his garrison could prepare an adequate defense. Perhaps he can be excused for misreading his enemy's intentions. Originally, American planners had contemplated the capture of Eniwetok around 1 May 1944. Based on the rapid success of the Kwajalein operation and the availability of reserves that had not been committed, however, Admiral Nimitz decided to attack Eniwetok immediately.

When U.S. forces arrived at Eniwetok in February 1944, they found the atoll largely defenseless. Large amounts of fortification material were on hand, coastal defense guns were waiting to be emplaced, and land and beach mines were stored in dumps, but the Japanese had not completed the hard work of constructing a defense. General Nishida's defense order, which was captured during the battle, showed that he had correctly anticipated a landing from the lagoon and was preparing his defenses accordingly. Twenty-eight moored contact mines were found in the lagoon, a first in the central Pacific.[32] The defenders were learning. The question was whether they were learning fast enough to stay ahead of U.S. advances in amphibious warfare.

Observations

The operations in the Gilberts and Marshalls illustrate the naval character of amphibious operations. Both sides regarded the landings as an integral part of a larger naval campaign. The Americans saw the atolls as advanced naval and air bases required to support the naval advance toward Japan. The Japanese also regarded the islands as advanced naval bases. In their case, the bases were an integral part of an interception-attrition strategy designed to defeat a numerically superior fleet.

Because Japanese garrison commanders almost invariably died while defending their islands, detailed after-action reports were virtually nonexistent, but some commanders managed to send out useful reports during the fighting. The defenders of Kwajalein and Eniwetok, for example, had originally anticipated an attack from the sea but, based on information from Tarawa, began to reorient their defenses to the lagoon beaches. The Japanese policy of fighting to the death also prevented the defenders from creating a pool of experienced veterans, as did the Americans. As the war progressed, U.S. amphibious commanders found themselves conducting landings for a second or third time. Many of the troops were also veterans of several landings. In the central Pacific, long distances between islands, coupled with U.S. sea control, generally eliminated any possibility of escape and doomed Japanese units to only one attempt to defeat a landing.

Although delay favored the defender, the Japanese were denied much of that advantage by the rapid tempo of the U.S. advance. A later D-day for Tarawa would have allowed the 2d Marine Division to accumulate more LVTs and might have coincided with more favorable tidal conditions during the landing. Had they delayed, however, the Marines would have faced a more thoroughly prepared defense, one that probably would have included mines along the lagoon beaches. Any delay at Tarawa also would have given the Japanese more time to complete their defenses in the Marshalls.

Japanese plans called for a naval defense of the Gilberts, but a combination of factors prevented them from executing their plans. One factor was MacArthur's southwest Pacific drive that drew Japanese naval forces away from the central Pacific immediately before the Tarawa landing. The other factor was U.S. naval and air superiority that prevented the Japanese from sending back forces from the SWPA to the central Pacific after the landings started there. As important as sea control and air superiority are to the success of an amphibious landing, however, they did not prevent the Japanese from very nearly defeating the landing at Tarawa.

Precluded by the size of Betio Island from using a mobile defense, Admiral Shibasaki conducted what must be considered the classic defense at the water's edge. Its failure resulted from a combination of factors, not the least of which were the specialized training and equipment of the 2d Marine Division and the bravery and skill of its officers and men. Given the force ratios of the two opponents, the attackers cannot be said to have overwhelmed the defenders. Although naval gunfire is considered by many to have been a failure at Tarawa, it was nevertheless a factor in the U.S. victory there. Improved by the lessons of Tarawa, naval gunfire played a significant role in overcoming Japanese defenses in the Marshalls and, increasingly, became one of the most serious problems for Japanese planners. To solve the problem, they began to explore other defensive concepts.

9

Japanese Defense in Transition:
Saipan to Iwo Jima, 1944–1945

The power of American warships and aircraft makes every landing operation possible on whatever beachhead they like and preventing them from landing means nothing but great losses.

Lt. Gen. Tadamichi Kuribayashi, Iwo Jima, 1945 (quoted in Yoshitka Horie, "Japanese Defense of Iwo Jima")

The Japanese faced a drastically changed situation in the central Pacific after their loss of the Marshalls. When Imperial General Headquarters redrew the main defense lines in September 1943, it designated the newly created area an "absolute national defense sphere."[1] The obvious implication of this designation was that the islands within the zone could not be written off as expendable outposts, as were the Gilberts and Marshalls. This made sense in that most of the designated islands had been Japanese mandates since World War I. They included the Marianas and Carolines and even older Japanese possessions, such as the Bonin and Ryukyu Islands. Guam, which the Japanese had captured from the United States at the start of World War II, was also in the new defense sphere. The Japanese realized that loss of these possessions would not only send a drastic psychological shock through the nation but would have serious strategic consequences as well. Emperor Hirohito himself told the garrison of Saipan that if Japan lost the island, frequent American air raids on Tokyo would result.[2]

The physical nature of the islands in the new sphere offered the Japanese some defensive advantages that were not available on the coral atolls of the Gilberts and Marshalls. Many of the islands in the new zone were large enough to give the defenders room to maneuver and conduct a defense in depth if the attackers broke through a defense at the water's edge. Saipan's area, for example, is approximately seventy-two square miles, compared with Tarawa's twelve miles. These larger islands also have hills and mountains that afforded the defenders not only observation but the opportunity to construct extensive underground defensive positions.

To take advantage of these conditions, the Japanese reinforced the islands' naval garrisons with much larger army units. With the army forces came an army perspective on ground combat. Japanese army tactical doctrine was overwhelmingly offensive in nature, even in defensive situations. Compliance with such doctrine tended to lead army commanders away from a static defense at the water's edge and toward a more mobile counterattack-oriented style of defense. This offensive orientation placed some army commanders at odds with the official doctrine for defending against landings. In April 1944, Imperial General Headquarters issued a document titled "Explanation of the Combat Guidance for Garrison on Islands" to amplify the earlier "Combat Guidance for Garrison on Islands" and incorporate the lessons of the Marshalls.[3] This new doctrine still called for the defender to deploy along the beach and defeat the enemy there.

The large-scale introduction of army units into the central Pacific presented command problems for the Japanese Combined Fleet's commander in chief, who remained responsible for the area. Realizing that the task was beyond the capability of the Fourth Fleet, Admiral Toyoda, who had replaced Admiral Koga as commander in chief of the Combined Fleet after Koga died in an airplane crash, created a new organization, the Central Pacific Area Fleet. This new command, not a fleet in the usual sense, was placed under the command of Vice Adm. Chuichi Nagumo, who had led Japanese carrier forces at Pearl Harbor, in the Indian Ocean, and at Midway. Out of favor since the defeat at Midway, Nagumo was assigned the job of overseeing the defense of the absolute national defense sphere against American amphibious attacks. Because the army would have a large number of units subordinate to Nagumo, it established the Thirty-first Army as its component of the Central Pacific Area Fleet. Commander of the Thirty-first Army was Lt. Gen. Hideyoshi Obata, a cavalry officer who had spent most of the war commanding army aviation forces.

Experience had taught the Japanese the need for unified command similar to that exercised by their enemies. In theory, the Central Pacific Area Fleet commanded forces from both the army and the navy. In practice, however, Nagumo and Obata could not overcome long-standing animosities between their services. The two commanders agreed to make the senior officer on each island responsible for its defense regardless of the officer's service, but this agreement was disregarded in many cases.

Another problem facing the Japanese after the Marshalls was determining where the Americans would strike next. Japanese planners both anticipated and hoped that the answer would be the western Carolines, specifically the Palau Islands. Their anticipation was based on an assessment that the Philippines would be the next major American objective and that seizure of the Palaus would be a necessary prerequisite. The Japanese navy hoped for such a move because it would place the Combined Fleet, operating from the Philippines at the time, in a better position to implement the A-GO plan against the American attackers. Events would prove that the Japanese made a bad guess.

The Situation in the Marianas

Although they did not expect the Mariana Islands to be the next target, the Japanese nevertheless took steps to build up the area's troop strength. Between February and May 1944, two divisions, two independent brigades, two independent regiments, and three expeditionary groups were transferred from Japan or Manchuria to the Marianas. At the end of this shift and the reorganizations that followed, the Japanese garrisons included the headquarters of the Thirty-first Army, 29th and 43d Divisions, and a variety of smaller army and navy units, with 31,629 troops on Saipan, 8,039 on Tinian, and 21,000 on Guam.[4]

The final composition of these garrisons resulted from both deliberate planning and chance. American submarines played havoc with the Japanese effort to reinforce their island garrisons. When transports were sunk, rescued troops frequently ended up at locations other than those originally planned. American submarines and limited transportation also restricted the ability of the Japanese to move troops between islands. The resulting mix of units and the exceptions to the army-navy command agreement contributed to a command picture in the Marianas even more convoluted than normal. On Saipan, for example, General Obata was in charge of the island's defense, even though Admiral Nagumo was the senior officer present.

The mission of the Thirty-first Army was to hold the Marianas. Because of its importance to the defense of Japan, Saipan had been designated an "absolute strategic area" within the overall "absolute sphere of national defense."[5] Unlike other island outposts that could be sacrificed to gain time, Saipan was a keystone to the defense of the Japanese Empire. The Japanese navy also needed air bases in the Marianas in order to implement the A-GO plan against the U.S. fleet.

Admiral Spruance divided U.S. forces for the Marianas operation into a northern force for Saipan and Tinian and a southern force for Guam. For the northern operation, Spruance assigned Lt. Gen. Holland M. Smith's Northern Troops and Landing Force, consisting of the 2d and 4th Marine Divisions and the U.S. Army's 27th Infantry Division. Although the Americans had initially underestimated the Japanese strength on Saipan, Smith's 66,779 assault troops were adequate for the task.[6]

The Japanese Plan for Saipan

The battles for the Gilberts and Marshalls had been fought under an anti-landing doctrine that called for destruction of the invader at the beach. When Imperial General Headquarters issued its revised anti-landing doctrine in April 1944, it attributed earlier defeats not to faulty doctrine but to commanders who had failed to implement the doctrine properly.[7] Anti-landing planning for Saipan, therefore, continued to be based around a defense at the water's edge. General Obata considered Saipan's western beaches to be the most likely site of a landing and oriented his defenses there.

Unfortunately for the Japanese, the speed of the American advance through the Marshalls and a serious shortage of construction materials, caused in part by U.S. submarines, prevented Saipan's garrison from fully implementing Obata's defensive concept. Antiboat obstacles and beach mines were almost nonexistent, a situation described as "amazing" by the American engineer officer who surveyed the defenses after the battle.[8] Concrete gun positions were being constructed to cover the likely invasion beaches, but many of these were unfinished at the time of the landing. After the battle, the Americans discovered three 5-inch coastal defense guns, four 140-mm coastal defense guns, thirty-five 120-mm dual-purpose guns, and six 200-mm mortars waiting to be emplaced.[9] Captured Japanese artillery charts indicated that the Japanese had carefully registered artillery on the anticipated beaches and the nearby reefs.[10]

In spite of the doctrine, General Obata was unwilling to stake his entire defense on defeating the landing at the water's edge. Only three of the 43d Division's nine infantry battalions were emplaced at the beach; the others were held back for local counterattacks. Additional units, including Col. Takashi Goto's 9th Tank Regiment with forty-eight tanks, were held back from the beaches as a mobile counterattack force.

While the Japanese army was planning the defense of Saipan, the navy was still planning to strike the next American invasion with a powerful naval force under the A-GO plan. On 1 March 1944, the navy had reorganized to create the First Mobile Fleet, an organization similar to an American task force. Once the Japanese could determine the location of the next enemy landing, Vice Adm. Jisaburo Ozawa, the new fleet's commander, planned to use it in concert with all of the land-based planes that the Japanese could marshal to destroy the Americans.

The Battle for Saipan

On 11 June 1944, U.S. naval forces began final preparations for the invasion of Saipan, which would include air strikes on nearby airfields, naval gunfire bombardment of Japanese defenses, and underwater demolition team (UDT) operations to locate and destroy mines and obstacles off the landing beaches. Because these preparations were so extensive, the Japanese had no doubt that Saipan was the next target. On 14 June, Admiral Toyoda ordered the First Mobile Fleet north from its base at Tawi Tawi in the Sulu Archipelago to execute the A-GO plan. Aircraft previously sent south to attack the Americans off Biak were ordered back to the Marianas.

On Saipan, the Japanese defenders could do little more than wait out the bombardment in their bunkers. Unfortunately for them, they faced the coming invasion without their commander. General Obata was in the Palaus on an inspection trip when the invasion began. He attempted to return to Saipan, but American air superiority forced him to stop at Guam. In Obata's absence, Lt. Gen. Yoshisugu Saito, commander of the 43d Division, assumed command of Saipan's defense.

General Saito's first decision came on 15 June, D-day for the American landing. As Marines from the 2d and 4th Divisions were landing across southwest beaches near Charan Kanoa, U.S. ships were conducting a demonstration—a simulated landing—farther to the north near Tanapag harbor. The Americans hoped to make the defenders shift forces away from the site of the real landing. The distribution of naval gunfire prior to D-day and the propaganda leaflets dropped by U.S. aircraft had convinced General Saito that Charan Kanoa would be the site of the landing.[11] As a result, he refused to shift any troops, including the 135th Infantry Regiment located in reserve behind the northern beaches. Be-

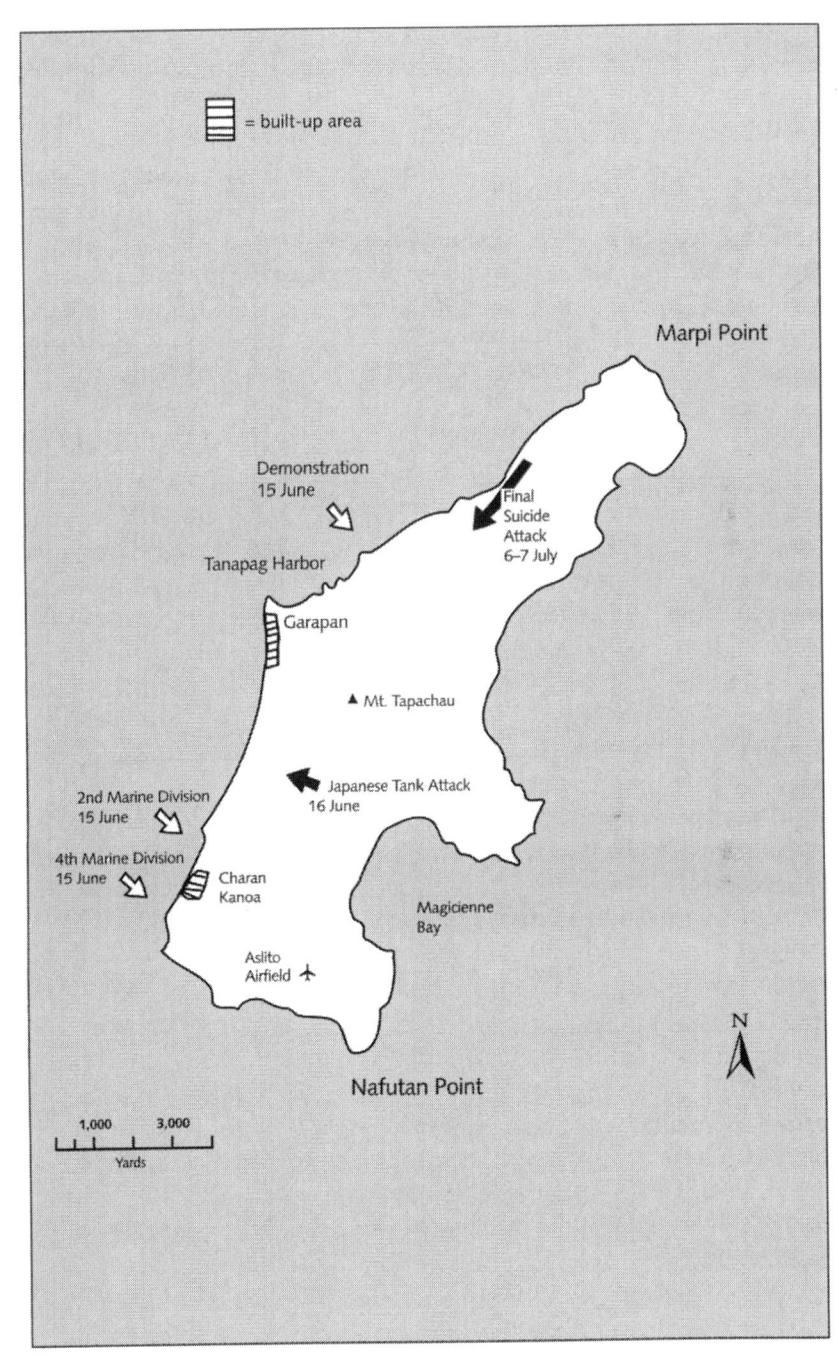

Saipan, 1944

cause the regiment was not ordered south to join the battle, the U.S. demonstration did have some effect. The Japanese also kept forces on the east coast until after D-day.

The relatively thin Japanese defense along the beaches was unable to stop the two-division American assault. The defenders hit the beachhead with accurate mortar and artillery fire, but the Japanese method of fire control did not allow them to mass the firepower of many units for greater effect.[12] In keeping with their plan, the defenders launched a series of local counterattacks against the beachhead that began on D-day and lasted through the night. The counterattacks were beaten back successfully, a feat attributed by the Japanese to American tanks and superior firepower.[13] One of the important roles of naval gunfire during these attacks was illuminating the battlefield at night by the use of star shells.

The following night, 16 June, the Japanese launched the largest tank attack of the island war in the Pacific. The attack force consisted of forty-four tanks from the 9th Tank Regiment, supported by troops from the 136th Infantry Regiment and the Yokosuka 1st SNLF. The Marines were ready, however, and defeated the attack by using every possible type of weapon, from rifle grenades and bazookas, to antitank guns and tanks, to artillery and naval gunfire. At daylight, most of the Japanese tanks were smoldering wrecks.

Unable to drive the Americans off the beach, General Saito reluctantly decided to carry out a delaying action by falling back on strategic areas in both the north and south of Saipan. In addition to inflicting casualties on the Americans, he also hoped to buy time for Admiral Ozawa's First Mobile Fleet to arrive and attack Spruance's force and for reinforcements to arrive from other islands.

On 19 June, the First Mobile Fleet was in position and Ozawa implemented the A-GO plan. The plan relied on land-based planes from Guam attacking the U.S. carriers, followed by more attacks from the fleet. Because Japanese planes had longer range than their American equivalents and also airfields were available on Guam where carrier planes could land, Ozawa should have been able to attack the American carriers while remaining out of range of U.S. reprisals. Instead, a combination of aircraft shortages, false reports by some commanders, and vastly better trained American aviators resulted in a decisive Japanese defeat at the Battle of the Philippine Sea. During the one-sided action, the Japanese lost two carriers and almost five hundred aircraft.[14]

Even though the Battle of the Philippine Sea was an overwhelming defeat for the Japanese, Admiral Ozawa's efforts did have some impact

Japanese tank out of action, Saipan, 1944. The Japanese unsuccessfully attempted to introduce more mobility into their defense when they launched the largest tank attack of the central Pacific war. Almost all of the tanks were destroyed by the U.S. Marines.
(U.S. Navy photo, No. 234302)

on the American invasion. When Admiral Spruance realized that a sizable enemy fleet was approaching, he ordered most of the transports to leave the beachhead area. This not only disrupted the landing of supplies but forced General Smith, the landing force commander, to land his reserve, the army's 27th Infantry Division, prematurely. Of even greater importance, Admiral Spruance postponed the invasion of Guam. Originally scheduled to be attacked simultaneously with Saipan, the Guam landing would have to wait until the situation on Saipan improved. The resulting delay gave the Japanese on Guam more time to prepare their defenses.

Frustrated by the lack of a Japanese naval victory, Saipan's defenders could do nothing more than buy time and force the attacking Americans to pay as high a price as possible for the island. Saipan's rugged, heavily wooded terrain aided the defenders greatly. On the night of 25 June, a unit from Tinian attempted to reach Saipan on eleven barges, but it was intercepted by American ships and forced to turn back.[15] An infantry regiment from Guam also tried unsuccessfully to reach Saipan by ship. By the end of June, organized resistance had ceased in the south and the Americans were closing in on the remaining Japanese defensive positions in the north.

Facing inevitable defeat, General Saito ordered a massive suicide attack by all remaining forces on the island. Just before dawn on the morning of 7 July, approximately three thousand Japanese soldiers and sailors, many unarmed, launched an attack in a long column down the coast near Tanapag. By sheer force, they broke through the U.S. lines at several points but eventually faltered in the face of superior firepower. Although some Japanese accounts indicate that Admiral Nagumo and General Saito died while leading the charge, witnesses have stated that they committed suicide at their headquarters while the attack was taking place.[16] Ultimately, this attack had no impact on the outcome of the battle, and Admiral Turner declared Saipan to be secure at 1615 on 9 July 1944.

The Battles for Tinian and Guam

Although the defenders of Saipan had failed to defeat the invasion, they had bought time for their counterparts on Tinian and Guam to learn from the experience at Saipan and prepare their defenses accordingly. Saipan had demonstrated once again the fragility of a thin defensive position at the beach. While the battle for Saipan was still raging, Thirty-first Army headquarters notified units on other islands, "Because fortifications built at the water's edge is [sic] extremely weak in strength, you are hereby ordered to have the key positions constructed in depth."[17]

The Japanese experience at Saipan had also demonstrated the power of American supporting arms, naval gunfire in particular, and had reemphasized the urgency of finding a way to overcome its effects. General Saito had attempted to pass this lesson on to his superiors by stating in a message, "If there were just no naval gunfire, we feel we could fight it out with the enemy in a decisive battle."[18] This particular lesson should have come as no surprise at this point in the war. A group established earlier at Imperial General Headquarters to study American amphibious techniques had estimated that a single U.S. battleship was the equivalent in firepower of five Japanese divisions.[19]

Although the defenders of Tinian and Guam clearly understood the weaknesses of the defenses on Saipan, they were unable to correct the

Japanese Defense in Transition ~ 143

problems before the Americans landed. As a result, the battles for the two islands followed the pattern set on Saipan with one major exception. By the time of the Tinian landing, the Japanese had accurately deduced the beach conditions required by the Americans for a large-scale assault. On Tinian, those conditions existed along the southwest coast near Tinian Town and across the island at Asiga Bay; therefore, the Japanese focused their defense on those two areas. In a surprise move, the 4th Marine Division landed in a column across two tiny beaches in northwest Tinian while conducting an amphibious demonstration off Tinian Town to fix the Japanese in that position. The demonstration was so successful that, when the landing craft turned around at the last minute, the defenders notified Tokyo that they had repelled the landing.[20]

Peleliu and the Lessons of Saipan

Within two weeks of the fall of Saipan, the Army Section of Imperial General Headquarters had analyzed the reports from the battle and disseminated combat lessons to forces in the field.[21] The Thirty-first Army had also submitted its own lessons during the battle.[22] The following were among the most important lessons listed by the two sources:

- Naval gunfire and tanks are the two biggest threats for which defensive measures are needed.
- Because beach positions cannot be relied on to stop a landing, defenses in depth are required.
- Banzai attacks, such as those conducted on Saipan, are wasteful and run counter to the mission of buying as much time as possible and causing the highest number of enemy casualties.
- Unity of command between the services is essential. To incorporate the lessons of the Marianas into anti-landing doctrine, Imperial General Headquarters issued "Defense Guidance on Islands" in August 1944. This document changed Japanese defensive doctrine from destruction of the enemy at the beach to destruction of the enemy within the larger area of the beachhead.[23]

Armed with the new doctrine and the lessons of the Marianas, Lt. Gen. Sadae Inoue, commander of the 14th Division, set about preparing the Palau Islands for the American assault, which he felt sure was coming. His division had arrived in the Palaus in April 1944 and established its headquarters on Koror. Most of the division remained on Babelthuap, also called Palau, immediately adjacent to Koror and the biggest island of the group. Although General Inoue believed that Babelthuap would be the principal target of any American invasion, he did transfer some forces to the southern part of the chain, including Peleliu Island, where the Japanese navy was constructing an airfield.

Col. Kunio Nakagawa, commander of the 2d Infantry Regiment, assumed command of Peleliu's defense in April. In addition to his own regiment, he had a tank unit, an additional infantry battalion, and a mix of naval personnel, for a total of 10,500 troops with which to defend Peleliu.[24] Unfortunately, he did not have the full cooperation of the senior naval officer on the island, an admiral who was more concerned with completing Peleliu's airfield than preparing its defenses. Partly to help Nakagawa deal with the navy, Inoue dispatched Maj. Gen. Kenjiro Murai to Peleliu in July 1944. Because Murai and Nakagawa both died at Peleliu, the former's exact role has remained unclear. General Murai's presence, however, points to the Japanese failure to insist on true unity of command for an island defense.[25]

In spite of his superior's presence on the island, Colonel Nakagawa appears to have remained in day-to-day control of Peleliu's defense. To accomplish his mission, Nakagawa formally planned a defense along the lines of the ones that had been improvised on Tinian and Guam. His intention was still to destroy the landing at or near the beaches, which he had correctly determined to be the southern beaches that gave quickest access to the airfield. The beaches were mined and covered with obstacles to such an extent that one U.S. admiral called them "the most formidable which we encountered in the entire Pacific."[26]

Additionally, the beaches were covered by automatic weapons and 47-mm guns to be fired from reinforced concrete bunkers and positions dug into coral ridges. Also, the Japanese might have planned some type of flame defense similar to that developed in 1940 by the British (see chapter 3). Earlier in 1944, the Japanese had planned to dump oil in a mangrove swamp adjacent to the beaches on Yap in the Carolines and set it alight if the Americans landed. A document captured on Peleliu indicated that perhaps Nakagawa had similar plans for Peleliu, but they were not carried out.[27]

If the Americans succeeded in getting a foothold on the beach, Nakagawa planned to counterattack with both tanks and infantry, although he realized that his tanks were no match for U.S. armor and antitank weapons. He also instructed his troops to use what has been called "passive infiltration." Rather than infiltrating the U.S. lines, defenders were instructed to hide in the ruins of defensive positions, allow the Americans to pass by them, and then attack from the enemy's rear. This tactic took advantage of the Marines' penchant for speedily consolidating a beachhead and bypassing isolated enemy pockets in the process.

The biggest change from the defensive tactics used in the Marianas, however, lay in Nakagawa's masterful use of Peleliu's broken coral terrain to create a defense in depth. For more than two years before the army arrived, the Japanese navy had been digging tunnels on the island, mostly for support facilities rather than fighting positions. Lacking time to duplicate the navy's effort, army troops looked to Peleliu's many natural caves and began to enlarge, reinforce, and adapt them to a defense in depth. The position included more than five hundred caves, but a lack of unified command prevented Nakagawa from combining the army and navy positions into a truly integrated defense system.[28]

On 15 September 1944, following a three-day naval gunfire bombardment, the 1st Marine Division landed on Peleliu. The defenders limited the effect of the bombardment by refusing to fire back, thereby preventing the gunfire ships from locating many of the Japanese gun positions. On D-day, the Americans were able to get ashore against heavy resistance, however, and then successfully withstood Colonel Nakagawa's counterattack that came, as he had planned, at the end of the day.

Although they could not prevent the landing, the defenders denied the Americans the speedy victory predicted by Maj. Gen. William H. Rupertus, commander of the 1st Marine Division. As the Marines were forced to dig their enemies out of Peleliu's extensive cave network, U.S. casualties became so high that his division bordered on the point of ineffectiveness. Rupertus reluctantly asked for reinforcement by the army, and the 81st Infantry Division was committed to the fight.

During the the battle, specially designated Japanese teams made "sacrificial" attacks with small arms and "suicidal" attacks with explosives, usually against the American tanks.[29] These attacks were made selectively, however, in keeping with efforts to avoid the mistakes of Saipan.

As the end became apparent, General Murai contemplated ordering a Saipan-like final suicide attack using all surviving defenders. On receiving word of this plan, General Inoue reminded Murai that Saipan was lost quickly because of such attacks and directed the defenders of Peleliu to forgo such an operation. Following this directive, the Japanese continued to resist until 24 November, when Colonel Nakagawa and General Murai committed suicide in their underground headquarters. In

Modified LVT spewing flames into cave at Peleliu. The Japanese defended the island at the water's edge and then employed the cave warfare tactics pioneered at Biak. Flame weapons were instrumental in overcoming the Japanese cave defenses.
(U.S. Marine Corps photo, No. 98259)

spite of holding off defeat for more than two months and inflicting one of the highest casualty rates of the war on the attackers, Peleliu's defenders had not found a method of turning back an American landing.

The Situation on Iwo Jima

Iwo Jima lies near the southern end of a long chain of islands, called the Nanpo Shoto, that extend south from Japan. In the Volcano group, Iwo Jima had been formally part of Japan since 1891 and was administered as part of the Tokyo Prefecture. For most of its history as a Japanese outpost, it was used to cultivate sugar cane and produce sulfur (Iwo Jima means Sulfur Island). The island came into importance in late 1944 because of its location halfway between the Marianas and homeland Japan. Airfields on Iwo Jima furnished a means for Japanese bombers to attack U.S. B-29 bases in the Marianas. With these airfields in U.S. hands, American fighters would be able to accompany the B-29s during their raids on Tokyo and other Japanese cities.

Understanding the importance of Iwo Jima, the Japanese high command had placed it under the command of the Thirty-first Army when that organization was created. To command the defense of the island, the Japanese chose Lt. Gen. Tadamichi Kuribayashi, a fifty-four-year-old cavalry officer with a distinguished record. Also, he was familiar with his enemy; he had served in the United States between the two world wars. To conduct the defense, General Kuribayashi had 13,586 army troops, including the 109th Infantry Division, the 2d Independent Mixed Brigade, and the 145th Infantry Regiment that had been slated for Saipan before that island fell.[30] These units were reinforced by the 26th Tank Regiment under the command of Lt. Col. Baron Takeichi Nishi, a flamboyant cavalryman who had won a gold medal as an equestrian in the 1932 Olympics at Los Angeles. On 26 June 1944, Imperial General Headquarters assumed direct control of Iwo Jima in place of Thirty-first Army Headquarters, which had been lost with the fall of Saipan.[31]

In addition to Army forces on Iwo Jima, the navy had 7,347 personnel commanded by Rear Adm. Toshinosuke Ichimaru, an aviator whose injuries from an airplane crash during the 1920s had kept him in rear-echelon assignments earlier in the war.[32] In spite of the lessons from the Marianas and Palaus about the need for unity of command, these naval forces were not fully under General Kuribayashi's control.

To better support his defense, Kuribayashi formed his five artillery battalions into a brigade that controlled the fire of 361 artillery pieces, 75-mm or greater; twelve 320-mm mortars; sixty-five smaller mortars; and seventy rocket launchers of various calibers.[33] A major concern for the defenders was dealing with American tanks. In addition to artillery, the Japanese had seventy antitank guns and twenty-three Type 97 tanks mounting 57-mm guns.[34] They also had ninety-four antiaircraft guns, 75-mm or greater, and two hundred smaller ones. Many of these guns also could be used in a ground defense role.

From documents captured on Saipan, the Americans had estimated that Japanese troops on Iwo Jima numbered between 13,000 and 14,000, an underestimation of as many as 7,000.[35] To deal with this situation, the Americans planned to attack Iwo Jima with three Marine divisions, the 4th and 5th in the assault and the 3d as a floating reserve. The three divisions and other assault units totaled 70,647 troops; Marine and army garrison and support forces brought the total expeditionary force strength to 111,308 troops.[36]

When General Kuribayashi assumed command of Iwo Jima's defense on 29 May 1944, he was concerned that the Americans might attack as early as the summer of 1944. His concern was heightened by U.S. carrier strikes during June. Had the United States invaded at that time, the attackers would have found the island essentially undefended. After careful consideration, Kuribayashi estimated that an invasion could come as early as October 1944 and set that time as a target for completing the island's defenses. Although the Americans had good reason for not attacking during the summer, they eventually paid dearly for the delay.

The Japanese Plan

The development of the defensive plans for Iwo Jima represents a case study of the evolution of the Japanese anti-landing concept as it moved away from defense at the water's edge. On 6 April 1944, General Obata, Thirty-first Army commander who later died on Guam, had inspected Iwo Jima and emphasized a defense based on destroying the enemy at the beach.[37] After inspecting the defenses in June, General Kuribayashi rejected the idea of a defense at the water's edge and halted construction of defensive positions at the beach. Instead, he planned a counterattack-oriented defense in depth. This concept also suited Baron Nishi, who considered his tanks to be the centerpiece of any counterattack.

As Kuribayashi began to implement his plans, several influences caused him to believe that neither a defense at the water's edge nor a counterattack-oriented defense would be successful against an American landing. In November 1944, he received a new anti-landing doctrine titled "Antiamphibious Operations."[38] This latest doctrine incorporated the lessons of the Marianas and Peleliu, particularly the success of defenses in depth. The doctrine was reinforced by reports from Peleliu that seriously exaggerated the success of the defenders there and at neighboring Angaur.[39] Based on Germany's defeat at Normandy, the German General Staff had also cautioned the Japanese against trying a defense at the water's edge.[40] American air and naval gunfire that bombarded Iwo Jima during 1944 also influenced Kuribayashi. The force of these bombardments convinced him that the intensity of American gunfire would prevent him from conducting any counterattack large enough to deal with a major landing.

At one point, Kuribayashi considered blowing Iwo Jima off the map with explosives or at least destroying the level areas that would be usable for American airfields. After being told by engineers that such a plan was impossible, he set about to make the island one of the most highly fortified places on earth. In doing so, he faced three major problems: lack of time, shortage of fortification materials, and reluctance by the navy to cooperate. Iwo Jima's volcanic rock was soft enough to be tunneled through with hand tools, but subterranean heat and a lack of water resulted in terrible working conditions and slow progress. Because of these problems, only seventeen kilometers of tunnels, out of a planned twenty-eight kilometers, had been completed when the Americans landed. One unfinished tunnel would have connected the positions inside Mount Suribachi, an extinct volcano that dominated Iwo Jima's exposed landing beaches, with the main defensive position to the north.[41]

Compounding Kuribayashi's problems were an almost total lack of barbed wire and a severe shortage of cement. Iwo Jima received only half the cement that Kuribayashi needed, and even that was not used entirely according to his plan. The navy insisted on constructing gun positions at the beach in spite of army predictions that they would be destroyed by any prelanding naval gunfire bombardment. As a result, more than half of Iwo's precious supply of cement was used for beach positions. The Japanese apparently constructed no underwater obstacles. They did emplace a wide variety of mines on the landing beaches that included anti-invasion, antipersonnel, and antitank mines, as well as depth charges and aerial bombs used as land mines.[42]

The Battle for Iwo Jima

The battle for Iwo Jima started on 16 February 1945 with the commencement of UDT operations and prelanding naval gunfire bombardment. General Kuribayashi had issued orders to all gun positions to hold their fire until the actual landing was in progress and the landing craft were immediately off the beaches. On the first day of the bombardment, however, navy coastal defense guns opened fire on U.S. rocket ships that were providing covering fire for UDT swimmers reconnoitering the southeastern landing beaches. The Japanese gunners apparently mistook the UDT activity for the start of the landing because, shortly thereafter, Admiral Ichimaru informed Tokyo that his forces had repulsed an American landing.[43]

The premature Japanese fire did not halt UDT operations, but it did expose the Japanese gun positions to counterbattery fire from American warships, exactly as General Kuribayashi had feared. As a result, twenty-three of the twenty-four Japanese naval gun positions along the beach were destroyed by naval gunfire before the first Marine units landed on D-day.[44]

Except for the premature opening fire, the Japanese defense was executed more or less as planned. Two Marine divisions landed on D-day in order to provide enough force to withstand the anticipated counter-attack that night. They afforded such a massive target that Japanese gunners could hardly miss them. In spite of the resulting casualties, the Marines captured Mount Suribachi in four days, sooner than the defenders had anticipated. The Americans then had to face Kuribayashi's main defensive position that had been dug across the center of the island in a way that it could not be outflanked. For almost a month, Marine frontline units engaged in the most brutal kind of close-quarter fighting as they overcame the hundreds of underground fighting positions that honeycombed the northern half of the island. At the beachhead, supporting troops continued to face a constant rain of artillery and mortar fire that made the rear areas only slightly less dangerous than the front lines. The Japanese government announced the fall of Iwo Jima on 17 March, but some resistance continued for several weeks.[45] Most of Iwo Jima's twenty thousand defenders, including their senior leaders, were killed in the battle or committed suicide. At this heavy cost, General Kuribayashi had caused more than twenty-five thousand U.S. casualties and bought a month for his comrades on Okinawa. He had not, however, solved the problem of defeating a landing.

Observations

Although the defense of the central and western Pacific nominally remained the responsibility of the Japanese navy, defense of the islands themselves became largely an army affair after the fall of the Marshalls. The nature of the defense against landings shifted slowly from trying to defeat the landing force at the water's edge, to driving it back into the sea after landing, and then to delaying and punishing the enemy force after it had become firmly established ashore. Although this final approach satisfied the strategic need to buy time to prepare for the defense of the homeland, it still did not succeed in defeating an amphibious operation. The Japanese were beginning to fear that such an achievement was beyond their capability.

By the fall of Saipan, the Japanese clearly understood the need for unity of command. Service rivalries and the apparent inability of the Japanese to confront this issue openly, however, seem to have made such unity impossible. The lack of a unified command caused several problems that persisted throughout the war. One such problem was the conflict of priorities between the services. During the period that island garrisons were preparing to meet American invasions, navy commanders generally gave priority of men, materials, and time to constructing airfields and associated facilities, even when airplanes were unlikely to be available. Army commanders, on the other hand, gave priority to constructing anti-landing defenses and inland fighting positions. Lack of unity by the defenders was in stark contrast to the unity of command exercised by U.S. Navy leaders in conducting the landings.

Japanese problems were also exacerbated by an anti-landing doctrine that changed frequently in reaction to American amphibious developments. The Japanese recognized the need for a formal anti-landing doctrine after their 1943 defeat at Attu in the Aleutians. Subsequently, the army and navy issued the first of a number of documents containing anti-landing doctrine. These publications contain general concepts; tactical and technical details; and, in some cases, historical examples. One navy manual issued in 1943, for instance, uses the German defense at Dieppe to illustrate the concept of defeating a landing at the water's edge.[46] As the war progressed, the Japanese changed their concept from one similar to the Dieppe defense to a counterattack-oriented defense within the beachhead and then to a delaying action in depth. Unable to find a workable doctrine, Japanese commanders were forced to rethink the basic concepts of defense as they prepared for each landing.

At first look, a comparison of the overall sizes of Japanese and American forces might lend credence to the idea that landing forces simply overwhelmed the defenders. The ratio at Iwo Jima, for example, was slightly more than five to one; however, the nature of an amphibious operation requires large numbers of supporting troops. This was particularly true on Iwo Jima, where everything, including drinking water, that was needed by the landing force had to be transported to the island and landed across the beach. If only the three assault divisions, with their own support units, are weighed against the defending garrison, the ratio becomes slightly more than three to one. The ratio is even less if only combat troops are counted.

Iwo Jima illustrates the way that delay can work to the advantage of a defender, but the speed of the American advance across the Pacific largely denied the Japanese the time required to construct adequate defenses. After the war, Adm. Kichisaburo Nomura, prewar ambassador to the United States, noted, "Everywhere, I think, you attacked before the defense was ready. You came far more quickly than we expected."[47]

The Americans feared that the Japanese were using chemical warfare several times during the central Pacific campaign. Gas scares occurred at both Saipan and Peleliu. At Saipan, Marines in a half-track fired their 75-mm gun into a cave that had been used to manufacture picric acid for explosives. Several Marines were temporarily overcome by fumes and a gas alarm was sounded.[48] A similar incident occurred on Peleliu when Japanese mortars fired yellow smoke rounds into an American position.[49] Although glass hand grenades containing hydrogen cyanide were found on Iwo Jima, the Japanese apparently had no overall plans to use chemical warfare in defending against amphibious operations. By the time of the Iwo Jima invasion, the Japanese were actually in the process of destroying their chemical warfare supplies, apparently to avoid giving the Americans any excuse for initiating chemical warfare against the Japanese homeland.[50] American planners had considered using chemical weapons against Iwo Jima but rejected the idea because of a U.S. policy that prohibited the first use of chemical weapons.[51]

Prior to the Iwo Jima operation, the Japanese had unsuccessfully tried the defense at the water's edge and the counterattack-based mobile defense. U.S. supporting arms were instrumental in overcoming both of these defenses. Given adequate time, a systematic naval gunfire bombardment could shatter any defensive line that could be constructed to protect a beach. At the same time, naval gunfire and air support made movement of counterattack forces on a large scale nearly impossible. As a result of these experiences, the Japanese were losing hope of establishing a successful defense against an American landing.

The Ultimate Naval Defense:
Okinawa and Japan, 1945

One Plane for One Warship
One Boat for One Ship
One Man for Ten of the Enemy
or One Tank
Battle slogan, Japanese Thirty-second Army, quoted in Nichols and Shaw, *Okinawa*

As the Japanese fell back toward Japan proper, the battles had progressed from their defense of islands captured early in World War II, to islands held by Japan under mandate since the end of World War I, and to Iwo Jima, a Japanese island since 1891. Okinawa marked another step in that progression. Associated with Japan since the 1500s, it had been a Japanese prefecture since 1879. Most Japanese regarded an invasion of Okinawa as only slightly less ominous than an invasion of Japan itself. Some of them viewed the defense of Okinawa as another opportunity to buy time for the defenders of mainland Japan, but others believed that Okinawa was their final chance to stop the American advance short of an invasion of the home islands. In either case, Okinawans feared that they were about to be sacrificed in an effort to protect Japan.

Their fears were well founded because the Japanese military had demonstrated a preoccupation with self-sacrifice since the days of the samurai. This preoccupation had manifested itself in several ways during the battles leading up to the invasion of Okinawa. One was the practice of suicide by defeated soldiers. In 1941, Japanese War Minister Hideki Tojo had prepared a set of battle ethics emphasizing that to be taken alive by the enemy was the ultimate form of dishonor.[1] The degree to which the military accepted this code of ethics was seen throughout the Pacific war as entire island garrisons fought to the death rather than surrender. Although senior officers sometimes committed ritual suicide with a sword, self-inflicted gunshots or hand grenades held against the body were more common means of suicide.

Although this uncompromising code ensured a determined defense against American attacks, it had some serious disadvantages for the Japanese. Because capture was unthinkable, soldiers killed themselves rather than risk capture should they continue to fight or attempt to escape the battle. Japanese soldiers who were taken alive had no idea of how to behave; they believed that further disgrace was impossible. Some gave vital information and assistance to their captors, actions that American prisoners would have considered treasonous.

Rather than waiting until no choice remained but to kill themselves, Japanese soldiers often took part in last-ditch attacks that had no chance of military success. Americans frequently called them banzai attacks, from the cry *tenno heika banzai* (ten thousand years for the Emperor!). The Japanese called such attacks *gyokusai*, which translates literally to "broken gem," referring to the line from an ancient poem: "Men of strength prefer to become gems to break into myriad fragments than to become roof tiles to live out their lives in idleness."[2] The accepted military translation of gyokusai was "honorable death," which came to mean deliberately seeking death in battle. The first large attack of this nature was carried out by survivors of the garrison on Attu. Such attacks often resulted in enemy casualties, but their purpose was to ensure honorable death for the attackers.

The final refinement of suicide as a tactic came with the introduction of the kamikazes in the Philippines. By the time the Japanese were faced with an imminent invasion of Okinawa, they had employed all three of these aspects of suicide in battle. The difference at Okinawa lay in the increased use of suicide tactics and the degree to which they formed the heart of the Japanese defense.

The Situation at Okinawa

The Thirty-second Army, activated on 1 April 1944, had responsibility for the defense of Okinawa. Its commander, Lt. Gen. Mitsuru Ushijima, reported to the commander of the 10th Area Army in Formosa. To defend Okinawa, General Ushijima had approximately 100,000 troops. The majority were in army units, including the 24th and 62d Infantry Divisions, 44th Independent Mixed Brigade, 5th Artillery Command, 11th Shipping Group, and 27th Tank Regiment.[3] The 9th Infantry Division also was part of the Thirty-second Army until its transfer to Formosa in December 1944. For better control, Ushijima placed all of his artillery under a single command. After the battle, U.S. intelligence accounted for 317 guns or mortars, 70-mm or greater. One Japanese source indicates that the artillery command had 470 pieces.[4] The 11th Shipping Group consisted of seven sea raiding squadrons, each of which had one hundred suicide boats with crews and support personnel. Three of these squadrons were located in the Kerama Retto, a group of islands ten to twenty miles west of southern Okinawa. In addition to army units, the Thirty-second Army also controlled an 8,825-man naval base force. Commanded by Rear Adm. Minoru Ota, a former commander of a special naval landing force in the SWPA, the Okinawa naval force included a midget submarine unit. The Thirty-second Army also included 23,350 Okinawans who had been impressed into the *Boetai* (Home Guard) and special "Blood-and-Iron-for-the-Emperor" units.

Because so few aircraft were available on Okinawa, General Ushijima's responsibility was limited to the ground defense of the island. Air operations, including suicide operations against the American fleet, were to be carried out from Japan by the Fifth Air Fleet and Sixth Air Army and from Formosa by the 8th Air Division.[5] To prosecute this effort, these air forces had assembled almost one thousand aircraft, more than half of them planned for suicide attacks. Although kamikaze tactics had proved to be an effective way of increasing the probability that a pilot with limited training could successfully attack an enemy ship, three serious problems remained. First, many of the aircraft were unable to fight their way through defending U.S. fighters to reach the targets. Second, experience in the Philippines showed that only one of every four kamikazes had actually hit its target.[6] Third, even a successful attack did not always sink a ship or put it out of action.

A kamikaze could, and did, cause fearful damage, particularly when it hit a smaller ship or the crowded flight deck of an aircraft carrier. The weight of bombs that could be carried by most suicide aircraft was not enough to sink a large ship under most conditions. To solve that problem, the Japanese navy had been working on a suicide bomb for a longer period of time than kamikaze tactics had been officially sanctioned. In mid-1944, a junior naval officer had proposed building a rocket-propelled winged bomb that could be guided to the target by a human pilot. After some debate, the navy adopted the concept and named the projected weapon *Oka* (cherry blossom). Production began in September.[7]

The Oka's 1,200-pound warhead and speed to 350 knots gave it an excellent chance of penetrating a large warship's armor and sinking it.

The Oka, a rocket-propelled suicide bomb. During the naval defense of Okinawa, the Japanese introduced this winged bomb, shown here under the twin-engine Betty bomber that would carry it to its target.
(Captured Japanese photo)

Although the Oka, at a length of six meters, was a much smaller target than a conventional aircraft, its method of delivery to the target area had a serious weakness. The Oka's limited range forced the twin-engine bomber carrying it to the target area to fly well inside the radius of the combat air patrols protecting the U.S. fleet. To perform this difficult new mission, the Japanese navy created a force called *Kaigun Jinrai Butai* (Navy Thunder Gods Corps), which became operational in November 1944.[8]

The submarine equivalent of the Oka was the *kaiten* (heaven shaker), a manned version of the Japanese Type 93 torpedo. Carried by a mother submarine, this weapon had been employed with limited success in November 1944 against the American fleet anchorage at Ulithi Atoll in the western Caroline Islands. At the time of the Okinawa landing, a number of kaiten-carrying submarines were standing ready in Japan.

In assessing the Japanese defense at Okinawa, U.S. intelligence was remarkably accurate with respect to the organization of the Thirty-second Army. The Americans correctly identified the two Japanese divi-

The Ultimate Naval Defense ~ 157

sions, the 44th Independent Mixed Brigade, and most of the supporting units. U.S. intelligence significantly understated total Japanese strength, however, in estimating 53,000 to 56,000 defenders compared with the roughly 100,000 actually present.[9] It also underestimated the amount of Japanese artillery on Okinawa. American planners correctly anticipated the general scheme of the Japanese defense, understood the potential for suicide boat attacks, and correctly predicted that the principal air threat would come from airfields on the island of Kyūshū, not from Okinawa itself.

To land against this considerable defense, the U.S. Tenth Army was organized into two corps, the XXIV Army Corps and the Marine V Amphibious Corps. The Tenth Army consisted of four army infantry divisions (7th, 27th, 77th, and 96th) and three Marine divisions (1st, 2d, and 6th). The 81st Infantry Division under Admiral Nimitz's control on New Caledonia was available, if needed. Overall strength of the Tenth Army was 180,000 troops, of which 116,000 were in five divisions committed to the initial assault.[10]

Okinawa is a sixty-mile-long island that varies in width from two to eighteen miles; it is most rugged in the north. Its cities, ports, and airfields are concentrated in the south below the narrow "waist" near the town of Ishikawa. On the west coast near Hagushi is a fifteen-thousand-yard stretch of beach, of which nine thousand yards are suitable for landings.

Based on their knowledge of earlier American amphibious assaults, the Japanese had expected their enemy to attack Okinawa by landing six to ten divisions across these beaches. Two of the island's most important airfields, Yontan and Kadena, were located on the flat ground inland from the Hagushi beaches. To the south of these airfields, coral ridges and plateaus running across the islands provided an almost ideal series of defensive positions. Okinawa's proximity to Japan also affected its defense. As the Pacific drive closed on Japan, the attackers' lines of communication lengthened, while those of the defenders became shorter. Only three hundred fifty miles from Japan, Okinawa was within range of aircraft operating from Kyūshū. The Japanese could use home airfields to make up for carriers that no longer existed.

As the Japanese began to prepare for the defense of Okinawa, the sacrifices made during earlier battles began to pay dividends. Initially, the Americans had planned to attack Okinawa on 1 March 1945, but continued fighting on Luzon had delayed the availability of amphibious ships. That, plus the prediction of bad weather during March, caused

U.S. planners to postpone the landing until 1 April. The defenders would take full advantage of the delay.

The Japanese Plan

Okinawa had remained relatively undefended during much of the war. After the Japanese began to draw in their defensive lines in 1943, Imperial General Headquarters came to regard the island primarily as an airfield to protect the new absolute national defense sphere. In August 1944, representatives from the high command inspected Okinawa to determine what progress was being made in the completion of airfields. As a result of pressure on the Thirty-second Army, airfields at Yontan and Kadena were essentially completed by September 1944.

After the Americans' successful penetration of the absolute defense sphere in the Marianas, the Japanese had realized that Okinawa would eventually come under attack. The Thirty-second Army had issued its first plan for the defense of the island on 19 July 1944.[11] In keeping with the doctrine of the time, General Ushijima intended to annihilate the landing at the water's edge. Failing in that, he planned to withdraw to defensive positions constructed in depth throughout the island. The general considered the three divisions and one brigade that were then available to be adequate for carrying out his defensive concept.

On 13 November, Imperial General Headquarters forced General Ushijima to completely reconsider his situation when it ordered him to detach his best division, the 9th, for duty in the Philippines.[12] Ironically, the division ended up in Formosa, where it contributed to the defense of neither the Philippines nor Okinawa. After losing the 9th Division, Ushijima decided to abandon northern Okinawa and defend only the area south of the island's central isthmus. Detailed staff planning, however, revealed that defending the entire southern part of the island was also too ambitious for the available forces. As a result, Ushijima decided to give up the Hagushi plain, where the most likely landing beaches were located, in order to establish a strong defensive position across the island north of Naha, Shuri, and Yonabaru. Any landings north of that position would be unopposed by the army. Landings south of the position would be met at the water's edge to prevent any opportunity for the enemy to attack the main defenses from the rear. In addition to forcing the Thirty-second Army to forgo a defense of the most likely landing beaches, the new plan also resulted in abandonment of the newly constructed airfields at Yontan and Kadena. Ushijima received permission to destroy the airfields in March 1945, and their destruction was completed by the end of the month.[13]

In many ways, southern Okinawa was an ideal place to make a stand. The ground was broken by ridges that would impede movement of the attackers. The area had many natural caves and, beneath a layer of coral from thirty to sixty feet deep, the red clay was conducive to tunneling. The coral afforded a level of protection that made up for the almost complete lack of cement available to the defenders. Timber for shoring up tunnels was available in the north, but the Japanese experienced great difficulties in transporting the logs to the south. Originally, General Ushijima had expected each unit to construct underground shelter adequate for three times its troop strength.[14] He abandoned this goal in November 1944, but the Thirty-second Army still managed to dig sixty miles of tunnels before the Americans landed.

Tactically, the defenders paid a great deal of attention to the location of their weapons, particularly antitank guns. Fighting positions were mutually supporting and generally had more than one opening. In many cases, the defenders organized their positions to accommodate a reverse slope defense. In earlier battles, the overwhelmingly offensive nature of Japanese tactical doctrine had hindered their planning to counter American attacks. The Japanese defended their positions fiercely but did not always lay them out well. On Okinawa, the Thirty-second Army managed to overcome those earlier weaknesses. In the words of a III Amphibious Corps document: "It was on Okinawa that the enemy had advanced his underground fortifications to the point where it was possible to discern fighting from within the earth as an established doctrine."[15]

While the Thirty-second Army waited for the invaders to come to them in their underground positions, the plan was for the Japanese navy to deal with the amphibious forces as they made the landing. By the time a landing on Okinawa became likely, however, the navy's surface forces had been almost totally destroyed. The battleship *Yamato* and a small number of cruisers and destroyers remained in Japan. Naval officers debated whether those ships should be used to attack a landing on Okinawa or saved to resist the anticipated invasion of the homeland. In any case, action against a landing on Okinawa would fall largely to suicide boats already in the landing area and to air attacks from airfields on Kyūshū and Formosa. In laying out this naval defense, Japanese planners once again had to wrestle with the issue of target priority. On 31 March 1945, the day before the landing on Okinawa, the Japanese Third and Fifth Air Fleets issued a directive stating that the first priority of attack would be warships. Only after they had been dealt with would attention be turned to the amphibious ships.[16] The navy's plan to lay aerial mines off Okinawa was foiled by a lack of aircraft.[17]

The Battle of Okinawa

On 14 March 1945, a Japanese reconnaissance plane from Truk reported that a U.S. task force was moving out of Ulithi. In response, Imperial General Headquarters placed air units in Japan on alert. When American carrier planes attacked airfields in southern Japan, the Japanese responded with conventional attacks against the carriers. On 21 March, the Fifth Air Fleet attempted to conduct the first special attack using Okas. Eighteen bombers took off; fifteen carried Okas.[18] U.S. Navy fighters intercepted the slow-moving bombers sixty miles from the American carriers and destroyed all of them in a matter of minutes.

On 26 March, the U.S. Army's 77th Infantry Division landed in the Kerama Retto and caught the Japanese by surprise. Unfortunately for the defenders, the commander of the local suicide boat unit was in Okinawa with many of his crews for an anti-landing exercise.[19] As a result, no order was given for the boats to attack the invasion fleet. Before securing the islands on 29 March, the 77th Division had captured or destroyed more than 350 of the Japanese craft.[20] Between 29 March and 3 April, the Japanese navy sent four submarines from bases in Japan to attack the invasion fleet with kaitens. The U.S. Navy sank two of the submarines before they reached Okinawa. The other two were unable to evade U.S. antisubmarine defenses and returned to Japan with their kaitens.[21] An effort to use kaitens from bases on Okinawa failed when the ship carrying eight weapons and their crews to Okinawa was sunk.

On 1 April 1945, two infantry divisions and two Marine divisions from Lt. Gen. Simon Bolivar Buckner's Tenth Army landed unopposed across Okinawa's Hagushi beaches. Simultaneously, the 2d Marine Division simulated a landing on Okinawa's southeast coast. When the amphibious force carrying the Marines retired, the Japanese mistakenly reported—as they had at Tinian—that they had repulsed the landing. Following the actual landing at Hagushi, the Marines turned north and the army moved south toward General Ushijima's defenses. In spite of his earlier decision to fight only a defensive battle, the Japanese general was pressured by his subordinates to conduct a large-scale counterattack in keeping with traditional Japanese views of combat and earlier anti-landing doctrine. Ushijima agreed and scheduled a counterattack

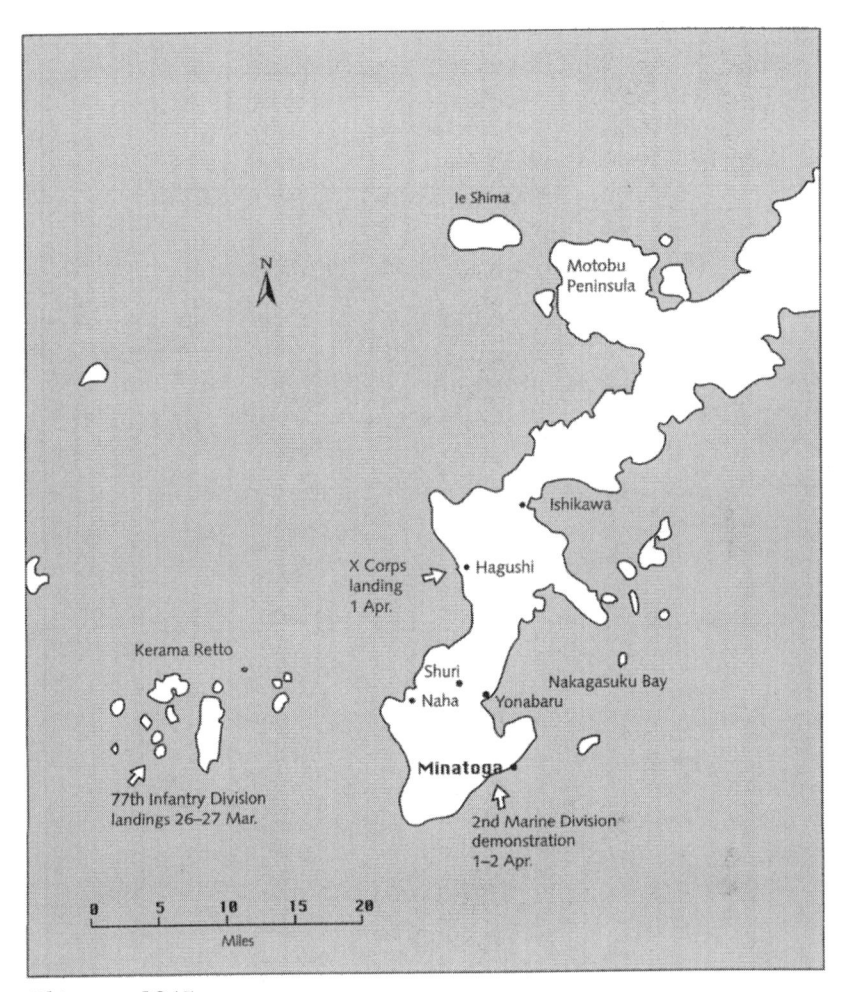

Okinawa, 1945

for the night of 6 April. When the Japanese detected an American task force south of Naha on 4 April, however, they feared a landing in their rear and canceled the counterattack.[22] They canceled another counterattack on 8 April for similar reasons. When the counterattack finally took place on 12 April, it was unsuccessful.

Off the invasion beaches, the Japanese navy launched a suicide operation of unprecedented scale. Imperial General Headquarters had ordered the Sixth Air Army to participate in the operation, with the agreement that army planes would attack the transports while the navy went

The Yamato, *the largest battleship in the world. While on a suicide mission to disrupt the American landing at Okinawa in April 1945, she was sunk by U.S. carrier planes.*
(U.S. Navy photo, No. 704702)

after the warships. The first of what would be nine general kamikaze attacks took place on 6 April. Aircraft from both Japan and Formosa took part in the attack. So much smoke filled the air over the U.S. ships that Japanese reconnaissance aircraft could not assess the situation accurately. The Thirty-second Army incorrectly reported observing thirty ships sinking and more than twenty others burning.[23]

The following day witnessed the most spectacular—and arguably the most futile—suicide attack of the war. After hearing arguments as to how best to employ its remaining surface forces, the Japanese navy made the decision to launch a special attack force led by the battleship *Yamato*. This magnificent ship, accompanied by an escort of destroyers and a cruiser, was ordered to proceed to Okinawa and attack U.S. naval forces there, if necessary by running aground and acting as an armored fortress on the beach. U.S. carrier aircraft sank the giant battleship and all but four of her escorts long before they were in position to threaten American forces on Okinawa. More than four thousand Japanese lost their lives in the action, including Vice Adm. Seichi Ito, the task force commander.[24]

Ashore on Okinawa, the Thirty-second Army continued to carry out its plan to delay the American attackers for as long as possible. By skillful use of the terrain, the defenders forced the Americans to fight their way through seemingly endless defensive positions that limited the U.S. advance to about one hundred yards per day. On 25 May, almost two months after the American landing, the Thirty-second Army began its final withdrawal to last-ditch positions on the southern tip of Okinawa.

While the Thirty-second Army was buying time ashore, the Fifth Air Fleet in Japan carried out an unprecedented aerial suicide effort off Okinawa against the U.S. fleet and Royal Navy ships that were reinforcing the Americans. Although figures vary greatly by source, the Japanese flew 1,900 to 3,000 kamikaze sorties and 5,000 to 6,300 conventional sorties against Okinawa's invaders.[25] Estimates of Japanese aircraft losses during the operation range from 4,100 to 7,830. For this terrible price, the Japanese sank 34 Allied ships and damaged 368. Although the damaged ships included battleships, cruisers, and aircraft carriers, no ship larger than a destroyer was sunk.

In spite of their potential lethality, the Okas—nicknamed *baka* (foolish) bombs by the Americans—sank only one ship, the U.S. destroyer *Mannert L. Abele*. More important, the Japanese generally failed to direct their attacks against the amphibious ships. Regardless of orders, the inexperienced kamikaze pilots often attacked the first ship they saw, usually a destroyer on picket duty between Japan and Okinawa. This situation posed a great hazard for the picket ships but furnished a welcome relief for the invasion fleet itself.

The kamikaze campaign exacted a heavy toll on the American fleet that resulted in the deaths of almost five thousand U.S. sailors, but it had no significant effect on the fighting ashore. By 19 June, the Americans had pushed the remaining defenders into a small pocket at the southern end of the island. That night, Lt. Gen. Isamu Cho, Ushijima's chief of staff, took an unusual step. Concerned that the policy of insisting on death rather than surrender had destroyed the Japanese officer corps, he ordered the surviving officers of the Thirty-second Army staff to try to escape through the American lines.[26] About twenty officers followed the general's order.

Around 0340 on the morning of 22 June, Cho and Ushijima committed suicide in the traditional manner by disemboweling themselves with daggers, after which they were decapitated by aides using samurai swords. A Japanese mortar shell had killed Ushijima's American counterpart, General Buckner, several days earlier. A ceremony on 22 June marked the official end of Japanese resistance, but mopping up continued until 2 July.

During the course of the fighting, the Americans captured 7,400

Japanese, many of them Okinawans who had been recently drafted. The remainder of the 100,000-man garrison died in the fighting. For that price, the defenders had delayed the American advance three months and killed or wounded almost 50,000 of their enemies. The Japanese had not succeeded in causing the Allies to reconsider the policy of unconditional surrender nor had they found a way to defeat an amphibious assault.

The Situation in Japan

With the fall of Okinawa, the Japanese could no longer avoid the fact that only Japan proper remained as the target of an Allied amphibious landing. Throughout the war, they had based their planning on the assumption that such an invasion was impossible and that the only real threat was air attack. The idea of invasion was unthinkable to most Japanese. No enemy had ever forcibly conquered Japan, a fact attributed by many Japanese to divine protection. American successes forced the Japanese to reconsider their assumptions, however, particularly after the fall of the Marianas.

A major problem for the Japanese had been allocation of resources. On one hand, they had been required to provide outposts, such as Iwo Jima and Okinawa, with troops and supplies necessary to delay the American advance, if not actually stop it. On the other hand, forces were needed in Japan proper to take advantage of any time gained to improve the defenses of the homeland.

After assessing the situation, Imperial General Headquarters concluded that the area around Tokyo, known as the Kanto Plain of Honshū, was the most critical for the survival of the nation. Accordingly, that region was given first priority for defensive planning. At the same time, years of experience dealing with American amphibious operations made the Japanese confident that their enemy would not strike directly at the Kanto Plain without first securing advanced naval and air bases to support an attack. Further assessment caused the Japanese to decide that the likely first stage of an American invasion of Japan proper would be an attack to seize southern Kyūshū and nearby smaller islands. As a result, the defense of Kyūshū became the immediate focus of Japanese planning, in spite of its second place to Honshū in overall importance.[27]

To defend Kyūshū and Honshū, the Japanese planned to raise a new 2 million-man army of forty divisions, twenty independent brigades, and supporting troops.[28] Some of the troops would be brought in from the Kwantung Army in Manchuria, but most would be mobilized in three phases starting in February 1945. The size of the new army and the scope of its mission required a new command structure to replace the one that had sufficed for most of the war. On 6 February, just before the landing on Iwo Jima, the high command had implemented a major reorganization under which Lt. Gen. Isamu Yokoyama's 16th Area Army became responsible for Kyūshū. Initially, General Yokoyama had split the responsibility by assigning the northern part of the island to the Fifty-sixth Army and the southern part to the Fifty-seventh Army. In June 1945, Fortieth Army Headquarters arrived from Formosa and assumed responsibility for Kyūshū's Satsuma Peninsula in the southwestern part of the island. This action left the Fifty-seventh Army responsible for the Miyazaki Plain and the Ariake Bay area.[29]

By the time U.S. forces secured Okinawa in July 1945, the 16th Area Army had more than 200,000 troops on Kyūshū and associated smaller islands. They were organized into fourteen divisions, seven independent mixed brigades, and three tank brigades. Eight divisions, three mixed brigades, and two tank brigades were located in southern Kyūshū under the command of the Fortieth and Fifty-seventh Armies.[30]

During the course of the war, Japan's air defense organization had changed several times in response to an increasing threat. As the possibility of invasion increased, Imperial General Headquarters had created the Air General Army to control the defensive effort of the army air force. As part of that effort, the Sixth Air Army became responsible for the air defense of Kyūshū.[31] Originally, Imperial General Headquarters had planned to place all defensive aircraft and antiaircraft guns in Japan under unified command regardless of service. This goal proved impossible to achieve in the time available, so the Fifth Air Fleet was made responsible for the navy's part of the air defense of the homeland. In May and June 1945, U.S. planners, using Ultra, counted 6,865 aircraft of various types in Japan, about half of which were fit for combat.[32]

The loss of the *Yamato* and its escort group had marked the end of the Japanese navy as a conventional fighting force. As a result, the navy focused its anti-invasion efforts on a wide variety of "special" (suicide) weapons. First in importance were the kamikaze aircraft. The navy planned to provide 2,700 of these, which would be reinforced by another 2,100 from the army.[33] The Japanese had also tested a variant of the Oka that could be launched from ramps on the shore. They planned to complete several hundred launchers by September 1945, with a total of ninety placed in Kyūshū and Shikoku.[34] The Japanese were also producing large numbers of suicide boats, kaitens, and midget submarines

Koryu type D midget submarines, Kure Naval Base, Japan, 1945. For the defense against a landing in Japan proper, the Japanese planned to use suicide weapons, including these submarines, on an unprecedented scale. (U.S. Navy photo, No. 495759)

for suicide attacks. After the surrender of Japan, the occupying forces discovered almost four hundred miniature submarines of various types.[35] In addition to these weapons, the Japanese had also created a corps of suicide frogmen called *fukuryu* (crouching dragons). Using underwater breathing devices, the divers would wait in underwater shelters off likely invasion beaches and attack the bottoms of landing craft with shaped charges attached to long poles. More than 1,000 fukuryu had graduated from training by the time the war ended, and 2,800 more were being trained.[36] The Japanese had even developed tracked amphibians armed with torpedoes to be used against landings. Earlier plans to use these vehicles at Bougainville, Saipan, and Peleliu had been aborted. When the war ended, the vehicles were found staged at Kure Naval Base for use during the expected invasion.[37]

Following the demise of the Japanese fleet, Imperial General Headquarters abolished the Combined Fleet and replaced it with the Navy General Command. Adm. Soemu Toyoda, previously commander of the Combined Fleet, assumed command of the new organization. In spite of discussing the need for unified command after every major defeat, the Japanese had failed to create such a command structure for the final defense of the homeland. Although it took steps to give command of some land-based naval forces to army commanders, Imperial General Headquarters never established a unified command for the defense of Kyūshū. Instead, Japanese orders stressed the need for cooperation between the services.

Thanks largely to Ultra, American planners had followed the Japanese buildup on Kyūshū with a great deal of accuracy. By 25 July, Ultra had correctly identified thirteen of the fourteen divisions on Kyūshū and all of the higher headquarters.[38] The Americans were also well aware of the vast array of suicide weapons that the Japanese planned to use in the defense of Kyūshū.

Lacking adequate intelligence sources, the Japanese used their experience with previous American landings to make remarkably accurate estimates about how the enemy would attack Kyūshū. They predicted that an American force of fifteen divisions would land simultaneously near Miyazaki on the southeast coast of Kyūshū (three to four divisions), at the head of Ariake Bay (five to six divisions), and near Kushikino on the Satsuma Peninsula (one or two divisions). The Japanese also believed that the Americans would precede the main landings with a smaller one on Tanegashima Island, land two divisions at Shikoku, and drop one or two airborne divisions on inland airfields.[39]

A brief look at the American plan for the invasion of Japan demonstrates the accuracy of the Japanese estimates. The overall plan, Operation Downfall, called for an invasion in two stages. A 1945 landing on Kyūshū (Operation Olympic) would set the stage for a 1946 landing on the Kanto Plain on Honshū (Operation Coronet).[40] Under General MacArthur, Lt. Gen. Walter Krueger's Sixth Army would assault Kyūshū with four corps, three army and one Marine. Similar to Japanese predictions, I Corps would assault Miyazaki with three divisions, XI Corps would land in Ariake Bay with three divisions, and V Marine Amphibious Corps would assault the Satsuma Peninsula with three divisions. Three more divisions were assigned to IX Corps, the Sixth Army's reserve, and the 11th Airborne Division was designated a follow-on force. The navy had enough amphibious ships available to lift all thirteen divisions simultaneously. No airborne operations were planned for the in-

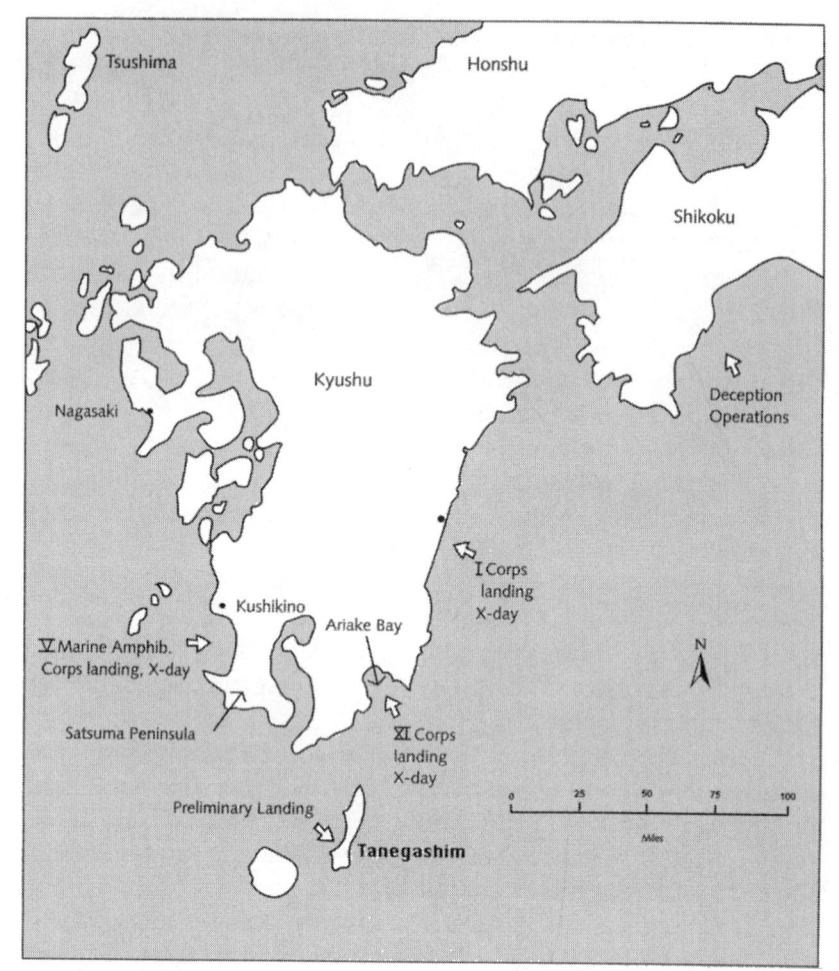

Kyushu, 1945

vasion, but the Americans played on Japanese fears of such operations through a deception plan titled Operation Pastel.[41]

The Japanese Plan

As the Japanese faced the prospect of invasion, two schools of thought developed within their military leadership regarding how to defend against a landing. One held that the delaying tactics used on Okinawa should be tried again on Kyūshū. The other school, in keeping with several doctrinal publications issued in 1945, proposed a decisive battle to stop the landing at the beach. In general, the publications returned antilanding doctrine to what it had been before Saipan, namely, defeating the attacker at or near the beach.[42]

The Japanese finally adopted a compromise plan. The main defense would be conducted from within a beachhead position but somewhat back from the shoreline. Army commanders would also hold back reserve forces that could counterattack the enemy beachhead once the site of the main landing had been determined. Opponents of this approach pointed to the German experience at Salerno to illustrate the difficulties of maneuvering a counterattack force in the face of American air and naval gunfire support. To overcome this problem, the 16th Area Army commander intended to have his units close with the American attackers in order to limit their ability to use supporting arms.

Defensive positions were connected by underground tunnels and laid out for all-around defense. The positions were located and constructed in keeping with three basic principles: (1) the positions should be located far enough inland to be beyond the effective range of naval gunfire; (2) they should be underground to provide protection from bombs and artillery; and (3) they should be in locations inaccessible to tanks, particularly flamethrowers.[43]

Tanks were a particular problem for the Japanese, whose lightly armored and under-gunned tanks were no match for American tanks. The largest Japanese antitank guns (47-mm) were only marginally effective against U.S. armor. The Japanese had developed an antitank rocket launcher similar to the American bazooka but had not produced it in significant numbers. The defenders sought to overcome this weakness by using suicide tactics. Infantrymen would attack tanks with explosive charges or shaped charges attached to the end of a long pole.

A shortage of materials, particularly cement, continued to hinder fortification efforts. By mid-August 1945, the Fifty-seventh Army had completed only half of its main defensive positions.[44] The Japanese planned a variety of mines and obstacles, but these plans remained largely unexecuted at the end of the war. The defenders erected poles and dug glider traps behind the Miyazaki beaches, however, to frustrate an airborne attack.[45] A unit of light tanks had the mission of attacking any airborne landing.

The Japanese navy believed that suicide tactics afforded the only chance of defeating the coming American landing. They planned to use these tactics off Kyūshū in two phases. Before the site of the landing became apparent, kamikaze aircraft would attack any enemy aircraft carriers that came within range. In the past, such an approach had diverted attention from American transports, which the Japanese now considered to be the highest-priority targets. Yet, if the carriers were allowed to operate unimpeded, their air groups would destroy many of the kamikaze aircraft before they could be used against the transports. Once a landing became imminent, however, all special attack forces would be directed against the enemy transports.

Given the number of aircraft, submarines, and boats available for suicide attacks, the Japanese navy estimated that it could sink 490 of an expected 2,000 American transports and landing ships. The Sixth Air Force held a map exercise in July and predicted an even more optimistic outcome. Using a 16.6 percent success rate calculated from the early phases of the Okinawa battle, it predicted the destruction of 625 transports, or 34 percent of the total American force. This figure indicated that the Japanese could destroy several American divisions at sea.

Predicted Outcome of the Battle

Operation Olympic would have been the largest amphibious operation in history if it had taken place. Instead, Japan surrendered on 15 August. Had the Americans landed on Kyūshū in November as scheduled, Japanese defenses would have been incomplete and the beaches free of mines. Given the number of naval gunfire ships and aircraft supporting the landing force, the defenders would have had little chance of preventing the attackers from establishing a beachhead. A November 1945 study by V Amphibious Corps reaches that conclusion: "From a wealth of experience, it may be assumed that, under the shock and destructive effect of preliminary and covering naval gunfire, the landing force would have carried the beach defenses."[46]

Japanese plans called for the divisions defending the beachhead positions to hold out for as long as a week in order for the mobile forces, limited to traveling at night, to position themselves for a counterattack. From a comparison of the relatively light nature of the counterattack forces with the expected forces of the attackers, a defeat of the landing force seems improbable. Even an all-out suicide effort against the U.S. fleet would seem unlikely to have succeeded in stopping the invasion.

The real question is how costly the Japanese could have made the invasion for the attackers. After the war, casualty figures as high as one-half million were thrown out to justify the use of the atomic bombs. Although such figures apparently have no basis in the military's invasion estimates, high casualties were predicted. In a 17 June 1945 message to Gen. George Marshall, for example, MacArthur predicted more than fifty thousand U.S. casualties in the first thirty days of a Kyūshū operation.[47] After observing the impact of Okinawa's casualties on the American public, President Harry S Truman was understandably reluctant to risk such high casualty rates again if he had the means to prevent them.

The end of the war in Europe on 8 May had complicated the situation for American planners. As the U.S. military began to demobilize, many combat-tested veterans in the Pacific were eligible for release from the service. Of the divisions slated for Operation Olympic, all but one had seen combat. Many of the troops, however, would be experiencing battle for the first time during an invasion of Japan. Undoubtedly, this factor would result in increased casualty rates.

Although the Japanese had failed to turn back a single landing during the war, they had inflicted such punishment on their enemy that Americans felt nothing but relief at being spared the necessity of another major amphibious operation. Commenting on the state of troop training that would have been available for the landing, a key operations staff officer with Army Ground Forces summed up American feelings by saying, "The capitulation of Hirohito saved our necks."[48]

Observations

After experimenting with several approaches to defending against a landing, the Japanese made nearly a full circle for the expected invasion of Japan. They had earlier abandoned the idea of a decisive battle at or near the beach, but they reverted to that concept for the defense of Kyūshū. Offshore, the Japanese navy intended to conduct a defense that would be concentrated on the attackers' amphibious ships. Ironically, the Japanese had been unwilling to give full support to that approach when their fleet might have been capable of destroying an American amphibious force.

Figures for total Japanese troops on Kyūshū at the end of the war vary greatly, but the numbers of divisions and other combat forces available to the two sides were roughly equal. As the attackers, the Americans would not have enjoyed the normally required three-to-one numerical superiority over the defenders. This shortcoming would have been counterbalanced, however, by an overwhelming preponderance of supporting arms at sea, in the air, and within the landing force itself.

Each side feared that the enemy would employ chemical warfare. The Japanese had no plans to use gas for the defense. Not knowing this, the Americans planned to have their troops carry gas masks and protective underwear, gloves, and socks. Full protective suits would have been available to the assault force.[49] The U.S. Chemical Warfare Service had tested chemical weapons against fortified positions similar to those used by the Japanese, and provisions for chemical warfare were built into the plans for Operation Olympic. Within the U.S. military, however, opinion was divided over whether chemical weapons should be used to overcome a stubborn Japanese defense.[50] General Marshall had also considered the possibility of employing atomic bombs in a tactical role during the landings for this purpose.[51]

Developed as a last-ditch measure, the special attack weapons, if used as part of a naval defense concept, showed the greatest potential of all Japanese attempts actually to defeat an American landing. Fortunately, the Japanese initiated this form of warfare too late in the war to develop the concept fully and to build the weapons needed to implement it as planned. Had they been able to do so, this concept might have succeeded where all others had failed. In its summary report of the Pacific war, the U.S. Strategic Bombing Survey notes that suicide tactics were "a measure of desperation, but the results obtained were considerable and, had they been much greater, might have caused us to withdraw or to modify our strategic plans."[52]

A Poor Man's Naval Defense:
Inchon and Wonsan, 1950

They caught us with our pants down.
Adm. Forrest Sherman

As the Americans prepared for Operation Olympic, the Red Army was getting ready to join the war against Japan. The Soviet Union had promised to take that step within two or three months of the end of the war in Europe. On 6 August 1945, a U.S. Army Air Force B-29 dropped the world's first atomic bomb on Hiroshima, Japan. Some historians now say that the bomb was unnecessary and its use was prompted largely by a desire to end the war before the Russians came in or, failing in that, to impress them with the power of the United States. If so, the first objective was a failure. The Japanese did not surrender, and the Soviet Union entered the war, as promised, on 8 August. Only after another atomic bomb destroyed the Japanese city of Nagasaki the following day did Japan make its first overtures toward surrender. By that time, eleven Soviet armies had attacked on three fronts in Manchuria to crush the Japanese Kwantung Army.

The country of Korea lay between the Soviet forces in northeast Asia and the U.S. occupation troops in Japan. The United States initially accorded little strategic importance to the Korean peninsula. As the Red Army began to move into Manchuria, however, the United States hastily agreed to divide Korea at the thirty-eighth parallel into U.S. and Soviet zones of postwar occupation. In the five years that followed, Korea became a microcosm of the Cold War division of the world into Communist and anti-Communist camps.

In the north, Kim-Il-Sung, aided by the Soviet Union and the People's Republic of China, created the Democratic People's Republic of Korea, a model of hard-line Stalinism. When the Soviet Army departed Korea in 1948, it left behind a well-trained 60,000-man army and even larger paramilitary forces.[1] In two years, the North Korean People's Army (NKPA) grew to a 135,000-man force of seven regular and three reserve divisions and a tank brigade equipped with Soviet T-34 tanks.[2] The North Koreans also formed a small air force armed with Soviet equipment.

Faced with a dearth of acceptable alternatives in South Korea, the United States chose to support the authoritarian regime of Dr. Syngman Rhee. The army of Dr. Rhee's Republic of Korea (ROK), started in 1946 as eight constabulary regiments, had grown by 1950 to eight divisions of 115,000 troops. These divisions were poorly trained and lacked the tanks and heavy artillery of their NKPA counterparts. U.S. forces were not much better prepared for war. Following the surrender of Japan, the United States had dismantled its World War II forces. Military personnel shrank from 12 million to 1.6 million, and the defense budget dropped from $82 billion to $13 billion.[3]

On 25 August 1950, North Korea's army ripped across the thirty-eighth parallel in an offensive aimed at conquering the Republic of Korea. President Truman responded with promises of American forces. He was also able to gain United Nations (UN) support for military action against the aggressors. American units rushed to Korea from Japan, but they were no more successful in stopping the North Koreans than the ill-trained South Koreans had been. Some units fell back; others broke and ran. By early August, the Americans and South Koreans had been forced back into a small perimeter around the South Korean port city of Pusan. The U.S. Eighth Army, under command of Lt. Gen. Walton H. Walker, was fighting for its life and the life of the Republic of Korea. While General Walker and most other American military leaders were worried about simply maintaining the tenuous foothold on the peninsula, Walker's boss had other ideas.

In July, General of the Army Douglas MacArthur, commander in chief of U.S. forces in the Far East, had assumed command of both UN forces and those of the Republic of Korea. Well versed in amphibious warfare and a master of the spectacular gesture, he decided to reverse the course of the war in Korea with a bold amphibious turning movement. Rather than commit additional reinforcements into the perimeter at Pusan, MacArthur wanted to insert them far behind the North Korean front lines and force the NKPA either to withdraw or to risk destruction. The geography of Korea limited the places where such a move could be made. Kunsan was too close to the perimeter to have the dramatic effect

MacArthur wanted. Chinnampo, the port for North Korea's capital, Pyongyang, was too far north to be feasible. A landing at Inchon, on the other hand, would achieve two important goals in addition to forcing the NKPA to withdraw from the area around Pusan. Capture of the port would position U.S. forces to seize the South Korean capital of Seoul, twenty-five miles inland. Capture of Seoul would not only give the Americans control of a vital transportation network that included Kimpo Airfield but would allow MacArthur to return the city to the South Koreans, an important political gesture.

The Situation at Inchon

Geography alone made Inchon an unlikely target for an amphibious assault. The greatest advantages that the North Koreans possessed there had been created by the forces of nature. Inchon's tidal range of more than thirty-two feet is one of the world's greatest. The harbor itself must be approached by one of two narrow channels swept by rapid currents. Easily blocked by mines, the channels were potential death traps for a fleet of amphibious ships. In addition, Inchon had no landing beaches in the conventional sense. At high tide, the invaders would encounter stone seawalls along the port's waterfront. Low tide, on the other hand, exposed a mud flat that was two miles wide in places and impassible by vehicles or troops on foot. To make matters even worse, the seawalls that would have to serve as beaches were dominated by Wolmi-do, a small island in the harbor that was connected to the mainland by a causeway.

Determined to destroy the enemy pocket at Pusan, the North Koreans appear to have given little thought to defending Inchon against an amphibious assault. In the vicinity of Seoul, the NKPA had approximately 44,000 troops consisting of the 18th Rifle Division and a large number of independent units.[4] Approximately 2,200 troops from the 226th Marine Regiment and elements of the 918th (Coast) Artillery Regiment defended Inchon. The 400 troops on Wolmi-do had emplaced Soviet 76-mm guns in bunkers overlooking the harbor. In the five years since the end of World War II, the Americans had failed to gather even basic information about the conditions at Inchon. In an effort to correct this oversight, Lt. Eugene F. Clark, USN, and a small group of Americans and Koreans landed on the nearby island of Yonghung-do on 1 September. Working with local guerrillas, Lieutenant Clark's group gathered badly needed intelligence about Inchon's tides and beaches.

As the landing force for his amphibious end run, General MacArthur selected the U.S. X Corps, under command of Maj. Gen. Edward M. Almond, who had been MacArthur's chief of staff in Tokyo when he received the Korean assignment. Two divisions would make up X Corps for the landing. The 1st Marine Division, minus one of its own regiments but reinforced by a regiment of ROK Marines, would conduct the assault. The division's third regiment would join up as soon as it arrived from the United States. The U.S. Army's 7th Infantry Division would land after the Marines as a follow-on force. Total strength, including ROK reinforcements and Marine Corps aviation units, was just over 71,000 troops.[5] Compared with North Korean units at Inchon and Seoul, X Corps was not an overwhelming force.

A bigger problem for MacArthur, however, was assembling the naval forces needed to conduct a division-size amphibious assault. Although the British contributed two cruisers to the naval gunfire support group, the task of transporting the troops fell largely to the U.S. Navy. In the five years since the end of World War II, the U.S. Navy had dismantled what had been the greatest amphibious fleet ever assembled. The state of the navy's amphibious force in 1950 is illustrated by the problems of Rear Adm. James H. Doyle, commander of Amphibious Group One, in obtaining a minimum of forty-seven LSTs to carry out the plan. Unfortunately, the navy that had employed more than two hundred LSTs for the invasion of Okinawa in 1945 could muster only seventeen in time for the landing at Inchon. MacArthur solved Doyle's problems by recalling thirty LSTs that the United States had given the Japanese government after World War II to use in coastal trade. The ships were in bad condition and had Japanese crews, many of whom were former members of the Imperial Japanese Navy. U.S. Marines thus had the strange experience of being carried to war by their previous enemies.

In developing his landing plan, Maj. Gen. Oliver P. Smith, commanding general of the 1st Marine Division, insisted on seizing Wolmi-do before landing in the city of Inchon. This meant that, if the Marines were to land on Wolmi-do on the morning high tide, they would have to wait until 1700 before the tide was again high enough for the main landing at Inchon. Because the ebbing tide would then leave the Marines stranded in Inchon without the possibility of being resupplied until the next morning, Marine logisticians conceived a daring plan. As soon as the Marines had seized a beachhead at Inchon, the navy would beach eight LSTs, each loaded with five hundred tons of equipment and supplies.[6] Because the tide would recede before the LSTs could be unloaded, they would remain beached on the mud flats overnight. Filled with fuel and explosives, the stranded ships would be sitting ducks for enemy gunners, but no alternatives were available.

Having assembled an adequate amphibious force, MacArthur faced another enemy: time. Beaching the LSTs over Inchon's mud flats required a high tide of at least twenty nine feet. The next tide at that depth would occur on 15 September. If the Americans missed that date, they would have to wait until the middle of October, too long to help relieve the pressure on the Eighth Army. The need for speed dictated that D-day at Inchon be 15 September.

The Inchon Landings

Between 5 and 10 September, U.S. and British carrier aircraft struck targets on both of Korea's coasts. Wolmi-do received a particularly thorough working over. British ships also shelled the island during that period. Meanwhile, U.S. planners were having a debate, much like the one that had taken place before Normandy, regarding the balance between adequate naval gunfire preparation and the need for surprise. To avoid revealing the location of the coming landing, UN forces carried out air strikes, naval bombardments, and other operations at a number of possible invasion sites. During the night of 12–13 September, for example, U.S. Army troops and British Royal Marines made an amphibious raid on the waterfront at Kunsan. That morning, U.S. and British ships began a naval gunfire bombardment of North Korean positions at Inchon.

By that time, security of the landing was already suspect. The atmosphere in Tokyo appears to have been similar to that in Cairo before the British landing at Gallipoli. Speculation about an imminent landing was so widespread that correspondents dubbed the landing Operation Common Knowledge.[7] In spite of the open speculation in the American press and two days of naval gunfire preparation, the North Koreans made no significant effort to reinforce the garrison at Inchon or add to the small number of mines laid in response to an earlier British bombardment. North Korean documents captured at Inchon indicate that the North Koreans did expect some type of landing there but took only minimal steps to prepare for an attack.[8]

Mines had been spotted in Korean waters as early as 4 September, but they had claimed no ships by the time of the Inchon landing. Vice Adm. Arthur D. Struble, commander of Joint Task Force 7, of which the amphibious forces were part, was nevertheless concerned about mines. Having commanded minesweepers in World War II, he was thoroughly familiar with both the threat presented by mines and the limited capability of his task force to deal with them. The U.S. Navy had almost eliminated its mine countermeasures forces. The navy had deployed more than one hundred minesweepers in the Okinawa landings. For Inchon, Admiral Struble had fourteen minesweepers, seven American and seven Korean.[9]

Admiral Doyle had not planned to sweep at Inchon before the assault, so the minesweepers were scheduled to arrive with the transports, rather than with the advance force. When the possibility of meeting mines arose, Admiral Struble estimated that his force could probably deal with a limited number of moored contact mines, but that magnetic ground mines might cause insuperable problems.[10] With respect to this new threat, Inchon's tides did the invaders one favor. Because of the large tidal range, moored mines were exposed at low tide, and the Americans were able to destroy them by gunfire.

After being pounded by air and naval gunfire for two days, the defenders of Wolmi-do were in no mood to put up a stiff resistance when the 3d Battalion, Fifth Marines, began landing at 0633 on 15 September. After a brief fight, during which 17 Marines were wounded, the island was in American hands. North Koreans who refused to surrender were sealed in their underground bunkers by Marine bulldozers. Marines on Wolmi-do reported that the island was officially secured at 0800. From then until 1730, both sides waited. The disadvantage of seizing Wolmi-do before the main landing was that it would give the North Koreans more than nine hours to reinforce Inchon before the tide was again high enough to allow the Marines to make their main assault. The North Koreans took no such action, however, and, at 1730, the 1st and 5th Marines landed on schedule at Inchon to the southeast and northeast of Wolmi-do, respectively.

The landing force overcame problems of the tide and seawalls, as well as sporadic resistance by the enemy, to achieve a shallow but solid foothold in the city of Inchon by nightfall. During the next two days, the 1st and 5th Marine Regiments linked up and began to push toward Seoul. Casualties for the first two days had been relatively light; 24 killed, 196 wounded, and 2 missing.[11] Only then did the North Koreans choose to react; they sent a small force of tanks and infantry down the Seoul-Inchon road toward the beachhead. This belated reaction was dealt with quickly by the U.S. Marines using air strikes, tanks, and infantry antitank weapons. In the meantime, ROK Marines were mopping up in Inchon. On the evening of D + 1, General Smith assumed command of operations ashore, which marked completion of the amphibious operation.[12]

The 7th Infantry Division came ashore on 18 and 19 September to take part in the advance toward Seoul. Although Admiral Struble had good reason to be pleased with the success of the landing, he also had reason to worry. On Wolmi-do, the Marines had found unassembled Russian magnetic mines.[13] Had the North Koreans been able to lay those mines, they well might have delayed the American landing beyond the critical 15 September deadline set by the tides. Discovery of the mines also indicated what American forces might face during any future landings in Korea.

The Situation Between Inchon and Wonsan

The day after the 1st Marine Division landing at Inchon, the Eighth Army began its offensive to break out of the Pusan perimeter. The army's advance was so imperceptible at first that MacArthur worried that his great strategic gamble had failed. In the worst case, the situation could have developed into another Anzio (see chapter 4), with the Inchon beachhead drawing resources from the battle to the south rather than supporting it. The North Korean commander proved to be no Kesselring, however, and the Eighth Army was soon driving its opponents northward. On 27 September, forward elements of the 1st Cavalry Division linked up with the 7th Infantry Division, thus joining the breakout from Inchon to the ground offensive from the south.

With the North Koreans in full retreat, the UN and the United States paused to debate the legality and desirability of pursuing the enemy beyond the thirty-eighth parallel. MacArthur, a strong proponent of destroying the NKPA while he had the chance, used the time to plan his next move. South Korean forces were already moving north across the thirty-eighth parallel by the time UN forces received approval to cross it and began to move on 9 October. Because of the spine of mountains that runs down the center of Korea and a general lack of east-west roads, MacArthur envisioned advancing along two parallel axes. The U.S. Eighth Army would attack west of the mountains and the ROK I Corps along Korea's east coast. MacArthur would then use X Corps, fresh from its victory at Inchon, to conduct an amphibious operation ahead of the South Koreans. After landing, X Corps would push west to link up with the Eighth Army and trap the remnants of the NKPA in the process. Geography dictated that the landing would be at the port of Wonsan. D-day was set for 20 October.

The North Korean Plan

Just as the Red Army had given tanks to the North Koreans and taught them the rudiments of armored warfare, Soviet naval officers were to do the equivalent with respect to mine warfare. The Russians had a long history of using mines; as early as 1840, they had established a factory for their production and used mines extensively in the Baltic during the Crimean War. Since then, the Russians (and later the Soviets) had used them successfully in six wars, including the Russo-Japanese War and both world wars.[14] More concerned with protecting its nation's coasts than operating around the world, the Russian/Soviet navy found the mine to be an ideal weapon.

If the Soviets were the experts, Korea was a perfect place for them to use their expertise. Beginning in mid-July, they shipped more than four thousand mines by rail to Wonsan for use there and at other likely invasion sites. Between 16 July and 17 August, the Soviet naval mine experts taught the Koreans to assemble and lay both contact and magnetic mines.[15] The main effort took place at Wonsan. The method of laying was crude. The Koreans loaded ten to fifteen mines at a time on wooden barges and then rolled the mines over the sides by hand to create a minefield. By the time the American minesweepers arrived off Wonsan on 10 October, the North Koreans had laid more than three thousand mines to protect the port. More than five lines of mines blocked the seaward approaches to Wonsan's beaches. To hamper enemy minesweeping efforts, the Koreans emplaced artillery on nearby islands.

The Landing at Wonsan

Also on 10 October, troops from the ROK I Corps entered Wonsan. By the next day, the city was in South Korean hands, thus obviating the need for an amphibious assault. General MacArthur decided to continue as planned, even though X Corps would face no opposition on landing. In his operation order, Admiral Doyle had evaluated a number of potential enemy courses of action, including the possibility that the North Koreans might employ suicide boats against the landing.[16] In Doyle's view, the most serious threat was a defense at the water's edge combined with naval mines. The first part of the threat disappeared when the South Koreans captured Wonsan, but the mines remained a very real threat.

Immediately after arriving at Wonsan, the minesweeping force, which eventually included twelve American, nine Japanese, and three

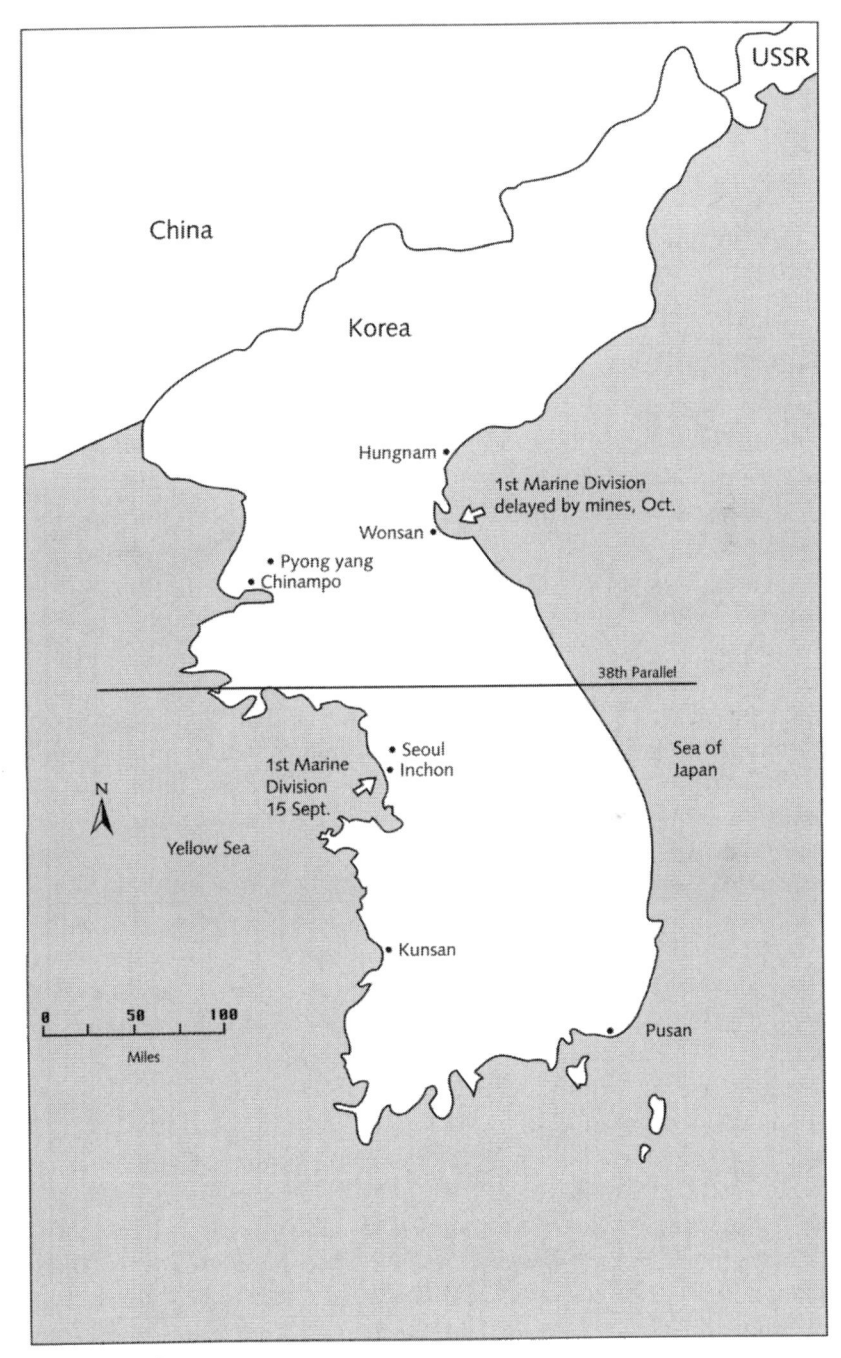

Korea, 1950

ROK minesweepers, began the work of clearing the way for a landing ten days later.[17] Intelligence was limited to the knowledge that a helicopter from the cruiser USS *Worcester* had spotted a number of mines in the area earlier. On the first day of operations, the minesweepers destroyed twenty-one moored contact mines in the process of clearing a path three thousand yards wide from the 100-fathom curve to the 30-fathom curve. By that time, however, *Worcester*'s helicopter had discovered five more lines of mines between the 30-fathom curve and the beach. Aware that his minesweeping force was too small to accomplish its mission by the designated D-day, Admiral Struble tried an alternate method to clear a path through the minefield. On 12 October, carrier planes bombed the field to determine if sympathetic explosions could destroy the mines. The experiment failed, however, and the navy reverted to more traditional methods. UDT swimmers, low-flying aircraft, and, occasionally, local fishermen located the mines for the minesweepers to destroy. The process was slow and dangerous. Two U.S. minesweepers were sunk with significant casualties.

On 18 October, the small minesweeping force had nearly completed its task when it received another setback so characteristic of the operation. The Korean minesweeper *YMS-516* disintegrated in one of three explosions that announced the presence of some previously undiscovered type of mine. The Americans suspected magnetic ground mines, a suspicion soon confirmed. Lt. Cmdr. Donald C. DeForest, a mine expert who had flown in from the Atlantic Fleet, went ashore to find the location where the mines had been assembled. It proved to be a fortunate move, albeit one that could not be taken in most amphibious operations. DeForest found the search coil from a 1,800-pound magnetic mine, which gave him the necessary information for sweeping the minefield.[18] The task required seven more days, however, and was not completed until the evening of 25 October, two weeks after the minesweepers had arrived.

While the minesweepers were carrying out their dangerous work, Admiral Doyle's amphibious task force, with X Corps embarked, was sailing back and forth off the coast in what the troops called Operation Yo-Yo. Marines began to land at Wonsan on 25 October. To their chagrin, they found they had been beaten there not only by the ROK I Corps and the 1st Marine Aircraft Wing but also by a Bob Hope USO show. These groups had all arrived while the amphibious assault force was delayed by mines. The North Koreans had not actually defeated an amphibious assault force, but, with virtually no defense ashore, they had delayed its

Destruction of the South Korean minesweeper YMS-516, 1950. The North Koreans delayed a landing at Wonsan for more than two weeks with the use of mines. During the sweeping operation, three minesweepers were sunk.
(U.S. Navy photo, No. 423625)

landing for almost a week. Adm. Forrest Sherman, chief of naval operations at the time, admitted later that he could easily think of circumstances when such a delay could mean losing a war.[19]

The Korean War continued for more than two and one-half years, but UN forces made no more major amphibious assaults. They did conduct a large-scale amphibious withdrawal from the port of Hungnam to evacuate the 1st Marine Division and other forces after the entry of Chinese troops into the war. Mines continued to plague UN naval forces. They caused 70 percent of all U.S. Navy casualties during the first two years of the war and accounted for all U.S. ships lost in Korean waters during the entire war.[20]

Observations

The Korean War was the first major war in which the threat of nuclear weapons was a consideration for both sides. Gen. Omar Bradley, chairman of the Joint Chiefs of Staff, had such weapons in mind when he made his well-known prediction in October 1949 to the House Armed Services Committee that there would never be another large-scale amphibious invasion.[21] The Soviet Union had exploded its first nuclear device that same year and was in the process of creating a strategic bombing force. Had the Soviets possessed an actual nuclear weapon in 1950 and been able and willing to drop it on Inchon on D-day, it would have undeniably defeated the landing. The Soviet Union understood this and developed its strategic bombing forces with a mission that included the defense of the homeland against amphibious assaults.[22]

The United States took the nuclear threat seriously and developed such concepts as helicopter assaults and dispersed amphibious task forces, in part, to limit the effects of nuclear weapons. The use of nuclear weapons in Korea was discussed by American military leaders, but the concept was never adopted. Although nuclear weapons, like chemical ones, are self-deterring to a large degree, a nation faced with utter defeat might use such weapons as a last resort. The British threatened to use gas against a German invasion in 1940. Given earlier Japanese willingness to use chemical and biological weapons, it is difficult to imagine that the Japanese would not have used an atomic bomb to defeat an Allied invasion of Japan had their efforts to develop that weapon been successful. When asked whether they would have employed an atomic bomb, one of Japan's leading World War II aviators replied, "Why wouldn't we have?"[23] In any case, the decision to take such a drastic step would be based on national strategic considerations, rather than on strictly tactical or operational factors, such as defeating an amphibious landing.

By using mines, which are weapons at the other end of the spectrum of technical sophistication from atomic bombs, the North Koreans seriously disrupted an amphibious operation at Wonsan. In doing so, they demonstrated the potential of what might be called a poor man's naval defense, one waged without the large ships of a major navy. Frustrated by the effects of mines in delaying the landing at Wonsan, Rear Adm. Allen E. Smith, commander of the amphibious advance force, sent the chief of naval operations a message stating that the United States had lost control of the sea off Korea. Initially, Admiral Sherman responded that the claim was exaggerated, but he later admitted, "If you can't go where you want to, when you want to, you haven't got command of the sea."[24]

The Wonsan landing demonstrated vividly the threat that mine warfare presents to a landing. After the Korean War, the U.S. Navy improved its capability to deal with enemy mines, but competing requirements have again reduced the priority given to mine warfare. In peacetime, the U.S. Navy typically has been unwilling to maintain the mine countermeasures forces needed to preclude a recurrence of the problems that delayed the landing and might have caused a disaster at Wonsan in 1950.

12

Lessons Learned and Unlearned:
The Falkland Islands, 1982

What the hell are you talking about?
Brig. Gen. Mario Menéndez, when told he would be defending the Falklands

More than enough opposed landings took place during World War II and the Korean War to furnish an adequate historical base from which to draw lessons about both amphibious and anti-landing operations. The British recapture of the Falkland Islands from Argentina in 1982 makes a good case study for reviewing some of those lessons and investigating the state of amphibious warfare and anti-landing defense since the Korean War.

Following the end of World War II, Britain greatly reduced its military establishment, including its amphibious forces. The commando mission was given to the Royal Marines, and the Royal Navy maintained a small amphibious fleet to land the Marines. In spite of their small sizes, the two services joined the U.S. Navy and Marine Corps in developing the concept of using helicopters in amphibious operations. The British made amphibious history in 1956 when they landed 45 Commando, a Royal Marine unit, by helicopter during the Anglo-French assault on Suez. U.S. Marines had employed helicopters in combat during the Korean War, but Suez marked their first use as amphibious assault vehicles.

In spite of this impressive record, the British government, by the beginning of the 1980s, was ready to discontinue amphibious warfare. The Royal Navy had decommissioned the *Intrepid*, one of its two amphibious assault ships, and planned to do the same to her sister ship, the *Fearless*. Similar to the U.S. Navy's LPDs (amphibious transport, dock), these two ships were used to carry landing craft to the landing site.[1]

At about the same time, the British made another decision that also would have a great impact on their amphibious capability. Because their North Atlantic Treaty Organization (NATO) commitments would never require British forces to operate outside the range of land-based aircraft, they decided that a role for aircraft carriers no longer existed in the Royal Navy. Although it had pioneered the use of such concepts as jet aircraft on carriers, the steam catapult, and the angled flight deck, the Royal Navy had already scrapped its last conventional carrier. Its two remaining carriers, the *Hermes* and *Invincible,* were light carriers, with neither catapults nor arresting gear. They carried helicopters and Harrier VSTOL (vertical/short takeoff and landing) fighters. The Harriers used a ski jump to take off with heavier bomb loads than they could lift vertically. By 1982, the British had decided that even a limited carrier force was no longer needed and had arranged to sell both the *Hermes* and the *Invincible.*

The Argentines also had a marine corps, an amphibious navy, and a carrier force. Although the Argentine Marine Corps was small, it was equipped with American-made LVTs that provided an assault capability no longer available to the British Royal Marines. For landing the marines, the Argentine navy had a former American LST, the *Cabo San Antonio,* that had been built subsequent to World War II. To support the marines and carry out other naval missions, the navy had the carrier *Veinticinco de Mayo.* Commissioned in 1945 as HMS *Venerable,* the carrier's air wing included a squadron of A-4Q Skyhawks that had been reduced, through accidents, to eight aircraft by 1982.[2] In April of that year, these naval forces were the principal means of achieving an Argentine national dream, the return of the Malvinas from Great Britain.

The Malvinas, or the Falklands, as they are known in the English-speaking world, are a small group of islands lying four hundred miles east of Argentina in the South Atlantic. In 1833, the British had reestablished, by force, a claim to the islands that had been made in 1765. Since that time, most Argentines had considered this a blot on their national honor and return of the Malvinas to Argentine sovereignty had been on the agenda of every Argentine government. For the most part, the attempts to achieve that aim involved negotiations. When negotiations began to stall in 1982, the military junta that ruled Argentina resolved to take matters into its own hands. Spurred perhaps by the desire to deflect public attention away from many serious domestic problems, the junta decided to retake the islands by force.

Named Operation Rosario, the invasion was planned in such secrecy that most military leaders were unaware of it until the junta announced its successful completion. That secrecy also precluded much of the planning that might have been made for the defense of the islands after their capture. Using an incident in which the British had expelled an Argentine scrap dealer from South Georgia (another British island in the South Atlantic claimed by Argentina) as the immediate pretext for action, Argentine marines landed there and in the Falklands on the night of 1–2 April 1982.

Army Brig. Gen. Mario B. Menéndez assumed control of the islands as military governor, and troops began to arrive to establish an Argentine presence. As captured British military personnel and government officials were released for their return to Britain, the Argentine junta still hoped that the British government would accept the loss of the islands and negotiate accordingly.

The Situation in the Falklands

The junta's expectations that the British would react only diplomatically to the takeover of the Falklands should have been dashed on 5 April, when the *Invincible* and *Hermes*, their decks loaded with helicopters and Sea Harrier fighters, sailed from Portsmouth, England. Within several days, the Argentines accepted the possibility of having to defend the Falklands and began to reinforce them. By the end of April, they had established a ground force of three infantry brigades and a battalion of marines, supported by two artillery groups with 105-mm howitzers and two armored cavalry squadrons with French-made wheeled armored cars mounting 90-mm guns.[3]

The Argentine army did not have a divisional structure, but the thirteen thousand soldiers on the Falklands were equivalent in number to a division.[4] This force alone would eventually defend the islands because the arrival of the British task force off the Falklands on 29 April effectively prevented Argentine reinforcement by either sea or air. The greatest weakness of the Argentine force was not its size but the ability of its soldiers. Most were conscripts, and many of them had just begun their one-year term of service. With the exception of the marines and soldiers who had participated in Operation Rosario, none of the Argentine defenders had seen combat.

The Argentine army, air force, and navy each contributed aircraft to the defense of the Falklands. The army had nineteen helicopters, a mix of utility, heavy lift, and attack types.[5] The air force added four helicopters and twelve Pucara light-attack aircraft; the navy, eight light-attack aircraft; and the Coast Guard, one helicopter and two small transports. A total of forty-six aircraft operated from the Falklands; most of these were based at the Stanley airfield, a 4,000-foot strip of aluminum matting. The Argentines also established grass fields on Pebble Island and at Goose Green on East Falkland. Neither of the outlying fields was capable of handling high-performance fighters or attack planes. The Argentines test-landed a Super Etendard at Stanley and considered the use of Skyhawks, but they decided that the field's short length and slippery condition when wet made it unsafe for normal operations by these planes. Although pressed by the need to use the Stanley airfield for resupply and reinforcement, the Argentines took no steps to lengthen the runway enough for high-performance aircraft to use it safely.[6] In Argentina itself, the air force fielded eighty-two combat aircraft. Most important of these were thirty-two American A-4 Skyhawks, twenty-four Israeli Daggers, and eight French Mirage IIIEAs.[7] The navy added eight more Skyhawks and five of the Super Etendards that had been ordered from France in 1979 to replace the aging Skyhawks. For each of the Etendards, the navy had one Exocet AM-39 antiship missile. At the request of the British, the French government held up delivery of the five Super Etendards remaining on the 1979 order and more missiles.

The navy Skyhawks constituted the attack capability of Argentina's only carrier, the *Veinticinco de Mayo*. In British eyes, the carrierborne Skyhawks and the Exocet-armed Super Etendards, which were not able to operate from the carrier, presented Argentina's greatest threat to the task force that would deliver a landing force to the Falklands.[8] The Argentine navy had two other capabilities that concerned the British: (1) its submarine force of two American Guppy-class submarines and two modern German Type 209 boats, and (2) the light cruiser *General Belgrano* (the former USS *Phoenix*), which could be escorted by modern British Type 42 destroyers similar to those that the Royal Navy planned to deploy to the South Atlantic.

The Argentines realized that they would have to reorganize their peacetime command structure for adequate control of a war in the Falklands and set about doing so.[9] On 7 April, the Argentine junta created a South Atlantic Theater of Operations under the command of Vice Adm. Juan J. Lombardo. Reporting directly to the junta, the admiral commanded the navy's operational forces and a joint military garrison in the Falklands under the direct command of General Menéndez. General Menéndez had three service-component commanders for the forces stationed in the Falklands: Brig. Gen. Oscar L. Jofre, army; Brig. Gen. Luis G. Castellano, air force; and Rear Adm. Edgardo A. Otero, navy. Air force units other than those on the Falklands were not controlled by the South Atlantic Theater but through a separate Air Force South, whose commander reported to a newly created Strategic Air Force. Only at the level of the junta itself was unity of command achieved between the air force and navy.

Responding to the Argentine invasion, the British organized their forces to accomplish four basic missions: (1) recapture South Georgia, (2) isolate the Falklands, (3) gain sea control and air superiority around the islands, and (4) recapture the Falklands. As a means of displaying resolution in the face of adversity, the British government assembled the necessary forces to carry out the missions and dispatched them from British ports as rapidly as possible, even though some of them would have to stage at an intermediate base to reorganize.

The first British forces to reach the South Atlantic were three nuclear submarines with the mission of enforcing the two-hundred-mile exclusion zone around the Falklands declared by the British on 8 April, which became effective four days later. In addition to reaching the Falklands rapidly, the submarines had another advantage over surface ships. The Argentines probably would not be able to detect the submarines, but they would have to assume that submarines were present to enforce the exclusion zone as soon as it became effective.

The British had organized a task force, under Rear Adm. John ("Sandy") Woodward, around the carriers *Invincible* and *Hermes*, whose sale had been shelved when the Argentines invaded the Falklands. Woodward's mission was to gain air and sea control around the islands in preparation for an amphibious operation. Twenty Royal Navy Sea Harriers on the two carriers held the key to gaining air superiority over the islands and protecting the task force from Argentine air attacks. Escorting the carriers was a group of destroyers and frigates of various classes that averaged in number about seven or eight during the operation.[10] Several of these ships would carry a small party of marines and special forces to South Georgia for the landing there. When that operation was completed, the ships would rejoin the main task force off the Falklands.

An amphibious task force, under Commodore Michael C. Clapp, carried the landing force for the Falklands operation. The task force included two assault ships, the *Fearless* and *Intrepid*; six logistics landing ships (LSLs) from the Royal Fleet Auxiliary; and requisitioned merchant ships, including the cruise liner *Canberra*. The *Canberra* was one of fifty ships that had been taken up from trade for the Falklands conflict and modified rapidly to serve in a variety of military roles, from hospital ships to minesweepers.[11] The initial landing force would be 3 Commando Brigade under the command of Brigadier Julian Thompson, Royal Marines. The brigade, whose first mission was to seize a beachhead in the islands, was built around five battalions: 40, 42, and 45 Royal Marine Commandos and the 2d and 3d Battalions of the Parachute Regiment.[12] These battalions were backed up by a variety of combat and support units, including artillery, antiaircraft artillery, tracked reconnaissance vehicles, and logistics. Special forces personnel from the 22d Special Air Service Regiment (SAS) and the Royal Marines' Special Boat Squadron (SBS) added their unique capabilities to the landing force. Total strength of the brigade was about 5,500, with more than half of that number infantry.[13] Once the brigade had secured a beachhead, it would be joined by 5 Infantry Brigade, with two battalions of Guards and one of Gurkhas. Maj. Gen. Jeremy Moore, Royal Marines, would command the combined force of about 10,000 troops in the effort to take back the Falklands from a slightly larger number of Argentine defenders.[14]

The British troops were all professionals, many of whom had served in Northern Ireland. Adm. Sir John Fieldhouse would command the overall operation from Royal Navy Fleet Headquarters at Northwood, just north of London. The principal component commanders, Admiral Woodward, Commodore Clapp, and Brigadier Thompson (until the arrival of General Moore), all reported directly to Admiral Fieldhouse, as did other supporting RAF and navy commanders. The British had no unified commander in the South Atlantic. As they had done at Gallipoli and during World War II, they relied on cooperation between the commanders at the scene of the action. Some friction did occur, but problems were resolved because modern equipment made rapid communication possible between Admiral Fieldhouse and his subordinates thousands of miles away. Admiral Woodward, senior officer on the scene, believed that his lack of control over the British submarines around the Falklands posed potential problems and tried unsuccessfully to have the command arrangements changed.[15]

Three factors involving terrain and weather had a particularly significant impact on the British operations and the Argentine efforts to defend against them. The first was the location of the islands. The Falklands are approximately eight thousand miles from Britain and more than three thousand miles from Ascension Island, the location of the nearest British support base. This incredibly long supply line placed an immense logistics burden on British forces and limited their ability to react to unanticipated situations. Although the islands are only four hundred miles off the Argentine coast, that distance became critical with respect to air operations. Argentina's Daggers and Mirage fighters lacked the capability to be refueled in flight. Their maximum range allowed them to reach the islands but afforded them as little as two or three minutes over a target before they were forced to return to their bases.

The second factor was the nature of the Falklands themselves. The group consists of two major islands, East Falkland and West Falkland, which are separated by Falkland Sound, and numerous smaller islands. The approximately 2,500-mile coastline of the islands is broken by innumerable harbors and inlets. The Argentine defenders estimated that thirty beaches were suitable for a British landing.[16] The mountainous terrain of the islands favored defenders, and the marshy soil and lack of roads made cross-country movement difficult.

The third factor was the weather. By the end of June, winter gales in the South Atlantic would make naval and air operations impossible. As much as anything, nature set the timetable for the British operation. Admiral Woodward estimated that if his force did not capture the islands by the end of June, it would have to withdraw. To allow adequate time for the landing force to defeat the Argentine defenders, D-day could be no later than 25 May.[17]

The Argentine Plan

In planning his defense, General Menéndez faced the same questions that had concerned numerous other commanders threatened by enemy landings. His initial priority was to determine where the British might land. After considering a number of possibilities, including Cow Bay, Low Bay, and Fitzroy, he concluded that the greatest threat would come from a landing at Stanley, the Falklands' capital, where the Argentine marines had landed during Operation Rosario. He dismissed San Carlos because it lacked naval maneuver room and was sixty miles from Stanley, which the British would have to capture before they could claim victory.[18]

Regardless of where the British landed, Menéndez needed a plan to deal with them. Argentine army defensive doctrine dictated either a zone defense or a mobile defense.[19] After considering the composition of his force, its state of training, and the nature of the terrain, Menéndez rejected a mobile defense. The number of possible landing beaches precluded the possibility of covering them all with defenses at the water's edge. By elimination, Menéndez decided to create a static defensive position around Stanley. To execute his plan, he created two tactical sectors.

He assigned the X Brigade and a marine battalion to defend the area around Stanley and dispersed the remainder of his forces to cover the rest of East Falkland and the other islands. If necessary, reinforcements could move from the Stanley sector by helicopter to assist outlying units.[20]

Troops from the Stanley sector dug in along the mountain line protecting the capital. Engineers laid thirty-seven thousand antipersonnel and six hundred antitank mines to hinder British troop movement.[21] To discourage a landing, the Argentines laid naval mines in the waters off Stanley and mounted a shipborne version of an Exocet missile launcher on a trailer for use as coast artillery.[22] Rather than go after the British when they landed, the defenders would wait for the attackers to come to them.

Since the British victory, the Argentine defenders generally have been derided for failing to react aggressively to the British landing. On closer look, however, perhaps General Menéndez's concept made more sense than he is given credit for. In many respects, the Argentine situation was similar to that of the Japanese at Okinawa. Once the Japanese had decided they could not stop an American landing, they waited for the enemy to come to them. In the process, they hoped to delay the enemy ground attack long enough for the Japanese navy and air force to inflict a decisive defeat on the American invasion fleet. The Japanese ultimately failed, but they inflicted terrible punishment on the ships off Okinawa. The Argentine navy and air force planned a similar defense. At the first indication of a landing, they intended to throw everything they had against the British task force in a coordinated air attack.[23]

The Battle for the Falklands

Any hope the Argentines might have had that the British would not resort to force was dashed on 25 April when Royal Marines landed on South Georgia and reclaimed the island after a short fight with the Argentine defenders. That morning, off South Georgia, British helicopters from the ice patrolship *Endurance* and the frigate *Brilliant* attacked the Argentine submarine *Santa Fe* with rockets. Damaged and unable to submerge, the submarine made it to King Edward Harbor, where she sank in shallow water. In this opening move, the British gained an advance base less than eight hundred miles from the Falklands, eliminated one fourth of the Argentine submarine threat, and obtained an important, albeit small, victory.

At 0340 on 1 May, the garrison at the Stanley airfield awakened to the sound of explosions caused by twenty-one 1,000-pound bombs that were dropped from a single RAF Vulcan bomber. It had made the 3,750-mile flight from Ascension Island and fueled during flight in accordance with a complex plan requiring the support of sixteen aerial tankers.[24] Only one of the bombs hit the runway, but others damaged aircraft and airfield facilities. The attack put the garrison's antiaircraft units on alert, a move that prevented them from being caught off guard when British Harriers attacked the field just after daylight. These events started a day of intensive but largely inconclusive air and naval actions.

The dual intent of Admiral Woodward's operation was to provoke a reaction from the Argentine air force on the mainland and to keep the attention of the Falkland's garrison focused on Stanley's beaches while special forces units landed at other locations. By a combination of Harrier attacks and naval gunfire, he wanted to make the defenders believe that a landing at Stanley was under way. The attempt apparently worked because at least one Argentine source notes that the Stanley garrison repelled two landings on 1 May.[25]

Apparently, the Argentine air force also believed that a landing was taking place. It reacted, as planned, with an all-out effort against the British task force. Beginning in the morning, the air attacks increased in the afternoon with sorties by Skyhawks, Daggers, Mirages, and Canberras. Only the Canberras had adequate range to carry out the mission with any margin for error, but their slow speed made them the most vulnerable to British defenses. On reaching the British beachhead, the Daggers and Mirages lacked the ability to loiter because they could not be refueled in the air. The Skyhawks and Etendards could be refueled, but the air force had only two KC-130 refuelers. This limitation made strike planning difficult and restricted the ability of the Argentines to launch massive, coordinated air strikes. By the end of the day, the Argentines had lost several aircraft, including one to their own antiaircraft fire. In return, they had damaged two British ships that had been shelling Stanley.

The raids gave the British some idea of Argentine capabilities and reinforced Admiral Woodward's view that he needed to keep his two carriers far enough east to be out of range of airplanes flying out of bases in Argentina.

Although it limited the threat from land-based aircraft, repositioning of the carriers did not solve the problem posed by the Argentine navy. Admiral Woodward's greatest concern was the Exocet missile that could be launched either by air or by Argentine destroyers. Two of those destroyers were escorting the *General Belgrano* just outside the British exclusion zone southwest of the Falklands, where they were being trailed by the British nuclear submarine *Conqueror*. The *Veinticinco de Mayo*, with her air wing, was also at sea north of the British task force, but she had so far managed to elude detection by the British. In addition, Woodward had to contend with the threat from the remaining Argentine submarines. Argentine sources claim that the German-built *San Luis* fired several torpedoes at an unidentified target on 1 May, but technical problems caused the weapons to miss or fail to explode.[26]

Concern for the safety of his carriers caused Admiral Woodward to make the most controversial decision of the conflict. He requested and received permission from London to have the *Conqueror* sink the *General Belgrano*, even though the cruiser and her escorts were outside the British exclusion zone. The *Conqueror* carried out that mission on 2 May with the resulting loss of 368 Argentine lives. The sinking caused an international dispute over the legitimacy of the action, but it gave Woodward an immediate operational benefit. The remaining surface ships of the Argentine navy, including the *Veinticinco de Mayo,* returned to port and stayed there for the remainder of the conflict.

The Argentine navy's air arm still packed a powerful punch, however, and it was about to make itself felt. Using radar tracks from Port Stanley and information taken from the flight plan found on the body of a British pilot, the Argentines believed that they had located the two enemy carriers. On 4 May, they launched two Exocet-armed Super Etendards on a mission against the carriers. The Argentine aviators had to fly just above the waves in order to avoid detection by the radar picket ships stationed between the carriers and the Argentine bases. The two planes popped up periodically to allow their radars to search for a target. When they located one, they fired their missiles and ran for home.

Unlike the German missiles used at Salerno and Anzio, the Exocets homed in on their targets without the need for human guidance. The Argentine aviators had no way of knowing that their missiles had locked on the British destroyer *Sheffield* instead of a carrier. In effect, they had made the same mistake made by many of the kamikazes at Okinawa. They had attacked the first available target, which happened to be a picket ship. One missile damaged the *Sheffield* badly enough that she eventually sank—the first Royal Navy ship lost to enemy action since World War II. The sinking also heightened Admiral Woodward's concern about the vulnerability of his ships to air attack.

For the next two weeks, both sides prepared for an amphibious landing. Having decided on San Carlos as the site, the British began to consider possible Argentine reactions to a landing there. The defenders had established two positions in the area that were of particular concern: the airfield on Pebble Island and Goose Green, also with an airfield, that was thirteen miles from the possible landing beaches. Woodward was also worried that the defenders might have mined the sound. To determine whether they had, he sent the frigate *Alacrity* into Falkland Sound during the night of 10–11 May. Lacking any special equipment to locate mines, the frigate's hazardous mission was simply to sail through the sound to determine if the channel was apparently clear. The *Alacrity* made the passage safely and sank a small Argentine supply ship in the process.

Alarmed by the British activity, General Menéndez ordered the garrison at Goose Green to send a small detachment to San Carlos.[27] The detachment established an outpost on Fanning Head overlooking both San Carlos and the northern entrance to Falkland Sound, through which the amphibious ships would have to pass to reach the landing beaches. About 0250 on the morning of 21 May, the Fanning Head outpost detected ships sailing into San Carlos Bay. Shortly afterward, the Argentine troops found themselves under fire from the ships and began to withdraw down the peninsula to safety. Instead, they ran into a small British force that had been landed by helicopter. Some of the Argentines escaped after a brief fight, but others surrendered. About 0810, as the morning mist began to clear, the defenders at San Carlos could see that a landing was in progress, but they decided that they would be unable to stop it and withdrew.

As General Menéndez began receiving reports of the activities at San Carlos, he was also informed that the garrison at Goose Green was being shelled by naval gunfire and attacked by ground forces. He then found himself in a position, shared by many other defensive commanders, of having to determine which, if either, of these two operations was the actual landing. Initially, he believed that the San Carlos activity was a diversion.[28] After changing his mind, he notified the commander of Air Force South at about 1030. An Italian-built Macchi 339 from the Stanley airfield had already struck a spontaneous first blow when it strafed HMS *Argonaut* in Falkland Sound shortly after 1000, and the air force was already preparing for a major response to the landing. At 1235, an attack by three Daggers marked the start of a series of periodic raids by mainland-based aircraft that continued for the next three days. The Argentine attackers generally came in low over West Falkland, popped up over the sound, and bombed the first targets that they could find.

Given the amount of antiaircraft fire faced by the aviators and their

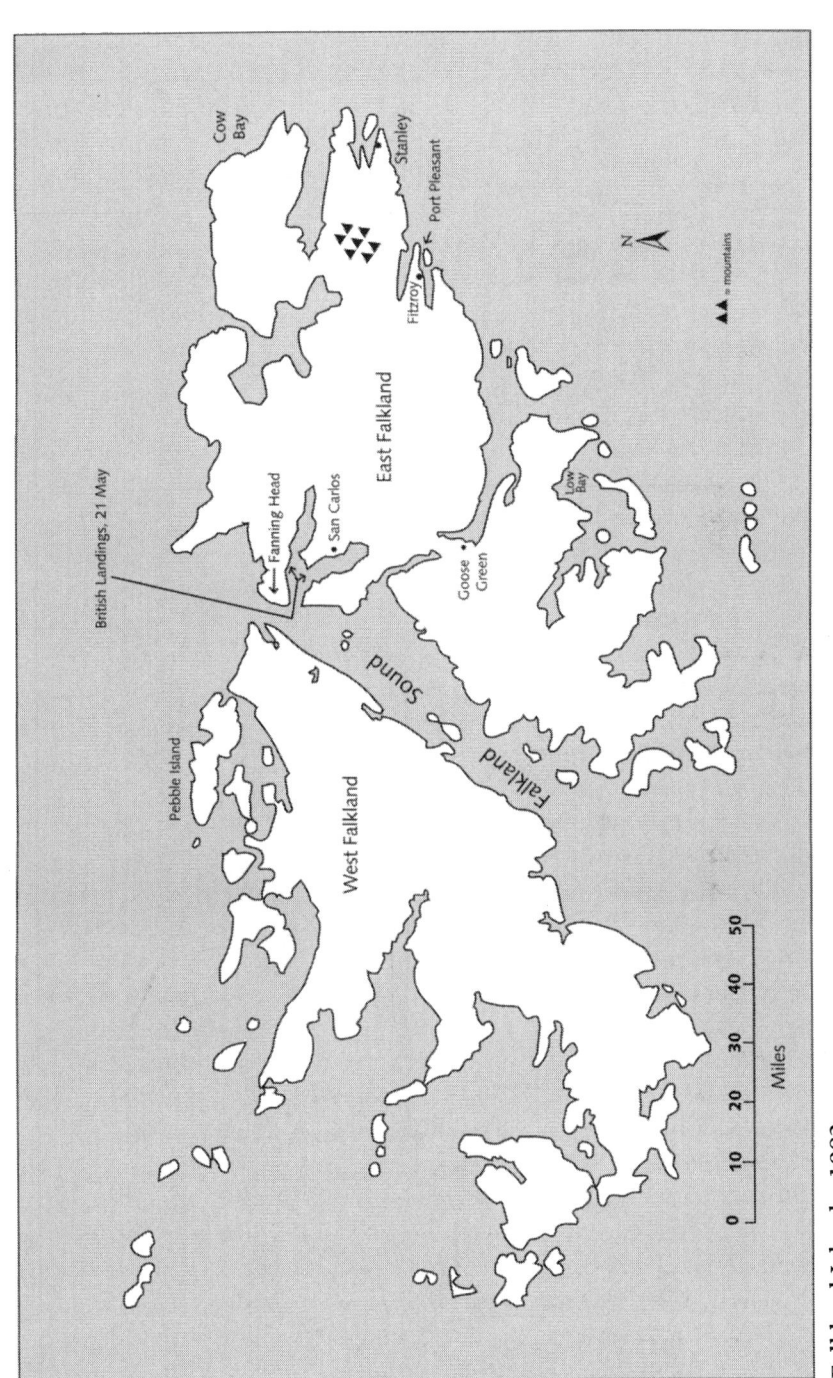

Falkland Islands, 1982

limited time over the target because of fuel, the temptation to hit the first available target is understandable. The British positioned their destroyers and frigates accordingly. Regardless of the Argentines' understandable reasons for haste, their tactics allowed the amphibious ships, with their important passengers and vital supplies, to escape all but limited damage. Unbelievably, the 44,000-ton *Canberra*—conspicuous in her all-white paint scheme—remained unmolested off the landing beaches all day. By the end of D-day, the landing force was ashore, essentially without casualties, but the Argentine aviators had forced the Royal Navy to pay a high price for that accomplishment. The frigate *Ardent* was sinking, and four other warships were damaged. Two of the damaged ships might have sunk if some bombs had not failed to explode.

On D-day and the three following days, Argentine aircraft sank a total of two British ships and damaged six others, but the focus of operations had passed ashore to the landing force and the actions that General Menéndez might take against it. Initially, both sides remained static, the Argentines in positions at Stanley and Goose Green and 3 Commando Brigade in its newly won beachhead. During this period, a difference of opinion arose among the British commanders over the need for action by the landing force. Historically, naval commanders involved in amphibious operations have demanded rapid action by the landing force in order to reduce the time that their ships are tied to the shore and vulnerable to enemy attack. Such a demand was made by Royal Navy officers in the Falklands because of the punishment being taken by their ships at San Carlos.

Brigadier Thompson, on the other hand, resisted an early move because his orders directed him to establish a beachhead and wait for the arrival of General Moore and 5 Infantry Brigade at approximately D + 7 before starting the land campaign.[29] Concerned about the effect that the lack of an early land victory would have on British public opinion, Admiral Fieldhouse, on 25 May, ordered Brigadier Thompson to move out of the beachhead toward Stanley without waiting for 5 Infantry Brigade to arrive. To implement this new order, the landing force staff began planning a move across the island with the use of six Wessex and four Chinook helicopters waiting offshore on the container ship *Atlantic Conveyor*, which had been converted to a makeshift carrier for Harriers and helicopters.

The day that Thompson received his new orders was Argentina's national day, and the Argentine air force used the occasion to demonstrate its ability still to influence the battle for the Falklands. Before 3 Commando Brigade could begin its move, the Argentine navy had sent two Super Etendards on a circuitous route north of the Falklands to attack the British carriers from an unexpected direction. At the time, the *Atlantic Conveyor* was stationed with the carriers east of the islands while her captain waited for darkness to cover the move to San Carlos. When the two Super Etendards acquired a radar target, they launched their Exocets. The closest British ships were the frigates *Ambuscade* and *Brilliant*, which launched chaff as soon as they detected the two incoming missiles. The two Exocets were deflected from the frigates by the chaff cloud but soon reacquired the *Atlantic Conveyor*, which had no means of protection. Both missiles hit and started fires that ultimately caused the loss of the ship. Before she was hit, the Harriers had flown to the *Invincible* and *Hermes*. Of the helicopters, all but one Wessex and one Chinook were still on the *Atlantic Conveyor* when she sank. As a result, the marines and paratroopers had to walk across the island with everything they needed to attack Stanley.

When Admiral Fieldhouse informed Brigadier Thompson about the loss of the helicopters, he also told him that immediate action on the ground was still required. Thompson ordered the 2d Parachute Battalion to seize the Argentine position at Goose Green. This was accomplished after a tough fight, in which the British battalion commander was killed while leading an attack. In the meantime, 45 Commando and the 3d Parachute Battalion had started on their cross-country trek to Stanley.

The loss of the helicopters on the *Atlantic Conveyor* would have another impact on the battle for the Falklands. Being in superb physical condition, the marines and paratroopers were able to make the march across the island in bad weather and remain in condition to fight when they reached the Argentine defensive positions overlooking Stanley. The troops from 5 Infantry Brigade, who did not arrive at San Carlos until 1 June, however, were not in condition to follow the marines and paratroopers across country. Concerned that his troops would miss the fight for Stanley, Brigadier Tony Wilson, commander of 5 Infantry Brigade, managed to move part of the 2d Parachute Battalion, which was now part of his brigade, by helicopter to Fitzroy.

General Moore had not been informed of the move in advance. When he discovered what had taken place, he was unwilling to leave the paratroopers isolated where they might be cut off by an Argentine counterattack. Accordingly, he asked the navy to move the remainder of the brigade to Fitzroy by sea. What followed was a series of missteps of the type common in war, particularly when inexperienced troops first go into combat. When efforts to shuttle the troops by landing craft from the two assault ships proved unsatisfactory, the remaining men of the 1st Battalion, Welsh Guards, embarked on the LSL *Sir Galahad* for what they thought was a move to Bluff Cove. Although they should have been landed after dark, another series of foul-ups caused them still to be on board the ship, in Port Pleasant inlet off Fitzroy, after 1200 on the following day.

An Argentine observation post had spotted the *Sir Galahad* and her sister ship, *Sir Tristram*. On receiving this information, the Argentine air force launched eight Skyhawks and six Daggers to attack the ships. Three Skyhawks and one Dagger dropped out with mechanical problems. Before they reached Port Pleasant, the remaining Daggers came across the frigate *Plymouth* and chose to attack her, rather than continue on to their assigned targets. Because the Skyhawks had not found the LSLs, they headed for home but then spotted the two ships and attacked them with bombs. The *Sir Tristram* was hit but escaped serious damage. Three bombs hit the *Sir Galahad*, which was still crowded with soldiers waiting to be taken ashore. About fifty men died in the attack, and an equal number were wounded. This was the single most costly incident of the conflict and also the final attack on the amphibious ships.

The defenders ashore, however, had one more weapon to use against the Royal Navy. British ships supported the landing force throughout the battle with naval guns firing a total of eight thousand rounds against ground targets.[30] Because the naval guns outranged most Argentine artillery, the defenders had little chance to reply. They managed to mount a naval Exocet system on a trailer and waited for one of their tormentors to sail within the missile's thirty-mile range. That occurred on the morning of 12 June, when the destroyer HMS *Glamorgan* came within range while returning to the task force after a gunfire mission. The missile hit the *Glamorgan* and caused extensive damage, but it failed to sink her.

The night before, General Moore had begun his final move against Stanley with an attack by 3 Commando Brigade against the Argentine positions on Mount Longdon, the Two Sisters, and Mount Harriet. Similar attacks two nights later against Tumbledown Mountain and Wireless Ridge gave the British possession of the high ground overlooking Stanley. On 14 June, General Menéndez surrendered in spite of orders from Gen. Leopoldo Galtieri, chief of staff of the army and a member of the junta, to continue fighting. The British had won their race against winter by the narrowest of margins. At the end of the day, a heavy snow was falling and the wind was gusting at speeds up to one hundred miles per hour.[31]

Observations

The Falklands conflict illustrates vividly how the fighting ashore during an amphibious operation is linked inextricably to the naval aspect of the operation. Constructing a scenario in which General Menéndez's army, consisting mostly of conscripts, could have defeated General Moore's professionals, who were better trained and led, is difficult at best. This advantage on the ground would have become irrelevant, however, if Argentine air attacks or the onset of winter had prevented the Royal Navy from supporting the fighting ashore. To achieve that end, the troops defending the Falklands had only to delay the British invaders, not necessarily defeat them.

The British created part of the delay themselves by lacking the amphibious capability to land across a defended beach. Apparently not understanding this shortcoming, the Argentines feared a British landing at Stanley. In speculating about why the Argentines held this view, Admiral Woodward takes a somewhat gratuitous swipe at the U.S. Marine Corps. He reasons that the Argentines were influenced in amphibious matters by U.S. Marines, "whose instinct in the field of amphibious assault has usually been to go straight through the front door, kicking it down whether or not it happens to be locked."[32]

In the Falklands, the British did not have the option of going through the "front door," locked or not. Their forces did not have the amphibious assault vehicles and other specialized equipment needed to make an opposed landing. Had they been able to make such a landing, however, it might not have been a bad idea. Although the landing force suffered only 3 casualties on D-day by going through the "back door," British casualties were 253 men killed and 777 wounded during the conflict.[33] What their losses would have been if the British forces had been able to land at Stanley and chosen to do so can be only conjectured. Certainly, a case can be made that a short, violent assault at Stanley at the start of the operation would have cost fewer British casualties than did the drawn-out land campaign. The strength of that case depends on whether one believes an Argentine defense at the water's edge at Stanley would have been more like bloody Tarawa, where the Japanese severely punished the landing force, or Utah Beach at Normandy, where the defending Germans were able to inflict only 197 casualties on the U.S. 4th Infantry Division on D-Day.

The British delay in landing at San Carlos gave the Argentines time to employ their air force against the invading fleet. In some ways, they found themselves in a position analogous to that of the Japanese at Guadalcanal. Their enemy relied totally on carrier-based aircraft to support the initial landings. The Argentines, on the other hand, employed land-based aircraft operating at their maximum ranges.

The Argentines were also confronted by a problem that had confounded the Japanese throughout World War II: target priorities. Argentine Operations Plan 2/82 of 7 April 1982 assigned the highest priority for air attack to landing craft and troops on the beach. The second priority was troop transports.[34] At some point, top priority was shifted to the two British carriers. Ten years after the war, Gen. Basilio Lami Dozo, commander in chief of the Argentine air force during the war and a member of the military junta, expressed the opinion that making the carriers a priority had been a mistake.[35] He had a good historical basis for his opinion, but the Falklands War might be an exception to the hard-learned lesson that amphibious ships should be the highest-priority targets. Given the utter reliance that the British had placed on their two carriers to gain air superiority and the absence of any alternatives, assigning them top priority made sense. Admiral Woodward has since admitted that loss of the *Invincible* would have severely jeopardized the operation and loss of the larger *Hermes* would have caused it to fail.[36]

When they failed to mine the entrances to Falkland Sound, the Argentines missed an obvious chance to delay the invasion and buy more time for their air force to attack the British ships. The British had no minesweepers at the time of the landing and would have been in an even worse position than the one in which the Americans had found themselves at Wonsan during the Korean War. Commenting on the mine problem at Wonsan, the U.S. chief of naval operations said, at the time, that he could think of situations where a delay of eight days in making a landing might cause a war to be lost.[37] General Menéndez came close to proving the point. According to Woodward, the Argentines would have won had they managed to drag the battle out for ten more days.[38]

In the end, the Argentine defense proved incapable of buying those crucial ten days. In defiance of conventional wisdom, the outnumbered British had successfully landed and taken back the Falklands. When he surrendered, Menéndez joined a distinguished group of military commanders who had been unable to defeat modern amphibious assaults.

Anti-Landing Defense and the Implications for Future Amphibious Operations

It is more difficult to defend a coast than to invade it.
Sir Walter Raleigh

Since the beginning of modern amphibious warfare at Gallipoli, defenders have searched for a way to defeat a landing. With the exception of three small Japanese landings during World War II, the defenders have been unsuccessful. During this search, defenders have tried virtually all of the possible approaches to anti-landing defense. In the estimates of the attackers, all of the basic approaches have come close to succeeding on occasion. The fierce Japanese defense at the water's edge at Tarawa made the outcome of that landing uncertain during most of D-day. The same can be said of the German water's edge defense on Omaha Beach at Normandy. The German mobile defense at Salerno forced U.S. Gen. Mark W. Clark to consider evacuating the Americans from the beaches. Japanese attempts at naval defense at Guadalcanal, Leyte Gulf, and Okinawa clearly demonstrate the potential of that approach. In spite of these close calls, no major anti-landing defense has ever succeeded.

Sketching the characteristics of an anti-landing defense that would have the greatest chance of succeeding is not difficult. Such a scheme would commence with a naval defense combining the following actions:

- more extensive version of the minefields employed by the North Koreans at Wonsan
- all-out aerial assault against the invasion fleet that is patterned after the Japanese defense of Okinawa, with "smart" weapons replacing the kamikazes
- coordinated D-day attack on the naval forces conducting the

landing by midget submarines, fast-attack craft, assault swimmers, and other special units, such as those envisioned but never employed by the Germans at Normandy
- naval attack by major fleet units against the ships carrying and supporting the landing force, such as the operation attempted by the Japanese fleet at Leyte Gulf

The naval defense would be backed up by a defense at the water's edge, which combines the most lethal aspects of the Japanese defense at Tarawa and the German defense at Normandy. Once an enemy landing force had committed itself to assault one of these beaches, it would be counterattacked by heavy armored forces like those that nearly succeeded during the German mobile defense at Salerno. This defense would also include a counterlanding from the sea by specially trained amphibious forces along the lines that the Japanese planned several times during World War II but were never able to carry out.

The entire defense would be coordinated by a single individual who commanded all air, land, and naval forces committed to the defense from a headquarters near the scene of the action. This single commander would have the authority to make any decision needed to implement the defense except the use of chemical or nuclear weapons.

The ease of outlining this defense raises the obvious question of why no one has ever fielded such a defense. One answer might be that it requires a greater commitment of resources than most nations are willing to provide, particularly in peacetime. Historically, even where a defender has made the effort to construct impressive anti-landing defenses—the Atlantic Wall, for example—the amphibious attacker has nevertheless prevailed. Common to many of the failed attempts to defeat a landing are a number of factors that help to explain the overall failure of this particular operation of war. The steps that a potential defender might take to correct these past shortcomings also have important implications for the future of amphibious operations.

The Naval Character of Amphibious Operations

The basic requirement for a successful anti-landing defense is the recognition that an amphibious operation is a naval operation. As obvious as that conclusion is to some military planners, it appears to have escaped most of the commanders who have attempted to defend against landings. Commanders of ground troops participating in a landing are forced to accept the naval character of the operation by the very circumstances in which they find themselves. An amphibious assault requires both navy officers and ground officers to cooperate fully and to recognize the capabilities and limitations of the others' services. The navy must transport the landing force to the invasion site, sometimes against opposition, and deliver the troops to the shore. The landing force contributes little to the operation until it has reached the beach and can commence fighting.

Defending commanders face a quite different set of circumstances. They can act, and frequently have, as if defending against an amphibious operation were simply an operation of ground warfare not unlike the defense of a river line. In many cases, defending army commanders have treated their own naval forces as auxiliaries, rather than as one of the principal means of defeating a landing. General Senger und Etterlin attributed German anti-landing failures during World War II, in part, to the army's failure to understand the naval dimension of modern warfare. In his view, this weakness in the Germans' military thinking consistently caused them to overestimate the ease with which they could either prevent a landing or throw an invasion force back into the sea.[1] Admiral Ruge, in echoing this view, commented on its universal application and noted that naval officers appear to be able to apply their thinking to the land battle easier than army officers can do the reverse.[2]

Other German officers have taken issue with this view, but the record of World War II seems to support Senger und Etterlin's thesis.[3] The Japanese, on the other hand, fully understood the naval character of amphibious warfare, yet they could never bring themselves to act resolutely on that understanding with respect to defending against Allied landings. Instead, they chose to give precedence to forcing a decisive naval engagement with the U.S. fleet.

The danger for the U.S. military today is that it will lose sight of the essential naval character of amphibious operations. Emphasis is overwhelmingly focused on joint operations, with the result that single-service capabilities are not always fully appreciated. In spite of this emphasis on "jointness," an amphibious operation remains primarily a naval operation, even when forces from the army and air force participate. Perhaps the distinction seems academic, but it is an important one.

Command Relationships

The very nature of an amphibious operation requires ground and naval commanders to acknowledge one another's participation in the enterprise and demands a minimum level of cooperation. Because the navy must carry the landing force to the objective area and deliver it to a beach from which it can carry out its mission ashore, navy planners must at least consider the landing force's needs when planning the navy's part in the operation. The basic nature of a defense against a landing, on the other hand, exerts no corresponding pressure on commanders from different services to cooperate or consider the requirements of the other services. In many cases, naval and ground commanders defending against an enemy landing virtually have acted independently of one another.

This difference between conducting a landing and defending against one works to the advantage of the amphibious attacker by increasing the chances that the attacker's plan will reflect both unity of command and unity of effort. Defenders are not precluded from achieving such unity, but the nature of anti-landing defense does not demand it the way an amphibious operation does.

Historically, landings have been commanded at the operational level by admirals and defended against by generals. Notable exceptions to this rule were the Japanese island defenses in the Gilberts and Marshalls, which were commanded by admirals. Formal command relationships between commanders conducting landings have usually followed one of two patterns. Most of the central Pacific landings in World War II were conducted with command of all air, sea, and land forces in the hands of a naval officer who commanded a numbered fleet. Command relationships in the European landings, on the other hand, were generally based on the British concept of cooperation. Even then, the naval commanders normally exercised control over the landing force until the situation ashore reached the point where ground commanders could take control of the operation. Unlike those in the Pacific, however, air commanders in European operations refused to place their forces under naval command.

Given the record since Gallipoli, one salient lesson stands out. At the operational level, command of a defense against an expected landing should be placed in the hands of a single officer who controls all the forces available to oppose the landing. Most defenders have accepted this concept, at least in theory, but have been unable to achieve it in practice. The few exceptions include the defenses of Wake and Midway Islands early in World War II. The overall record not only supports a defensive organization based on the principle of unity of command but also suggests that the individual in command be a naval officer. Mirroring the command structure of the forces conducting the landing, command of the defense should shift to an army officer only when the enemy's landing force has established itself ashore to the degree that the operation has clearly changed from an amphibious operation to a land battle. Commanders planning a landing have no influence over how a defending enemy force chooses to structure its command relationships. By the wrong choice of their own command relationships, however, amphibious planners could inadvertently give up one of their greatest operational advantages: unity of command under naval leadership.

Sea Control and Air Superiority

For the most part, those who have had to defend against major landings have enjoyed neither sea control nor air superiority in the vicinity of the landing. This reality, which has been a major factor in the failure of most anti-landing defenses, has two related causes. First, virtually all practitioners of amphibious warfare have considered sea control and air superiority to be prerequisites to landing. Second, the amphibious attacker has the initiative. If control of the sea and air is not gained at least in the immediate area of a landing, the attacker can postpone or cancel the landing. The defender has no such option. The corollary, of course, is that a defender can usually deter a landing by maintaining air and sea control.

One trap into which amphibious commanders can easily fall involves their interpreting sea control and air superiority to mean absolute sea control and undisputed supremacy in the air. Ideally, an attacker would like to eliminate the enemy from the air over the projected beachhead before commencing the landing. Tarawa, Normandy, and Inchon are good examples where air supremacy was gained by the attackers under widely different conditions. Such absolute control is not always possible, however, and perhaps not even necessary. The landings at Salerno, Leyte Gulf, Okinawa, and the Falklands all succeeded in spite of determined opposition from the defenders' air forces. To insist on completely eliminating any air opposition before landing could unnecessarily deter some future landing.

A similar situation exists with respect to sea control during an amphibious assault. By the time of the Normandy invasion, the Allies had largely destroyed the German navy. The Germans were reduced to responding with mines, submarines, and small attack craft. Had the invasion of Japan taken place, the Japanese navy would have had no large surface ships to use in opposing the landings. Earlier, however, it had actively opposed or threatened most of the Allied landings in the SWPA and some in the central Pacific. The landings at Guadalcanal,

Leyte, and Saipan were all carried out under naval threats that resulted in the sea battles of Savo Island, Leyte Gulf, and Philippine Sea, respectively.

Doctrine

Doctrine is another issue that has distinguished amphibious attackers from defenders. The British and Americans, who have conducted most of the large-scale landings in this century, have had formal doctrine for amphibious operations since the period between the two world wars. Most of those who have defended against landings have had no formal doctrine to guide them. The Japanese were one exception. They recognized the need for anti-landing doctrine relatively late in World War II and then spent the rest of the conflict trying to develop a doctrine that worked. The result was a series of documents laying out a doctrine that evolved from a defense at the water's edge to a defense in depth and, by the end of the war, back to a defense at the water's edge.

The reason for the disparity between attackers and defenders with respect to the perceived need for formal doctrine is not clear. It may relate to two factors, both of which reflect the naval character of amphibious operations. First, naval officers have generally recognized both the special problems associated with conducting landings and the status of amphibious operations as a distinct form of naval warfare. Most defenders, army officers, for the most part, seem to have regarded their defensive efforts as simply ground operations and applied standard land warfare defensive doctrine.

Second, most attackers have considered landings to be operations of choice that can be used to advantage when the proper circumstances arise. Anticipating such circumstances in advance, they thought through the problems associated with amphibious warfare and created appropriate doctrines. Defenders, on the other hand, have generally found themselves in positions that were never anticipated. Had war plans of the Germans, Japanese, North Koreans, and Argentines succeeded, as they obviously anticipated, they never would have needed defenses against enemy landings. The lesson for defenders in the future is that anti-landing doctrine is essential. Developing such doctrine requires a potential defender to consider the many problems of the defense ahead of time, instead of waiting to confront them at some beachhead. Amphibious planners today should be aware that future opponents might not be as remiss in this respect as have many past defenders.

Opposing Force Ratios

In dismissing the importance of Allied landings during World War II, Soviet Admiral Gorshkov noted that the success of those operations could be reduced to a matter of arithmetic. He thought that amphibious attackers simply overwhelmed the defenders. Refuting this assertion involves an analysis of at least three complex factors: (1) numbers of troops and units on each side, (2) the weapons available to the opposing forces, and (3) the relative quality of their troops and leaders. Details of such an analysis would require a book of its own, but a few basic observations can be made.

Conventional wisdom holds that an amphibious attacker, like its land counterpart, requires a strength advantage of about three to one over the defender at the point of attack. The overall attacking force does not necessarily have to be three times larger than the overall defending force. Part of the art of the attacker is skill in concentrating the needed force at the point of attack. In spite of this, modern amphibious assaults have succeeded with a wide range of force ratios at the point of attack. At Tarawa, one of the most fiercely opposed landings in history, the 2d Marine Division succeeded with a numerical advantage of about two to one over the Japanese. At Sicily, a landing that one Soviet author called "an operation without risk," the Allies assaulted with nine divisions against a defending force of eleven.[4]

The landing on Sicily, however, points out the effect that varying qualities of troops can have on a battle. General Guzzoni, the Axis commander, estimated before the battle that an American division represented the combat power of two German divisions or four Italian divisions.[5] The outcome of the landing seems to have proved General Guzzoni right. Field Marshal Kesselring, overall German commander in Italy, said later that the armored attacks against the American beachhead at Gela would have succeeded had it not been for the determined resistance of a small number of American paratroopers from the 82d Airborne Division. Similarly, it is difficult to imagine that less skilled and determined troops than those of the U.S. Marine Corps would have been able to prevail at such heavily opposed landings as those on Tarawa, Peleliu, and Iwo Jima. At the same time, the history of modern amphibious warfare provides examples of forces of all calibers, elite to undistinguished, landing successfully against defenders of greatly varying quality.

During World War II, the attackers had the advantage of learning from firsthand experience. Three American divisions—1st and 4th Marine Divisions and 3d Infantry Division—each took part in four major landings. A number of others participated in more than one. Obviously, not every member of those divisions made every landing, but the collective experience of each division improved from operation to operation. The defenders, on the other hand, experienced quite different circumstances. With the major exception of some German divisions during the Italian campaign, each division of the defenders generally opposed only one landing.

The implications of opposing force ratios are particularly important to the future of U.S. amphibious operations. Since the Vietnam War, the requirement to apply overwhelming force has become an article of faith for American military planners. Although not precisely defined, overwhelming force would imply something greater than the three-to-one superiority normally accepted as necessary for a successful attack. This perceived need for overwhelming force, combined with the limited number of amphibious ships in the U.S. Navy, has the potential to deter operational commanders from making future landings against all but the weakest of opposing forces.

Risk and Casualties

Amphibious operations have the reputation of being particularly risky and costly in terms of casualties. Unfortunately, the reputation is based largely on a few landings that match this popular perception. Certain landings have produced exceptionally high casualty rates for the attackers; Dieppe, Tarawa, and Omaha Beach at Normandy come to mind. At Guadalcanal and Okinawa, landing forces same ashore unscathed because the enemy chose not to contest the landings. In the land battles that followed these two landings, the attackers suffered casualties, with particularly large numbers at Okinawa. The high casualty rates resulted from a variety of factors, however; only a few were related specifically to the nature of amphibious warfare.

The American public has always been sensitive to casualties in war. Realizing this, the Japanese attempted to exploit this sensitivity in their plans to defend against U.S. landings. The Japanese continued to hope that if they could inflict high enough casualties on American landing forces, the United States would reconsider its policy of unconditional surrender. That strategy failed during World War II, but it might well succeed today. An enemy of the United States, if anticipating a possible amphibious operation against its shores, might be able to deter it by creating the specter of massive American casualties.

The solution to this potential problem is psychological, not technical or tactical. U.S. military leaders must be able to calculate realistically the risks of military operations and then be willing to press civilian decision makers to authorize those operations in which the potential benefits outweigh the risks, including the risk of casualties. MacArthur did exactly that at Inchon. Although one pessimistic general rated the operation as a "5,000-to-1 shot," MacArthur informed the disturbed joint chiefs of staff that he regarded the chance of success to be "excellent."[6] The mood of the American public today and the precedent of the Gulf War of 1991, with its extremely low casualty rate, have made the U.S. military averse to all but the slightest risk. Unfortunately, these two factors also give an enemy a perfect strategy for deterring or defending against an American amphibious operation.

The Impact of Delay

In the past, delay on the part of an attacker in carrying out a landing has almost always worked to the advantage of the defender. The reason for this is not entirely clear, but part of the explanation might be that the timing of a landing is frequently dictated by periodic conditions involving tide, daylight, and weather. An attacker who misses one opportunity could be forced to wait a month or more for the appropriate conditions to recur. If the attacking force has reached a peak of physical and psychological readiness, any delay could cause its readiness to diminish, rather than increase. A defender, on the other hand, would regard any delay as a temporary reprieve and take advantage of it to lay more mines, build more obstacles and fortifications, and generally improve the defense. Although the timing of a landing is largely in the hands of the attacker, an astute defender might find ways of frightening an opponent suspected of preparing a landing into delaying its execution.

The Impact of Improved Weapons

In the past, the advent of important new weapons, such as the machine gun, the quick-firing cannon, the airplane, and precision-guided weapons usually has been accompanied by predictions of the resulting demise of amphibious warfare. Invariably, these predictions have been proved wrong. There is no apparent reason to believe that similar predictions in the future will be any more accurate with respect to conventional weapons. The issue remains unresolved, however, regarding two special types of weapons: chemical and nuclear.

Chemical weapons have been a factor in warfare since World War I. Although banned by several international conventions, chemical weapons remain a potential threat to amphibious operations. Despite this, no defenders have attempted to defeat a landing by resorting to chemical warfare. Their reasons probably involve factors that are not strictly related to amphibious warfare, including the fear of retaliation and the reluctance of most nations to violate international laws of war. The question of chemical warfare arose during the Gulf War because Iraq was known to have chemical warfare capability. Iraq did not overtly employ chemical warfare forces during the war and might not have used gas against a landing had the United States conducted one.

In spite of the record, prudence requires that amphibious planners take chemical warfare into consideration. Protective measures for a landing force are necessary, but they deal with only half the problem. An amphibious attacker who lacks the capability of responding in kind to the use of chemical weapons by an enemy gives that enemy a powerful advantage. By selective use of chemical weapons, the defender could force the attacking forces to land in full protective suits, while the defender's troops remain free of such encumbrances. Because the United States is in the process of dismantling its retaliatory chemical warfare capability, the use or threat of chemical warfare will become more attractive to future defenders. The implication for amphibious planners is twofold. First, U.S. amphibious forces must be capable of operating in a chemical environment. Second, lacking a retaliatory chemical capability, the United States must decide how to deter a future enemy's use of chemical warfare and how to respond if deterrence fails.

A similar set of uncertainties applies to the use of nuclear weapons to defeat a landing. In a narrow sense, nuclear weapons could have solved a variety of tactical problems since the end of World War II, but the cost of unleashing nuclear warfare far outweighs any potential benefits from doing so. The United States briefly considered their use during the Korean War and again at Dien Bien Phu to prevent a French defeat in Indochina. The reason why these weapons have not been used since World War II involve high-level strategic, political, legal, and moral considerations, not tactical or operational ones. So far, these high-level considerations have deterred the use of nuclear weapons by the few nations that possess them. Whether such restraint will continue as smaller, perhaps less responsible, nations develop nuclear capability is an open question.

Rather than allow a nuclear threat to deter future amphibious operations, the United States can pursue two courses of actions. The first course is to continue the development of dispersed amphibious operations that began with the use of helicopters after World War II. Such techniques offer the potential for a landing to succeed in spite of the use of a small number of low-yield tactical nuclear weapons by a defender. The second course is a statement by the United States that clearly delineates a policy regarding nuclear retaliation if nuclear weapons are ever used against American forces.

Mine Warfare

In a practical sense, naval mines constitute a much greater threat to amphibious operations today than either chemical or nuclear weapons. By modern standards, even the most sophisticated mines are relatively simple devices. They can be stockpiled during peacetime and laid with relative ease when needed. In spite of their relative simplicity, mines cause disproportionate problems for an attacker. Clearing a minefield for a landing is a slow process at best. An enemy could use the time gained to reposition forces and improve defenses. The damage to two U.S. warships off Kuwait by Iraqi contact mines during the Gulf War demonstrated the power of even a small-scale mine defense. Any nation threatened by amphibious attack today should clearly place naval mines high on its list of defensive priorities.

The lessons for the U.S. Navy are equally clear. Mine countermeasures must be considered an integral part of any amphibious operation. Unless the navy develops and maintains the ability to locate and sweep mines rapidly and on a relatively large scale, potential enemies will be able to deter the world's most powerful amphibious force. Some military planners might argue that the use of helicopters and air cushion landing craft (LCAC) has largely obviated the threat of mines to a landing. Although these two developments have reduced the threat, they have not eliminated it. For some time, the limited number of available LCACs will require amphibious forces to rely on conventional landing craft to deliver heavy equipment, such as tanks and self-propelled artillery, to a landing beach. Unless they are cleared, mines also can restrict the ability of amphibious ships to position themselves to launch amphibious vehicles or helicopters and can reduce the effectiveness of naval gunfire support by keeping ships far offshore.

Naval Gunfire

In the view of defenders against landings, naval gunfire, of all the weapons and techniques employed by amphibious attackers in modern landings, stands in a class of its own. The tremendous power of naval gunfire has been a common thread running through the accounts of defenders, including those from Turkey, Germany, Japan, and Argentina. Some military historians argue that this professed respect for naval gunfire is simply an excuse offered by defenders to deflect attention from their poor performance in other aspects of the defense. If so, it has been a recurrent, widely used excuse. Field Marshals Liman von Sanders, Kesselring, and Rommel and Generals Saito, Westphal, and von Senger und Etterlin, to name a few, highlight naval gunfire in their memoirs and after-action reports as an important factor in their defeats.[7]

In the past, naval gunfire has played a role in neutralizing defensive troops on beaches; smashing coastal defense batteries, pillboxes, and other emplacements; and breaking up counterattacks, including those by armored forces. Today, however, defenders are largely free from worry about dealing with an attacker's naval gunfire. The largest gun currently in the U.S. Navy's arsenal is the 5-inch/54 caliber. Other navies are in no better shape. Gone are the 8-inch guns that were available through Vietnam and the 16-inch battleship guns that fired their last rounds during the Gulf War. Modern developments, such as base-bleed and rocket-assisted shells to extend range, along with "smart" munitions to increase accuracy, ostensibly have allowed the 5-inch gun to carry out missions that previously required larger calibers. Unfortunately, that argument is only partially true. Regardless of its accuracy, a 5-inch shell can pack only a limited punch.

During World War II, the Germans and Japanese both constructed concrete coastal fortifications that could be destroyed only by repeated hits from naval guns of the heaviest caliber. Once again, the absence of such guns could make a defense at the water's edge a practical option for a defender willing to invest in coastal fortifications.

Missiles, such as the Tomahawk, could assume the point-destruction role of naval gunfire, but their use poses an economic question. In the past, American amphibious forces have landed against defenses that included hundreds of concrete emplacements. In the Pacific, naval guns systematically reduced these positions to rubble before a landing. Given the cost of modern missiles, the U.S. Navy is unlikely to maintain enough of them to use in the role previously performed by heavy naval gunfire.

World War II landings also demonstrated the need to neutralize enemy forces defending a beach before H-hour. To accomplish this mission, the British and Americans both developed vessels that could blanket a beach with tons of explosives delivered by rockets. The U.S. Navy lost this capability in the 1970s when it broke up or sold its few remaining rocket ships. This lost capability might be regained by mounting rocket launchers on amphibious ships. The Soviet navy used this approach. In the U.S. Navy, this idea is still in the conceptual stage.

Along with marginal mine countermeasures, the lack of naval gunfire may be the greatest weakness of U.S. amphibious capabilities today. Some military theorists argue that the current lack of naval guns can be overcome by the increased use of air support, including support from air force bombers. The experience of World War II would indicate otherwise.

Target Priorites

One problem that has consistently confounded defenders who have attempted to use a naval defense against landings is the assignment of target priorities. In this respect, three classes of ships have generally vied for the highest priority: aircraft carriers, heavy naval gunfire ships, and transports and other amphibious ships that carry the landing force. More often than not, defenders have devoted their attention mainly to the first two categories. In some cases, this attention was an effort to reduce the impact of air strikes and naval gunfire on the defender. Two examples are Hitler's order for German forces to attack Allied battleships at Normandy and the Japanese navy's decision to use kamikazes against American carriers at Leyte Gulf. In other cases, defenders have chosen to attack the first available targets, which frequently were warships, not transports. This occurred regularly during the kamikaze attacks at Okinawa and Argentine air attacks against the British fleet during the Falklands operation. In still other cases, such target priorities have resulted from the belief—common in the Japanese navy during World War II—that warships are more worthy targets for attack than transports or other ships.

By the end of World War II, the Japanese had adopted a more pragmatic approach that could serve as the model for any anti-landing defense. In this model, the amphibious ships are by far the highest priority targets. When an amphibious ship, with its embarked landing force, is sunk, neither the ship nor the landing force can participate in a landing, irrespective of how much damage the supporting carriers and naval gunfire ships inflict on the defender. In Clausewitzian terms, the amphibious ships are the attacker's center of gravity. Destroying that center is the defender's most certain way of defeating the landing. There are exceptions; in the Falklands, for example, the British carriers were as crucial to the landing as the amphibious ships. Realizing their importance, Admiral Woodward protected both carriers and troop transports, even when this increased the risk to other elements of the task force.

Summary

The record of amphibious warfare in the twentieth century seems to validate Sir Walter Raleigh's assessment that defending against an amphibious operation is more difficult than conducting one. In spite of the record, many military theorists continue to hold that an assault landing against a defended beach is no longer a feasible operation of war and that the United States should rely solely on a MacArthur-like approach of landing where the enemy "ain't." Such an approach would reduce the equipment needs of the U.S. Marine Corps and naval amphibious forces and largely obviate the necessity to replace large-caliber naval gunfire.

Landing at a location that is not a strongly defended one has always been the preferred option. During World War II, the Germans and Japanese were frequently unwilling to make such an option available. Those theorists who dispute the need to conduct opposed landings in the future are saying, in effect, that because they cannot envision any circumstances that would require another Tarawa or Normandy, no such circumstances will ever exist.

The severe limitations of an amphibious force with the inability to conduct an opposed landing offer a critical advantage to a defender. Against such a force, a defender can use a defense at the water's edge to protect selected landing beaches. Knowing that the attacker will not be able to land at the defended beaches, the defender's mobile forces are free to concentrate on those "undefended" areas where the enemy might be able to land. A force trained and equipped to land across a defended beach can always land across an undefended one, but the reverse is not true.

In the final analysis, the amphibious attack has been proved a stronger operation of war than the anti-landing defense. Some of the reasons for this superiority, such as the initiative that accrues to any attacker and the superior mobility of naval forces, can be attributed to the nature of the amphibious operation itself. Most of the reasons are not inherent, however, but result from a nation's willingness to maintain the tools of this specialized form of naval warfare and to accept the risks of using it when necessary.

Americans can always refuse to pay the price for maintaining an amphibious capability, thereby giving up what Liddell Hart calls "the greatest strategic asset that a sea-based power possesses."[8] If Americans should choose to take such a step, they will have, in effect, accomplished what no enemy has managed to do: defeat a modern amphibious operation.

Notes

CHAPTER 1. Anti-Landing Defense: The Other Face of Amphibious Warfare

1. Fuller, J. F. C., *Second World War 1939–45,* 207.
2. Liddell Hart, *Defence of Britain,* 130.
3. Gorshkov, *Sea Power of the State,* 122.
4. Corbett, *Some Principles of Maritime Strategy,* 213.
5. Furse, *Military Expeditions,* 359.
6. Jomini, *Art of War,* 229.
7. Quoted in Furse, *Military Expeditions,* 363–64.
8. Clausewitz, *On War,* 528.

CHAPTER 2. The Search Begins: Gallipoli, 1915

1. Quoted in Marder, *Anatomy of British Seapower,* 495.
2. Liman von Sanders, *Five Years in Turkey,* 56.
3. Aspinall-Oglander, *Military Operations, Gallipoli,* vol. 1, 127.
4. Liman von Sanders, *Five Years in Turkey,* 64.
5. Aspinall-Oglander, *Military Operations, Gallipoli,* vol 1, 104.
6. Hamilton, *Gallipoli Diary,* vol. 1, 22.
7. Ibid., 96–98.
8. Trumpener, *Germany and Ottoman Empire,* 69.
9. "Turkish General Staff History" pt. 1, 352.
10. For a detailed terrain analysis of the campaign, see Miles, "Notes on the Dardanelles Campaign."
11. "Turkish General Staff History," pt. 1, 351–52.
12. Liman von Sanders, *Five Years in Turkey,* 59.
13. Ibid., 61.
14. Aspinall-Oglander, *Military Operations, Gallipoli,* vol. 1, 226.

15. Liman von Sanders, *Five Years in Turkey*, 63.
16. Ibid., 81.
17. Kannengiesser, *Campaign in Gallipoli*, 220.
18. Liman von Sanders, *Five Years in Turkey*, 97.
19. Ibid., 69, 77.
20. Mackenzie, *Gallipoli Memories*, 73.
21. Groos, *Lessons of Naval Warfare*, 61.
22. Dupuy and Dupuy, *Encyclopedia of Military History*, 954.
23. "Turkish General Staff History," pt. 2, 95.
24. United Kingdom (UK) Parliament, *Final Report of Dardanelles Commission*, 25.
25. Kannengiesser, *Campaign in Gallipoli*, 238.
26. Liman von Sanders, *Five Years in Turkey*, 71.
27. Hamilton, *Gallipoli Diary*, vol. 1, 135.

CHAPTER 3. Preparations for Invasion: Great Britain, 1940

1. Keyes, *Amphibious Warfare*, 53.
2. Quoted in Collier, *Defence of United Kingdom*, 134.
3. Liddell Hart, *Defence of Britain*, 130.
4. Collier, *Defence of United Kingdom*, 10.
5. UK Public Records Office (PRO), War Office (WO) 199/579, "Appreciation by Commander-in-Chief, Home Forces," 1 August 1941, para. 16.
6. UK PRO, Cabinet (CAB) 80/5, COS (39)125, 15.
7. UK PRO, CAB 80/5, COS(39)125, 6–13.
8. UK PRO, CAB 80/14, COS(40)533(JIC), 1.
9. Roskill, *War at Sea*, 1:256–60.
10. UK PRO, WO 190/891.
11. UK PRO, WO 199/569, 1.
12. UK PRO, WO 199/579, paras. 2, 32.
13. Trevor-Roper, *Blitzkrieg to Defeat*, 34–37.
14. For a recent account of the German plans and planning process for Sea Lion, see Schenk, *Invasion of England 1940*.
15. Schenk, *Invasion of England 1940*, 231.
16. UK PRO, WO 199/569, 4.
17. Fleming, *Operation Sealion*, 179.
18. For varying German estimates, see ibid., 179–80; Schenk, *Invasion of England 1940*, 235; and Shulman, *Defeat in the West*, 49.
19. Collier, *Defence of United Kingdom*, 106–07.
20. Grinnell-Milne, *Silent Victory*, 94–96.
21. Collier, *Defence of United Kingdom*, 162.
22. According to Bryant, *Turn of the Tide*, 159–60.
23. UK PRO, CAB 80/11, COS(40)395, 1–4.
24. UK PRO, CAB 80/14, COS(40)522, 1.

25. Halder, *Halder Diaries*, 490.
26. Quoted in Bryant, *Turn of the Tide*, 164.
27. Ismay, *Memoirs*, 179.
28. Liddell Hart, *German Generals Talk*, 152.
29. Collier, *Defence of United Kingdom*, 222–23.
30. Wheatley, *Operation Sea Lion*, 80.
31. Churchill, *Their Finest Hour*, 291–92.
32. UK PRO, Admiralty (ADM 234)/436, 85.
33. Collier, *Defence of United Kingdom*, 140.
34. UK PRO, CAB 80/13, COS(40)495.
35. Collier, *Defence of United Kingdom*, 132–33; UK PRO, WO 199/1712.
36. For details of these fortifications, see Wills, *Pillboxes*.
37. Details of the flame trap and other efforts of the Petroleum Warfare Department are described in Banks, *Flame over Britain*, chap. 3.
38. Quoted in Macleod and Kelly, *Time Unguarded*, 368.
39. UK PRO, CAB 80/13, COS(40)495.
40. Bryant, *Turn of the Tide*, 157–58.
41. UK PRO, WO 199/328.
42. Churchill, *Their Finest Hour*, 279.
43. Chalmers, *Full Cycle*, 109.
44. Spencer, *Battle of Britain Revisited*, 20, quotes Robert Wright, *Dowding and the Battle of Britain*, London: MacDonald and James, 1969, 146.
45. Collier, *Defence of United Kingdom*, 225–27.
46. Wheatley, *Operation Sea Lion*, 95.
47. Quoted in Collier, *Defence of United Kingdom*, 182.
48. Quoted in Mcleod and Kelly, *Time Unguarded*, 366.
49. Qouted in Plehwe, "Operation Sealion 1940," 52.

CHAPTER 4. German Mobile Defence: Sicily and Salerno, 1943

1. Senger und Etterlin, *Neither Fear nor Hope*, 128; Badoglio, *Italy in Second World War*, 98.
2. *Fuehrer Conferences on Naval Affairs*, 321.
3. Ibid., 327.
4. See Montagu, *The Man Who Never Was*.
5. Garland and Smyth, *Sicily and Surrender of Italy*, 45–46; *Fuehrer Conferences on Naval Affairs*, 324.
6. Garland and Smyth, *Sicily and Surrender of Italy*, 80; Faldella, *Lo sbarco e la difesa della Sicilia*, 399–417.
7. Garland and Smyth, *Sicily and Surrender of Italy*, 83.
8. Molony, *Mediterranean and Middle East*, 5:46.
9. Craven and Cate, *The Army Air Forces in World War II*, 2:445; Morison, *Sicily-Salerno-Anzio*, 56.
10. D'Este, *Bitter Victory*, 86.

11. Garland and Smyth, *Sicily and Surrender of Italy*, 87.
12. Kesselring, *Kesselring: A Soldier's Record*, 193.
13. *Fuehrer Conferences on Naval Affairs*, 322.
14. European Theater Historical Interrogations (ETHINT), Kesselring, "Concluding Remarks on Mediterranean Campaign," 32; Senger und Etterlin, *Neither Fear nor Hope*, 131.
15. Senger und Etterlin, *Neither Fear nor Hope*, 129, 150.
16. Kesselring, *Kesselring: A Soldier's Record*, 194.
17. Garland and Smyth, *Sicily and Surrender of Italy*, 111.
18. Mitcham and Stauffenberg, *Battle of Sicily*, 93; D'Este, *Bitter Victory*, 252.
19. Garland and Smyth, *Sicily and Surrender of Italy*, 119.
20. Bradley, *A Soldier's Story*, 128.
21. Mitcham and Stauffenberg, *Battle of Sicily*, 121–22.
22. ETHINT, Kesselring, "Concluding Remarks on Mediterranean Campaign," 31.
23. Ibid., 32.
24. Garland and Smyth, *Sicily and Surrender of Italy*, 534.
25. Bennett, *Ultra and Mediterranean Strategy*, 241.
26. Nowarra, *German Guided Missiles*, 17.
27. Hinsley, *British Intelligence*, 3: pt. 1, 337–42.
28. ETHINT, Kesselring, "Concluding Remarks on Mediterranean Campaign," 31.
29. Blumenson, *Patton Papers*, 2:344.
30. Blumenson, *Salerno to Cassino*, 79.
31. Ibid., 116.
32. Clark, *Calculated Risk*, 199.
33. Blumenson, *Salerno to Cassino*, 117.
34. Hinsley, *British Intelligence*, 3: pt. 1, 497–500.
35. See Bogart, "German Remotely Piloted Bombs."
36. ETHINT, Kesselring, "Concluding Remarks on Mediterranean Campaign," 32–33.
37. D'Este, *Fatal Decision*, 450.
38. ETHINT, Kesselring, "Concluding Remarks on Mediterranean Campaign," 30.
39. Maugeri, *From the Ashes of Disgrace*, 192.

CHAPTER 5. German Defense at the Water's Edge: Normandy, 1944

1. See, for example, Blumentritt, *Von Rundstedt*; Geyr von Schweppenburg, "Reflections on the Invasion"; Liddell Hart, *Rommel Papers*, chap. 21; Ruge, *Rommel in Normandy*; and Speidel, *Invasion 1944*.
2. *Fuehrer Directives 1939–1941*, 234–36.
3. See Campbell, *Dieppe Revisited*, 196–233, for a discussion of how both sides applied the lessons of Dieppe in preparing for Normandy.

4. For an overall account of the evolution of the Atlantic Wall, see Wilt, *Atlantic Wall*. For locations and detailed descriptions of individual positions, see Chazette, *1940–1944 Les batteries allemandes*; Rolf, *Atlantic Wall Typology* and *Der Atlantikwall*; and *German Seacoast Defenses, European Theater*. For the relationship between Organization Todt and the German Army in constructing the wall, see ETHINT, Ullersperger, "Nineteenth Army Fortress Engineer," and ETHINT, Schmetzer, "Report Regarding Construction of Atlantic Wall," Manuscript No. B-668, pt. 3.
5. Warlimont, *Inside Hitler's Headquarters*, 403.
6. Chazette, *1940–1944 Les batteries allemandes*, 3.
7. Warlimont, *Inside Hitler's Headquarters*, 409.
8. *Fuehrer Directives 1942–1945*, 35.
9. Hinsley, *British Intelligence*, 3: pt. 2, 74.
10. Shulman, *Defeat in the West*, 94.
11. Boyd, *Hitler's Japanese Confidant*, 114.
12. Harrison, *Cross-Channel Attack*, 459–63, quotes Fuehrer Directive 40 in full.
13. Ibid., 243. Also, see diagram illustrating the complexity of the German command structure in the west, 244.
14. Simpson, "A Close Run Thing?," 65.
15. For additional information about German naval anti-invasion forces, see Skinner, "Naval Threat on Western Flank."
16. *German Seacoast Defense, European Theater*, Appendix 7, enclosure 84, "Information on Operation of German Small Battle Units (KdK)," 1.
17. Howard, *British Intelligence*, 5:115.
18. Ryan, *The Longest Day*, 22.
19. *Fuehrer Directives 1942–1945*, 110–15.
20. Ruge, "With Rommel before Normandy," 614.
21. Geyr von Schweppenburg, "Reflections on the Invasion," pts. 1, 2; Ose, "Rommel and Rundstedt."
22. Harrison, *Cross-Channel Attack*, 141; Chandler and Collins, *D-Day Encyclopedia*, 66.
23. Carell, *Invasion—They're Coming!*, 10.
24. Wilt, *Atlantic Wall*, 121; Liddell Hart, *Rommel Papers*, 457.
25. Liddell Hart, *Rommel Papers*, 459.
26. Gilbert, *Hitler Directs His War*, 134–35.
27. ETHINT, Ruge, "Mines in the Channel," 2.
28. Hoyt, *Invasion before Normandy*, 99–112.
29. Kahn, *Hitler's Spies*, 503–13.
30. Stacey, *Canadian Army*, 177. For a German assessment of the damage see ETHINT, Schmetzer, "Report Regarding Construction of Atlantic Wall," pt. 4, 1–33.
31. For a description of these specialized vehicles, see Fletcher, *Vanguard of Victory*, and Futter, *The Funnies*.

32. Bradley, *A Soldier's Story,* 272.
33. Irving, *Trail of the Fox,* 321.
34. Ruge, "Invasion of Normandy," 33.
35. Skinner, "Naval Threat on Western Flank," 188–89.
36. O'Neill, *Suicide Squads,* 255.
37. Morison, *Invasion of France and Germany,* 170.
38. *Fuehrer Conferences on Naval Affairs,* 399.
39. Geyr von Schweppenburg, "Reflections on the Invasion," pt. 1.
40. Weigley, *Eisenhower's Lieutenants,* 46.
41. Harris and Paxman, *Higher Form of Killing,* 69.
42. Bradley, *A Soldier's Story,* 279.
43. Harris and Paxman, *Higher Form of Killing,* 57–73.
44. Ochsner, *History of German Chemical Warfare,* 23.

CHAPTER 6. The Americans Try Their Hand: Wake and Midway, 1941–1942

1. For a summary of the development of the advanced base mission in the U.S. Marine Corps, see Clifford, *Progress and Purpose,* 15–21.
2. Updegraph, *U.S. Marine Corps Special Units,* 62–63.
3. Director, War Plans Division, Secret memorandum to Chief of Naval Operations, 12 December 1935, quoted in McPoil, "Development and Defense of Wake Island."
4. Miller, Edward S., *War Plan Orange,* 242.
5. McPoil, "Development and Defense of Wake Island."
6. Heinl, *Defense of Wake,* 3–4.
7. U.S. National Achives, Record Group 127, ACC 63A-2534, Box 12. Letter from CinCPac to CNO of 18 April 1941, "Wake Island—Policy in Regard to Construction on and Protection of."
8. CinCPacFlt, Secret message, 11 October 1941, quoted in McPoil, "Development and Defense of Wake Island."
9. Heinl, *Defense of Wake,* 70.
10. Schultz, *Wake Island,* 39.
11. Heinl, *Defense of Wake,* 69.
12. Ibid., 10–11.
13. U.S. Strategic Bombing Survey (USSBS), *Interrogations of Japanese Officials,* vol. 2, interrogation No. 413, Koyama, 371.
14. *Tentative Manual for Landing Operations,* para. 3-104.
15. Ibid., para. 3-120.
16. Ibid., para. 3-217a.
17. Ibid., para. 3-122b.
18. Heinl, *Defense of Wake,* 16.
19. *Tentative Manual for Landing Operations,* para. 3-1003.
20. Heinl, *Defense of Wake,* 14–15.

21. Ibid., 25.
22. Ibid., 36.
23. Ibid., 61.
24. Bates, *Battle of Midway*, 41.
25. Fuchida and Okumiya, *Midway*, 217–19.
26. Ibid., 218.
27. USSBS, *Interrogations of Japanese Officials*, vol. 1, interrogation No. 252, Toyama, 250.
28. Cressman, "A Magnificent Fight," 11.
29. Heinl, *Marines at Midway*, 55–56.
30. CinCPac Operation Plan 29-42, 27 May 1942, para. 1(e).
31. Aircraft figures from Heinl, *Marines at Midway*, 24, and Bates, *Battle of Midway*, 13.
32. *Japanese Story of Battle of Midway*, 2.
33. Quoted in Cressman et al., *Glorious Page in Our History*, 35.
34. *Tentative Manual for Landing Operations*, para. 3-812.
35. CO, 6th Defense Battalion, letter to CO, Naval Air Station, Midway, 13 June 1942, and Robert C. McGlashan, "Historical Report on the Defense of Midway," 24, both in National Archives, Record Group 127, Acc 63A-2534, Box 11. Except as otherwise noted, details of the defense are from McGlashan.
36. Morison, *Coral Sea, Midway, and Submarine Operations*, 85.
37. U.S. Far East Command, *World War II Japanese Monograph Series*, No. 156, 4.
38. *Tentative Manual for Landing Operations*, para. 3-805.

CHAPTER 7. Japanese Naval Defense: The Southwest Pacific Area, 1942–1944

1. Frank, *Guadalcanal*, 43.
2. Ibid., 44.
3. Bates, *Battle of Savo Island*, 7–8.
4. Ibid., 5.
5. Frank, *Guadalcanal*, 50.
6. Hough, Ludwig, and Shaw, *Pearl Harbor to Guadalcanal*, 264.
7. Frank, *Guadalcanal*, 78–79.
8. Potter, *Sea Power: A Naval History*, 307.
9. Dull, *Battle History of Imperial Japanese Navy*, 253–59.
10. Hara, *Japanese Destroyer Captain*, 242.
11. Miller, John, Jr., *Cartwheel*, 259–60.
12. Smith, Robert Ross, *Approach to the Philippines*, 300–04.
13. Ibid., 347.
14. "War Game for the Sho-Go Operation," U.S. Army Center of Military History Files, Box 8-5.1 AN V.9 sec. 4.
15. Drea, *MacArthur's Ultra*, 155.

16. For a detailed comparison of U.S. and Japanese estimates of Japanese losses, see Bates, *Battle for Leyte Gulf,* vol. 1, 122.
17. Warner and Warner, *Sacred Warriors,* 83.
18. Cannon, *Leyte,* 26–27.
19. Drea, *MacArthur's Ultra,* 158–59.
20. Warner and Warner, *Sacred Warriors,* 96–97.
21. Cannon, *Leyte,* 93.
22. Dull, *Battle History of Imperial Japanese Navy,* 336–37.
23. Cannon, *Leyte,* 50.
24. Ibid., 23.
25. *Reports of General MacArthur,* vol. 2, pt. 1, 322.
26. Ibid., 319–20.
27. Field, *Japanese at Leyte Gulf,* 31.
28. Cannon, *Leyte,* 78.
29. Ugaki, *Fading Victory,* 485–86.
30. USSBS, *Interrogations of Japanese Officials,* vol. 2, interrogation No. 503, Fukudome, 504.
31. Warner and Warner, *Sacred Warriors,* 84.
32. Ibid., 94.
33. Ibid., 160.
34. Quoted in Koyanagi, "With Kurita in Battle for Leyte Gulf," 126.
35. USSBS, *Interrogations of Japanese Officials,* vol. 2, interrogation No. 378, Toyoda, 318.
36. Warner and Warner, *Sacred Warriors,* 97.

CHAPTER 8. Japanese Defense at the Water's Edge: The Gilberts and Marshalls, 1943–1944

1. Wilds, "How Japan Fortified Mandated Islands"
2. Ibid.
3. Miller, *War Plan Orange,* 247.
4. U.S. Far East Command, *World War II Japanese Monograph Series,* No. 161, 4–9.
5. Alexander, *Utmost Savagery,* 31.
6. Ibid., 19
7. Quoted in Potter, *Nimitz,* 254–55.
8. Alexander, *Across the Reef,* 3.
9. U.S. Far East Command, *World War II Japanese Monograph Series,* No. 161, 14.
10. Ibid., 16.
11. Alexander, *Utmost Savagery,* 95.
12. Holmes, *Double-Edged Secrets,* 143–144.
13. Crowl and Love, *Seizure of Gilberts and Marshalls,* 33.
14. Joint Intelligence Center, Pacific Ocean Areas (JICPOA) Item 7384. Quoted in USSBS, *Japanese Military and Naval Intelligence Division,* 77–78.

15. U.S. Far East Command, *World War II Japanese Monograph Series,* No. 161, Appendix I.
16. Ibid., Appendix III.
17. Ibid., Appendix IV.
18. Ibid., Appendix II.
19. U.S. Navy Historical Center, JICPOA, Item 3764.
20. Stockman, *Battle for Tarawa,* 5.
21. Morison, *Aleutians, Gilberts and Marshalls,* 148–49.
22. Dyer, *Amphibians Came to Conquer,* vol. 2, 653.
23. Naval Gunfire Training Section, Headquarters, Fleet Marine Force Pacific, letter reporting ammunition expenditures for various central Pacific operations, 4 August 1945, author's personal files.
24. For a detailed discussion about the tides at Tarawa, see Dyer, *Amphibians Came to Conquer,* vol. 2, 715–25.
25. Quoted in Alexander, *Across the Reef,* 26.
26. Smith, Julian C., "Tarawa."
27. Alexander, *Across the Reef,* 50.
28. Orita and Harrington, *I-Boat Captain,* 190–95.
29. Holmes, *Double-Edged Secrets,* 149.
30. USSBS, *Interrogations of Japanese Officials,* vol. 1, interrogation No. 139, Nakajima, 144.
31. U.S. Marine Corps University Archives, Engineer, V Amphibious Corps, "Letter Report, Kwajalein Atoll, Study and Report of Japanese Defenses," 15 February 1944, 1, Marshalls Files, Box 17, Folder 34.
32. Elliott, *Allied Minesweeping,* 156.

CHAPTER 9. Japanese Defense in Transition: Saipan to Iwo Jima, 1944–1945

1. Hayashi and Coox, *Kogun,* 72.
2. Northern Troops and Landing Force (NTLF) G-2 Thirty-first Army, incoming message file, No. 152, quoted in Shaw, Nalty, and Turnbladh, *Central Pacific Drive,* 295.
3. Kuzuhara, "Operations on Iwo Jima," 38.
4. Crowl, *Campaign in Marianas,* 453–54.
5. Hayashi and Coox, *Kogun,* 109.
6. Crowl, *Campaign in Marianas,* 36.
7. Kuzuhara, "Operations on Iwo Jima," 33–34.
8. U.S. National Archives, Expeditionary Troops Engineer, "Report on Japanese Defensive Plan for the Island of Saipan," 2. Record Group 127, Acc 65-4556, Box 76.
9. Ibid., 1.
10. Hoffman, *Saipan,* 45.

11. Shaw, Nalty, and Turnbladh, *Central Pacific Drive*, 266.
12. Crowl, *Campaign in Marianas*, 67–68.
13. Shaw, Nalty, and Turnbladh, *Central Pacific Drive*, 278–79.
14. Morison, *New Guinea and Marianas*, 320–21.
15. Shaw, Nalty, and Turnbladh, Central Pacific Drive, 322.
16. Love, *27th Infantry Division*, 434.
17. U.S. National Archives, U.S. 4th Marine Division, translations of Japanese documents captured on Saipan, Record Group 127, Acc 65A-4556, Box 86, Folder C-1-1.
18. Ibid.
19. Kuzuhara, "Operations on Iwo Jima," 34–35.
20. Shaw, Nalty, and Turnbladh, *Central Pacific Drive*, 378.
21. Kuzuhara, "Operations on Iwo Jima," 13.
22. Ibid., 28–29; Allied Translator and Interpreter Section (ATIS), Enemy Publication No. 328, *Lessons from Saipan Operation*.
23. Kuzuhara, "Operations on Iwo Jima," 37.
24. Garand and Strobridge, *Western Pacific Operations*, 499.
25. For varying explanations of General Murai's role, see "Interrogations of Lt. Gen. Sadae Inoue and Col. Tokuchi Tada," Box 8-5.1, AD 1, v.5, sections 36 and 37, U.S. Army Center for Military History; and Hough, *Assault on Peleliu*, Appendix F, 200–02.
26. Vice Adm. Jesse B. Oldendorf, letter to Brig. Gen. Clayton C. Jerome, 25 March 1950, quoted in Gailey, *Peleliu 1944*, 66.
27. Gailey, *Peleliu 1944*, 50.
28. Ibid., 43–45.
29. Kuzuhara, "Operations on Iwo Jima," 71–72.
30. Japanese strength figures are from the Japanese Defense Agency, as given in Garand and Strobridge, *Western Pacific Operations*, 458.
31. Kuzuhara, "Operations on Iwo Jima," 44–45.
32. Garand and Strobridge, *Western Pacific Operations*, 454.
33. Ibid.
34. Kuzuhara, "Operations on Iwo Jima," 89.
35. Garand and Strobridge, *Western Pacific Operations*, 475.
36. Ibid.
37. Kuzuhara, "Operations on Iwo Jima," 41–43.
38. Ibid., 50–51.
39. Ibid., 111–12.
40. Garand and Strobridge, *Western Pacific Operations*, 458.
41. Kuzuhara, "Operations on Iwo Jima," 56–63.
42. U.S. Marine Corps University Archives, "Japanese Mines on Iwo Jima," Iwo Jima File, Box 65, Folder 43.
43. Garand and Strobridge, *Western Pacific Operations*, 499.
44. Kuzuhara, "Operations on Iwo Jima," 80.

45. Newcomb, *Iwo Jima*, 193.
46. ATIS, Enemy Publication No. 415, *Combat Regulations*, 20.
47. USSBS, *Interrogations of Japanese Officials*, vol. 2, interrogation No. 429, Nomura, 387.
48. Shaw, Nalty, and Turnbladh, *Central Pacific Drive*, 293–94.
49. Gailey, *Peleliu*, 77.
50. Garand and Strobridge, *Western Pacific Operations*, 614.
51. Ibid., 612–14.

CHAPTER 10. The Ultimate Naval Defense: Okinawa and Japan, 1945

1. Hoyt, *Japan's War*, 197–98.
2. Warner and Warner, *Sacred Warriors*, 40.
3. Japanese strength figures are from Huber, *Japan's Battle of Okinawa*, 125–29.
4. Huber, *Japan's Battle of Okinawa*, 74–79.
5. Hayashi and Coox, *Kogun*, 141.
6. Warner and Warner, *Sacred Warriors*, 148.
7. Naito, *Thunder Gods*, 33–49.
8. Ibid., 70–74.
9. Appleman et al., *Okinawa*, 15–17.
10. Ibid., 25–26.
11. Ibid., 92.
12. Huber, *Japan's Battle of Okinawa*, 5.
13. Ibid., 25.
14. Ibid., 13.
15. Headquarters III Amphibious Corps, "Japanese Cave Warfare," letter, 3 July 1945, Author's collection.
16. Naito, *Thunder Gods*, 140.
17. USSBS, *Interrogations of Japanese Officials*, vol. 1, interrogation No. 34, Tamura, 268.
18. Naito, *Thunder Gods*, 113–15.
19. O'Neill, *Suicide Squads*, 112.
20. Appleman et al., *Okinawa*, 60.
21. Carpenter and Polmar, *Submarines of Imperial Japanese Navy*, 59..
22. Huber, *Japan's Battle of Okinawa*, 27–39, discusses the series of Japanese counterattack plans.
23. Yokoi, "Kamikazes in Okinawa Campaign," 464.
24. Spurr, *Glorious Way to Die*, 283.
25. O'Neill, *Suicide Squads*, 169–70.
26. Huber, *Japan's Battle of Okinawa*, 114–15.
27. Skates, *Invasion of Japan*, 118.
28. Ibid., 105.
29. Matsumoto, "Preparations for Decisive Battle," 34–35.

30. Ibid., 8–9; U.S. Far East Command, *World War II Japanese Monograph Series*, No. 17, 123; Skates, *Invasion of Japan*, 120.
31. Skates, *Invasion of Japan*, 107.
32. Ibid., 138.
33. Ibid., 109.
34. Naito, *Thunder Gods*, 186.
35. Skates, *Invasion of Japan*, 111.
36. O'Neill, *Suicide Squads*, 270–71.
37. Ibid., 271–72.
38. Drea, *MacArthur's Ultra*, 220–21.
39. Skates, *Invasion of Japan*, 103–04; Matsumoto, "Preparations for Decisive Battle," 26–27.
40. Details of the American plan for Operation Olympic are from Skates, *Invasion of Japan*, except as otherwise indicated.
41. For an account of the deception, see Huber, *Pastel*.
42. Matsumoto, "Preparations for Decisive Battle," 50–52; Kuzuhara, "Operations on Iwo Jima," 38.
43. U.S. Far East Command, *World War II Japanese Monograph Series*, No. 17, 105.
44. Matsumoto, "Preparations for Decisive Battle," 69–70.
45. Skates, *Invasion of Japan*, 122.
46. U.S. Marine Corps University Archives, Headquarters, V Amphibious Corps, "The Japanese Plan for the Defense of Kyushu," G-2 Report, Annex C, 30 November 1945, 34, Japan Files, Box 89, Folder 9.
47. Skates, *Invasion of Japan*, 80.
48. *Reports of General MacArthur*, vol. 2, 393–94.
49. Skates, *Invasion of Japan*, 95.
50. For a discussion of chemical warfare and the invasion of Japan, see ibid., 92–97, and van Courtland Moon, "Project Sphinx." Details of U.S. military thinking are also in "Use of Gas Warfare against the Japanese," memorandum for Chief, Strategy Section, Operations Division, War Department General Staff, 3 June 1945, Strategy Section Paper 387.
51. Skates, *Invasion of Japan*, 243; Gallicchio, "After Nagasaki."
52. USSBS, *Summary Report (Pacific War)*, 28.

CHAPTER 11. A Poor Man's Naval Defense: Inchon and Wonsan, 1950
1. Savada, *North Korea*, 214.
2. Summers, *Korean War Almanac*, 203.
3. Hastings, *Korean War*, 58.
4. North Korean order of battle is from Montross and Canzona, *Inchon-Seoul Operation*, 325–26.
5. Heinl, *Victory at High Tide*, 52.
6. Ibid., 47.

7. Ibid., 79.
8. U.S. Marine Corps University Archives, "Special Action Report on Inchon," Annex B to 1st Marine Division, 15 September 1950, Korean War Collection, Box 18, Folder 202.
9. Field, *United States Naval Operations: Korea*, 180.
10. Ibid.
11. Cagle and Manson, *Sea War in Korea*, 78.
12. Montross and Canzona, *Inchon-Seoul Operation*, 142.
13. Heinl, *Victory at High Tide*, 80; Cagle and Manson, *Sea War in Korea*, 133.
14. See Mitchell, "Russian Mine Warfare," for a summary of the Russian and Soviet use of naval mines.
15. Lott, *Most Dangerous Sea*, 277.
16. U.S. Marine Corps University Archives, Annex C [Intelligence] to ComPhibGru [Commander, Amphibious Group] One Op Order 16-50, 15 October 1950, Korean War Collection, Box 18, Folder 150.
17. Montross and Canzona, *Chosin Reservoir Campaign*, 27–28.
18. Lott, *Most Dangerous Sea*, 276.
19. Ibid., 277.
20. Ibid., 285.
21. Heinl, *Victory at High Tide*, 3.
22. Berman and Baker, *Soviet Strategic Forces*, 40.
23. Allen and Polmar, *Code-Name Downfall*, 272.
24. Admiral Smith's message and Admiral Sherman's response are in Cagle and Manson, *Sea War in Korea*, 142.

CHAPTER 12. Lessons Learned and Unlearned: The Falkland Islands, 1982

1. Woodward, *One Hundred Days*, 62; Brown, *Royal Navy and Falklands War*, 65.
2. Burden et al., *Falklands: Air War*, 39.
3. For Argentine ground order of battle, see van der Bijl and Hannon, *Argentine Forces in Falklands*, 11–13, and Jofre and Aguiar, *Malvinas*, 54, 321–24.
4. Middlebrook, *Fight for the "Malvinas,"* 63.
5. For detailed air order of battle for both sides, see Burden et al., *Falklands: Air War*.
6. Scheina, "Malvinas Campaign," 108–9.
7. Burden et al., *Falklands: Air War*, 21.
8. Woodward, *One Hundred Days*, 280–81.
9. For the Argentine command structure, see Burden et al., *Falklands: Air War*, 15–25, and Moro, *History of South Atlantic Conflict*, 78–79.
10. For the Royal Navy order of battle, see Brown, *Royal Navy and Falklands War*, 358–65.
11. For an account of the modification and employment of these ships, see Villar, *Merchant Ships at War*.

12. For the British order of battle, see Hastings and Jenkins, *Battle for the Falklands*, 357–59.
13. Middlebrook, *Task Force*, 78–79.
14. UK Parliament, *Falklands Campaign: The Lessons*, 6.
15. Woodward, *One Hundred Days*, 122–23.
16. Jofre and Aguilar, *Malvinas*, 52.
17. Woodward, *One Hundred Days*, 92–93.
18. Moro, *History of South Atlantic Conflict*, 211.
19. Jofre and Aguilar, *Malvinas*, 58.
20. Middlebrook, *Fight for the "Malvinas,"* 58–59; van der Bijl and Hannon, *Argentine Forces in Falklands*, 11–12.
21. Landaburu, *La guerra de las Malvinas*, 176.
22. Scheina, "Malvinas Campaign," 114–15.
23. Burden et al., *Falklands: Air War*, 21.
24. For an account of this operation, see Middlebrook, *Task Force*, 114–24.
25. Moro, *History of South Atlantic Conflict*, 102–03, 113.
26. Scheina, "Where Were Argentine Subs?," 117–19.
27. Middlebrook, *Fight for the "Malvinas,"* 143; Moro, *History of South Atlantic Conflict*, 183–84.
28. Moro, *History of South Atlantic Conflict*, 215.
29. Thompson, *No Picnic*, 73–74.
30. UK Parliament, *Falklands Campaign*, 23.
31. Woodward, *One Hundred Days*, 333.
32. Ibid., 132.
33. Middlebrook, *Task Force*, 383.
34. Moro, *History of South Atlantic Conflict*, 227.
35. D'Odorico, "Interview with General Lami Dozo."
36. Woodward, *One Hundred Days*, 99.
37. Lott, *Most Dangerous Sea*, 277.
38. Woodward, *One Hundred Days*, 336.

CHAPTER 13. Anti-Landing Defense and the Implications for Future Amphibious Operations

1. Senger und Etterlin, *Neither Fear nor Hope*, 147–48; ETHINT, Senger und Etterlin, "Liaison Activities," 59.
2. Ruge, *Rommel in Normandy*, 3.
3. See, for example, Hermann Burkhart Mueller-Hillebrand, "Comments on MS#C-095," in ETHINT, Senger und Etterlin, "Liaison Activities."
4. Sekistov, "Operation without Risk."
5. Senger und Etterlin, *Neither Fear nor Hope*, 128.
6. Manchester, *American Caesar*, 576; also, see MacArthur's message to the Joint Chiefs of Staff, quoted in Pirnie, "Inchon Landing."
7. Liman von Sanders, *Five Years in Turkey*, 71; ETHINT, Kesselring, "Con-

cluding Remarks on Mediterranean Campaign," 31–32; Liddell Hart, *Rommel Papers*, 477; U.S. National Archives, U.S. 4th Marine Division, translations of Japanese documents captured on Saipan, Record Group 127, Acc 65A-4556, Box 86, Folder C1-1; Senger und Etterlin, *Neither Fear nor Hope*, 148; Westphal, *German Army in the West*, 151.
8. Liddell Hart, "Value of Amphibious Flexibility and Forces," 492.

Bibliography

In addition to listing the sources cited in this book, the bibliography provides a reasonably comprehensive list of works in English on the subject of defending against amphibious operations. One notable omission is the body of Soviet writings on the subject. Although some of these works have been translated into English, most of them fall outside the scope of this book. Based on my own experience in researching the subject, I have organized the bibliography into three parts: (1) archival collections that contain material not generally found elsewhere; (2) orders, estimates, and other official documents that are more widely held than the material in the archival collections and, in many cases, are available through interlibrary loan; and (3) other books and articles.

Archival Collections

U.S. Marine Corps University Archives. Korean War Collection, Box 18.
U.S. Marine Corps University Archives. Miscellaneous World War II Files.
U.S. National Archives. Record Group 127. U.S. Marine Corps records from World War II.
U.S. Navy Historical Center. Joint Intelligence Center, Pacific Ocean Areas (JICPOA) Files.
United Kingdom Public Records Office (PRO). Miscellaneous documents from the following records: Admiralty (ADM), Cabinet (CAB), and War Office (WO).

Orders, Estimates, and Official Documents

Allied Translator and Interpreter Section (ATIS), Southwest Pacific Area. Available on microfiche, U.S. Army Military History Institute, Carlisle Barracks, Pa.:
    Enemy Publ. No. 224   *Use of Explosives on Beaches and in Raiding Attacks*, n.d.

Enemy Publ. No. 328 — *Lessons from the Saipan Operation,* 12 October 1944

Enemy Publ. No. 384 — *Manual for Defense against Landings (Provisional),* October 1944

Enemy Publ. No. 415 — *Combat Regulations for Island Garrison Forces and Study of Island Defense,* 25 December 1943

Assman, Kurt. "German Plans for the Invasion of England in 1940, Operation 'Sealion.' " London: Naval Intelligence Division (Section 24), Admiralty, 1947.

Bates, Richard W. *The Battle for Leyte Gulf, October 1944. Strategical and Tactical Analysis.* Vol. 1, Preliminary Operations until 0719 October 17th, 1944, Including Battle off Formosa. Newport, R.I.: Naval War College, 1953.

———. *The Battle of Midway Including the Aleutians Phase, June 3 to June 14, 1942: Strategical and Tactical Analysis.* Newport, R.I.: Naval War College, 1948.

———. *The Battle of Savo Island. August 9th, 1942. Strategical and Tactical Analysis.* Newport, R.I.: Naval War College, 1950.

Ellis, Earl. *Advanced Base Operations in Micronesia.* Washington, D.C.: Headquarters Marine Corps, 1921. Operation Plan 713H. Reprint, Washington, D.C.: Headquarters Marine Corps, 1992. Fleet Marine Force Reference Publication 12-46.

European Theater Historical Interrogations (ETHINT):

Kesselring, Albert. "Concluding Remarks on the Mediterranean Campaign," Manuscript No. C-014.

Ruge, Friedrich. "Mines in the Channel." Manuscript No. C-068.

Schmetzer, Rudolf. "Report Regarding the Construction of the Atlantic Wall." Manuscript Nos. B-668 and B-669.

Senger und Etterlin, Fridolin von. "Liaison Activities with the Italian Sixth Army." Manuscript No. C-095.

Ullersperger, Wilhelm. "Nineteenth Army Fortress Engineer (1943–Aug 1944)." Manuscript No. B-449.

Fuehrer Directives and Other Top-Level Directives of the German Armed Forces 1939–1941. Washington, D.C.: 1948.

Fuehrer Directives and Other Top-Level Directives of the German Armed Forces 1942–1945. Washington, D.C.: 1948.

German Seacoast Defenses, European Theater. 7 vols. N.p.: Seacoast Artillery Evaluation Board, European Theater, 1945. Copy in U.S. Army Military History Institute Library.

Japanese Defense against Amphibious Operations. Washington, D.C.: Military Intelligence Division, War Department, 1945.

The Japanese Story of the Battle of Midway. Washington, D.C.: Office of Naval Intelligence, 1947.

Ochsner, Herman. *History of German Chemical Warfare in World War II.* Pt. 1,

The Military Aspect. N.p.: Historical Office of the Chief of the Chemical Corps, n.d.

Tentative Manual for Landing Operations. [Quantico, Va.: U.S. Marine Corps Schools, 1934.]

United Kingdom (UK), Parliament. *The Falklands Campaign: The Lessons*. Cmnd. 8758. 1982.

———. *First Report of the Dardanelles Commission and Supplement*. Cd. 8490, 8502. 1917.

———. *Final Report of the Dardanelles Commission*. Cmd. 371. 1919.

U.S. Army Forces Pacific. *Survey of Japanese Coast Artillery*. U.S. Army Forces Pacific General Order 292 of 27 October 1945.

U.S. Far East Command. *World War II Japanese Monograph Series:*
  No. 17   "Homeland Operations Record"
  No. 44   "History of the Eighth Area Army, Nov. 1943–Aug. 1945"
  No. 48   "Operations in the Central Pacific"
  No. 49   "The Palau Operation"
  No. 51   "Air Operations on Iwo Jima and the Ryukyus"
  No. 52   "History of the 10th Area Army, 1943–1945"
  No. 156 "Historical Review of Landing Operations of the Japanese Forces"
  No. 161 "Inner South Sea Islands Area Naval Operations, Part I, Gilbert Islands"

U.S. Strategic Bombing Survey (USSBS). "Evaluation of Photographic Intelligence in the Japanese Homeland." Pt. 9 "Coast and Antiaircraft Artillery." N.p., 1946.

———. *Interrogations of Japanese Officials*. 2 vols. N.p.: Naval Analysis Division, n.d.

———. *Japanese Military and Naval Intelligence Division*. Washington, D.C.: Government Printing Office, 1946.

———. *Summary Report (Pacific War)*. Washington, D.C.: Government Printing Office, 1946.

U.S. War Department. *TM 30-480 Handbook on Japanese Military Forces*. N.p.: War Department, 1 October 1944. Reprint, Novato, Calif: Presidio Press, 1991.

Other Books and Articles

Alexander, Joseph H. *Across the Reef: The Marine Assault of Tarawa*. Washington, D.C.: History and Museums Division, Headquarters Marine Corps, 1993.

———. *Utmost Savagery: The Three Days of Tarawa*. Annapolis, Md.: Naval Institute Press, 1995.

Allen, Thomas B., and Norman Polmar, *Code-Name Downfall: The Secret Plan to Invade Japan—And Why Truman Dropped the Bomb*. New York: Simon & Schuster, 1995.

Appleman, Roy E., James M. Burns, Russell A. Gugeler, and John Stevens. *Okinawa: The Last Battle. United States Army in War II Series. Washington, D.C.: Historical Division, Department of the Army, 1948.

Aspinall-Oglander, C. F. *Military Operations, Gallipoli.* 4 vols. History of the Great War Series. London: William Heinemann, Ltd., 1929.

Badoglio, Pietro. *Italy in the Second World War.* London: Oxford University Press, 1948.

Banks, Donald. *Flame over Britain: A Personal Narrative of Petroleum Warfare.* London: Sampson Low, Marston & Co., n.d.

Bauer, K. J., and Alvin D. Coox. "Olympic vs. Ketsu-Go." *Marine Corps Gazette* 49 (August 1965): 32–44.

Baxter, William P. "Soviet Defense against Amphibious A Assault." *Marine Corps Gazette* 67 (February 1983): 24–26.

Bennett, Ralph. *Ultra and Mediterranean Strategy.* New York: William Morrow, 1989.

Berman, Robert P., and John C. Baker. *Soviet Strategic Forces: Requirements and Responses.* Washington, D.C.: The Brookings Institution, 1982.

Blumenson Martin. *The Patton Papers 1940–1945.* Boston: Houghton Mifflin Co., 1974.

———. *Salerno to Cassino.* United States Army in World War II Series. Washington, D.C: Office of the Chief of Military History, U.S. Army, 1969.

Blumentritt, Guenther. *Von Rundstedt: The Soldier and the Man.* London: Odhams Press, 1952.

Bogart, Charles H. "German Remotely Piloted Bombs." U.S. Naval Institute *Proceedings* 102 (November 1976): 62–68.

Boyd, Carl. *Hitler's Japanese Confidant: General Oshima Hiroshi and Magic Intelligence 1941–1945.* Lawrence: University Press of Kansas, 1993.

Bradley, Omar N. *A Soldier's Story.* New York: Henry Holt & Co., 1951.

Brown, David. *The Royal Navy and the Falklands War.* London: Leo Cooper, 1987.

Bryant, Arthur. *The Turn of the Tide: A History of the War Years Based on the Diaries of Field-Marshal Lord Alanbrooke, Chief of the Imperial General Staff.* Garden City, N.Y.: Doubleday & Co., 1957.

Burden, Rodney A., Michael I. Draper, Douglas A. Rough, Colin R. Smith, and David L. Wilton. *Falklands: The Air War.* London: Arms and Armour Press, 1986.

Cagle, Malcolm W., and Frank A. Manson. *The Sea War in Korea.* Annapolis, Md.: U.S. Naval Institute, 1957.

Callwell, C. E. "The Art of Repelling Landings." *Journal of the United States Artillery* 43 (March–April 1915):226–37.

Campbell, John P. *Dieppe Revisited: A Documentary Investigation.* London: Frank Cass, 1993.

Cannon, M. Hamlin. *Leyte: The Return to the Philippines.* United States Army in World War II Series. Washington, D.C.: Office of the Chief of Military History, Department of the Army, 1954.

Carell, Paul. *Invasion—They're Coming!* Translated by E. Osers. New York: Bantam Books, 1964.
Carpenter, Dorr, and Norman Polmar. *Submarines of the Imperial Japanese Navy.* London: Conway Maritime Press, 1986.
Chalmers, W. S. *Full Cycle: The Biography of Admiral Sir Bertram Home Ramsay.* London: Hodder & Stoughton, 1959.
Chandler, David G., and James Lawton Collins, eds. *The D-Day Encyclopedia.* New York: Simon & Schuster, 1994.
Chazette, Alain. *1940–1944 Les batteries allemandes de Dunkerque au Crotoy.* Tours: Editions Heimdal, 1990.
Churchill, Winston S. *Their Finest Hour.* Boston: Houghton Mifflin Co., 1949.
Clark, Mark W. *Calculated Risk.* New York: Harper & Brothers, 1950.
Clausewitz, Karl von. *On War.* Edited and translated by Michael Howard and Peter Paret. Princeton, N.J.: Princeton University Press, 1976.
Clifford, Kenneth J. *Progress and Purpose: A Developmental History of the United States Marine Corps 1900–1970.* Washington, D.C.: History and Museums Division, Headquarters Marine Corps, 1973.
Collier, Basil. *The Defence of the United Kingdom.* London: Her Majesty's Stationery Office, 1957.
Corbett, Julian S. *Some Principles of Maritime Strategy.* London: Longmans, Green & Co., 1918.
Craven, Wesley Frank, and James Lea Cate, eds. *The Army Air Forces in World War II.* 7 vols. Chicago: University of Chicago Press, 1948–1958.
Cressman, Robert J. *"A Magnificent Fight": The Battle for Wake Island.* Annapolis, Md.: Naval Institute Press, 1995.
Cressman, Robert J., Steve Ewing, Barrett Tillman, Mark Horan, Clark Reynolds, and Stan Cohen. *"A Glorious Page in Our History": The Battle of Midway 4–6 June 1942.* Missoula, Mont.: Pictorial Histories Publishing Co., 1990.
Crowl, Philip A. *Campaign in the Marianas.* United States Army in World War II Series. Washington, D.C.: Office of the Chief of Military History, Department of the Army, 1960.
Crowl, Philip A., and Edmund G. Love. *Seizure of the Gilberts and Marshalls.* United States Army in World War II Series. Washington, D.C.: Office of the Chief of Military History, Department of the Army, 1955.
Cunningham, W. Scott. *Wake Island Command.* New York: Popular Library, 1962.
Denfield, D. Colt. *Japanese Fortifications and Other Military Structures in the Central Pacific.* Saipan: Micronesian Archaeological Survey, 1981.
D'Este, Carlo. *Bitter Victory: The Battle for Sicily, 1943.* New York: E. P. Dutton, 1988.
———. *Fatal Decision: Anzio and the Battle for Rome.* New York: HarperCollins, 1991.

Devereaux, James P. S. *The Story of Wake Island.* New York: J. B. Lippincott Co., 1947.

D'Odorico, J. C. "An Exclusive AFJI Interview with General Lami Dozo." *Armed Forces Journal International* (September 1992): 48.

Drea, Edward J. *MacArthur's Ultra: Codebreaking and the War against Japan, 1942–1945.* Lawrence: University Press of Kansas, 1992.

Dull, Paul S. *A Battle History of the Imperial Japanese Navy (1941–1942).* Annapolis, Md.: Naval Institute Press, 1978.

Dupuy, R. Ernest, and Trevor N. Dupuy. *The Encyclopedia of Military History from 3500 B.C. to the Present.* Rev. ed. New York: Harper & Row, 1977.

Dyer, George C. *The Amphibians Came to Conquer: The Story of Admiral Richmond Kelly Turner.* 2 vols. [Washington, D.C.: Government Printing Office, 1972].

Eisenhower, Dwight David. *At Ease: Stories I Tell to Friends.* Garden City, N.Y.: Doubleday & Co., 1967.

Elliott, Peter. *Allied Minesweeping in World War 2.* Annapolis, Md.: Naval Institute Press, 1979.

Faldella, Emilio. *Lo sbarco e la defesa della Sicilia.* Rome: l'Aniene, 1956.

Field, James A., Jr. *History of United States Naval Operations: Korea.* Washington, D.C.: Government Printing Office, 1962.

———. *The Japanese at Leyte Gulf: The Shō Operation.* Princeton, N.J.: Princeton University Press, 1947.

Fleming, Peter. *Operation Sealion: The Projected Invasion of England in 1940.* New York: Simon & Schuster, 1957.

Fletcher, David. *Vanguard of Victory: The 79th Armoured Division:* London: Her Majesty's Stationery Office, 1984.

Frank, Richard B. *Guadalcanal.* New York: Random House, 1990.

Freiden, Seymour, and William Richardson, eds. *The Fatal Decisions.* New York: Berkley Medallion Books, 1958.

Fuchida, Mitsuo, and Masatake Okumiya. *Midway: The Battle That Doomed Japan.* Edited by Clarke H. Kawakami and Roger Pineau. New York: Ballantine Books, 1989.

Fuehrer Conferences on Naval Affairs 1939–1945. Annapolis, Md.: Naval Institute Press, 1990.

Fuller, J. F. C. *The Second World War 1939–45: A Strategical and Tactical History.* New York: Duell, Sloan & Pearce, 1949.

Fuller, Richard. *Shōkaen: Hirohito's Samurai, Leaders of the Japanese Armed Forces, 1926–1945.* London: Arms and Armour Press, 1992.

Furse, George Armand. *Military Expeditions beyond the Seas.* 2 vols. London: William Clowes & Sons, 1897.

Futter, Geoffrey W. *The Funnies: The 79th Armoured Division and Its Specialised Equipment.* Hemel Hempstead, Hertfordshire, UK: Bellona Books, 1974.

Gailey, Harry A. *Peleliu 1944.* Annapolis, Md.: Nautical & Aviation Publishing Co. of America, 1983.

Gallicchio, Marc. "After Nagasaki: General Marshall's Plan for Tactical Nuclear Weapons in Japan." *Prologue* 23 (Winter 1991): 396–403.

Garand, George W., and Truman R. Strobridge. *Western Pacific Operations.* Vol. 5, *History of U.S. Marine Corps Operations in World War II.* Washington, D.C.: Historical Division, Headquarters Marine Corps, 1971.

Garland, Albert N., and Howard McGaw Smyth. *Sicily and the Surrender of Italy.* United States Army in World War II Series. Washington, D.C.: Office of the Chief of Military History, Department of the Army, 1965.

"A German Staff Officer on the Dardanelles Expedition." *Journal of the Royal United Service Institution* 62 (May 1917): 342–48.

Geyr von Schweppenburg, Leo. "Reflections on the Invasion." Parts 1 and 2. *Military Review* 41 (February 1961): 2–11; (March 1961): 12–21.

Gilbert, Felix, ed. and trans. *Hitler Directs His War.* New York: Award Books, 1950.

Gorlitz, Walter, ed. *The Memoirs of Field-Marshal Keitel.* Translated by David Irving. New York: Stein & Day, 1966.

Gorshkov, Sergei G. *The Sea Power of the State.* Oxford: Pergamon Press, 1979.

Grinnell-Milne, Duncan William. *The Silent Victory: September 1940.* London: Transworld, 1958.

Groos, Otto. *Lessons of Naval Warfare in the Light of the World War: A Book for the Sailor, the Soldier and the Statesman.* Berlin: E. S. Mittler & Son, 1929. Typescript translation by Roland E. Krause. Newport, R.I.: Naval War College, 1936.

Halder, Franz. *The Halder Diaries: The Private War Journals of Colonel General Franz Halder.* Boulder, Colo.: Westview Press, 1976.

Hamilton, Ian. *Gallipoli Diary.* 2 vols. New York: George H. Doran Co., 1920.

Hara, Tameichi. *Japanese Destroyer Captain.* New York: Ballantine Books, 1961.

Harris, Robert, and Jeremy Paxman. *A Higher Form of Killing: The Secret Story of Chemical and Biological Warfare.* New York: Hill & Wang, 1982.

Harrison, Gordon. *Cross-Channel Attack.* United States Army in World War II Series. Washington D.C.: Office of the Chief of Military History, Department of the Army, 1951.

Hastings, Max. *The Korean War.* New York: Simon & Schuster, 1987.

Hastings, Max, and Simon Jenkins. *The Battle for the Falklands.* New York: W. W. Norton & Co.: 1983.

Hayashi, Saburo, and Alvin D. Coox. *Kogun: The Japanese Army in the Pacific War.* Quantico, Va.: Marine Corps Association, 1959.

Heinl, Robert Debs, Jr. *The Defense of Wake.* Washington, D.C: Historical Section, Headquarters Marine Corps, 1947.

———. *Marines at Midway.* Washington, D.C.: Historical Section, Headquarters Marine Corps, 1948.

———. *Victory at High Tide: The Inchon-Seoul Campaign.* Annapolis, Md.: The Nautical & Aviation Publishing Co. of America, 1979.

Hinsley, F. H. *British Intelligence in the Second World War.* Vol. 3, pts. 1 and 2. London: Her Majesty's Stationery Office, 1984.

Hirama, Yoichi. "Japanese Naval Preparations for World War II." *Naval War College Review* 44 (Spring 1991): 63–81.

Hoffman, Carl W. *Saipan: The Beginning of the End.* Washington, D.C.: Historical Branch, Headquarters Marine Corps, 1950.

Holmes, W. J. *Double-Edged Secrets: U.S. Naval Intelligence Operations in the Pacific during World War II.* Annapolis, Md.: Naval Institute Press, 1979.

Hoover, Karl D. "Commander Otto Hersing and the Dardanelles Cruise of S.M. U-21." *American Neptune* 36 (January 1976): 33–44.

Horie, Yoshitaka. "Defense Plan for Chichi Jima." *Marine Corpos Gazette* 37 (July 1953): 36–40.

———. "Japanese Defense of Iwo Jima." *Marine Corps Gazette* 36 (February 1952): 18–27.

Hough, Frank O. *The Assault on Peleliu.* Washington, D.C.: Historical Division, Headquarters Marine Corps, 1950.

Hough, Frank O., Verle E. Ludwig, and Henry I. Shaw. *Pearl Harbor to Guadalcanal.* Vol. 1, History of U.S. Marine Corps Operations in World War II Series. Washington, D.C.: Historical Branch, Headquarters Marine Corps, n.d.

"How the Guam Operation Was Conducted." Japanese Ground Self Defense Force (JGSDF) Paper. Translated copy in U. S. Marine Corps University Library.

Howard, Michael. *British Intelligence in the Second World War.* Vol. 5. New York: Cambridge University Press, 1990.

Hoyt, Edwin P. *The Invasion before Normandy: The Secret Battle of Slapton Sands.* New York: Stein and Day, 1985.

———. *Japan's War: The Great Pacific Conflict 1853 to 1952.* New York: Da Capo Press, 1986.

Huber, Thomas M. *Japan's Battle of Okinawa, April–June 1945.* No. 18 of Leavenworth Papers series. Leavenworth, Kans.: U.S. Army Command and General Staff College (USACGSC), 1990.

———. *Pastel: Deception in the Invasion of Japan.* Leavenworth, Kans.: USACGSC, 1988.

Inoguchi, Rikihei, and Tadashi Nakajima with Roger Pineau. *The Divine Wind: Japan's Kamikaze Force in World War II.* Annapolis, Md.: U. S. Naval Institute, 1958.

Irving, David. *The Trail of the Fox.* New York: E. P. Dutton, 1977.

Ismay, Hastings. *The Memoirs of General Lord Ismay.* New York: Viking Press, 1960.

Jacobsen, H. A., and J. Rohwer, eds. *Decisive Battles of World War II: The German View.* Translated by Edward Fitzgerald. New York: G. P. Putnam's Sons, 1965.

James, Robert Rhodes, ed. *Winston Churchill, His Complete Speeches.* 6 vols. New York: Chelsea House, 1974.

Jofre, Oscar Luis, and Félix Roberto Aguiar. *Malvinas: La defensa de Puerto Argentino.* Buenos Aires: Editorial Sudamericana, 1987.
Jomini, Antoine Henri. *The Art of War.* [1862?]. Translated by G. H. Mendell and W. P. Craighill. Reprint, Westport, Conn.: Greenwood Press, [1971?].
Kahn, David. *Hitler's Spies: German Military Intelligence in World War II.* New York: Macmillan, 1978.
Kannengiesser, Hans. *The Campaign in Gallipoli.* London: Hutchinson & Co., 1928.
Kesselring, Albert. *Kesselring: A Soldier's Record.* New York: William Morrow, 1954.
Keyes, Roger J. B. *Amphibious Warfare and Combined Operations.* New York: Macmillan, 1943.
Koyanagi, Tomiji. "With Kurita in the Battle for Leyte Gulf." Translated by Toshikazu Ohmae; edited by Roger Pineau. U.S. Naval Institute *Proceedings* 79 (February 1953): 119–33.
Kuzuhara, Kazumi. "Operations on Iwo Jima: Utility of Combat Lessons Learned." Paper presented to USA–Japanese GSDF [Ground Self Defense Force] Military History Exchange, U.S. Army Command and General Staff College, Fort Leavenworth, Kans., 1990.
Landaburu, Carlos Augusto. *La guerra de las Malvinas.* Buenos Aires: Circulo Militar, 1989.
Larcher, M. *The Turkish War in the World War.* N.p, n.d. Typescript translation by L. L. Pendleton. Washington, D.C.: Army War College, 1931.
Liddell Hart, B. H. *The Defence of Britain.* London: Faber & Faber Ltd., 1939.
———. *The German Generals Talk.* New York: William Morrow & Co., 1948.
———. "The Value of Amphibious Flexibility and Forces." *Journal of the Royal United Service Institution* 105 (November 1960): 483–92.
———, ed. *The Rommel Papers.* Translated by Paul Finlay. New York: Harcourt Brace & Co., 1953.
Liman von Sanders, Otto. *Five Years in Turkey.* Annapolis, Md.: U.S. Naval Institute, 1927.
Lofgren, Stephen J., ed. "Diary of First Lieutenant Sugihara Kinryu: Iwo Jima, January–February 1945." *Journal of Military History* 59 (January 1995): 97–133.
Lorey, Herman. *The War at Sea 1914–1918: The War in Turkish Waters.* N.p.: German Naval Archives, n.d. Typescript translation by H. S. Babbitt. N.p., n.d., Naval War College Library, Newport, R.I.
Lott, Arnold S. *Most Dangerous Sea: A History of Mine Warfare and an Account of U.S. Mine Warfare Operations in World War II and Korea.* Annapolis, Md.: U.S. Naval Institute, 1959.
Love, Edmund G. *The 27th Infantry Division in World War II.* Washington, D.C.: Infantry Journal Press, 1949.
Mackenzie, Compton. *Gallipoli Memories.* Garden City, N.Y.: Doubleday Doran & Co., 1930.

Macleod, Roderick, and Dennis Kelly, eds. *Time Unguarded: The Ironside Diaries 1937–1940.* New York: David McKay, 1962.

Manchester, William. *American Caesar: Douglas MacArthur 1880–1964.* Boston: Little, Brown & Co., 1978.

Marder, Arthur J. *The Anatomy of British Seapower: A History of British Naval Policy in the Pre-Dreadnought Era.* Hamden, Conn.: Archon Books, 1964.

Marietti, Giovanni. "Landing Operations and the Value of Mobile Defense." *Journal of the Military Service Institution of the United States* 60 (January–February 1917): 50–62.

Martienssen, Anthony. *Hitler and His Admirals.* New York: E. P. Dutton & Co., 1949.

Matsumoto, Keisuke. "Preparations for Decisive Battle in Southern Kyushu in Great East Asia War." Translated by Tokui Yanase. Paper presented to USA–Japanese GSDF [Ground Self Defense Force] Military History Exchange, Carlisle Barracks, Pa., 1987.

Maugeri, Franco. *From the Ashes of Disgrace.* Edited by Victor Rosen. New York: Reynal & Hitchcock, [1948].

Mavrogordato, Ralph S. "Hitler's Decision on the Defense of Italy." In *Command Decisions,* edited by Kent Roberts Greenfield. Washington, D.C.: Office of the Chief of Military History, U.S. Army, 1960.

McFarland, Stephen L. "Preparing for What Never Came: Chemical and Biological Warfare in World War II." *Defense Analysis* 2 (1986): 107–21.

McPoil, William D. "The Development and Defense of Wake Island, 1934–1941." *Prologue* 23 (Winter 1991): 361–66.

Middlebrook, Martin. *The Fight for the "Malvinas": The Argentine Forces in the Falklands War.* London: Viking, 1989.

———. *Task Force: The Falklands War, 1982.* London: Penguin Books, 1987.

Miles, Sherman. "Notes on the Dardanelles Campaign of 1915." *Coast Artillery Journal* (December 1924): 1–83.

Miller, Edward S. *War Plan Orange: The U.S. Strategy to Defeat Japan, 1897–1945.* Annapolis, Md.: Naval Institute Press, 1991.

Miller, John, Jr. *Cartwheel: The Reduction of Rabaul.* U. S. Army in World War II Series. Washington, D.C.: Office of the Chief of Military History, Department of the Army, 1959.

———. *Guadalcanal: The First Offensive.* United States Army in World War II Series. Washington, D.C.: Historical Division, Department of the Army, 1949.

Milner, Samuel. "The Battle of Milne Bay." *Military Review* 30 (April 1950): 18–29.

Mitcham, Samuel W., Jr., and Friedrich von Stauffenberg. *The Battle of Sicily.* New York: Orion Books, 1991.

Mitchell, Donald W. "Russian Mine Warfare: The Historical Record." *Journal of the Royal United Service Institution* 109 (February 1964): 32–39.

Mitsuru, Yoshida. *Requiem for Battleship Yamato*. Translated by Richard H. Minear. Seattle: University of Washington Press, 1985.

Molony, C. J. C. *The Mediterranean and the Middle East*. Vol 5, *The Campaign in Sicily 1943 and the Campaign in Italy 3rd September 1943 to 31st March 1944*. London: Her Majesty's Stationery Office, 1973.

Montagu, Ewen. *The Man Who Never Was*. Philadelphia: J. B. Lippincott Co., 1954.

Montross, Lynn, and Nicholas A. Canzona. *The Chosin Reservoir Campaign*. Vol. 3 of *U.S. Marine Operations in Korea*. Washington, D.C.: Historical Branch, Headquarters Marine Corps, 1957.

———. *The Inchon-Seoul Operation*. Vol. 2 of *U.S. Marine Operations in Korea*. Washington, D.C.: Historical Branch, Headquarters Marine Crops, 1955.

Morison, Samuel Eliot. *Aleutians, Gilberts and Marshalls June 1942–April 1944*. Vol. 7 of *History of United States Naval Operations in World War II*. Boston: Little, Brown & Co., 1975.

———. *Coral Sea, Midway and Submarine Actions May 1942–August 1942*. Vol. 4 of *History of United States Naval Operations in World War II*. Boston: Little, Brown & Co., 1959.

———. *The Invasion of France and Germany 1944–1945*. Vol. 11 of *History of United States Naval Operations in World War II*. Boston: Little, Brown & Co. 1968.

———. *New Guinea and the Marianas March 1944–August 1944*. Vol. 8 of *History of United States Naval Operations in World War II*. Boston: Little, Brown & Co., 1968.

———. *Sicily-Salerno-Anzio January 1943–June 1944*. Vol. 9 of *History of United States Naval Operations in World War II*. Boston: Little, Brown & Co., 1975.

Moro, Rubén O. *The History of the South Atlantic Conflict: The War for the Malvinas*. New York: Praeger, 1989.

Morris, Eric. *Salerno: A Military Fiasco*. New York: Stein & Day, 1983.

Naito, Hatsuho. *Thunder Gods: The Kamikaze Pilots Tell Their Story*. Tokyo: Kodansha International, 1989.

Newcomb, Richard F. *Iwo Jima*. New York: Signet Books, 1966.

Nichols, Charles J., Jr., and Henry I. Shaw. *Okinawa: Victory in the Pacific*. Washington, D.C.: Historical Branch, Headquarters Marine Corps, 1955.

Nowarra, Heinz J. *German Guided Missiles*. Atglen, Pa.: Schiffer Military/Aviation History, 1993.

Ohmae, Toshikazu. "The Battle of Savo Island." Edited by Roger Pineau. U.S. Naval Institute *Proceedings* (December 1957): 1263–78.

O'Neill, Richard. *Suicide Squads of World War II*. New York: Military Heritage Press, 1981.

Orita, Zenji, and Joseph D. Harrington. *I-Boat Captain*. Canoga Park, Calif.: Major Books, 1976.

Ose, Dieter. "Rommel and Rundstedt: The 1944 Panzer Controversy." *Military Affairs* 50 (January 1985): 7–11.

Pirnie, "The Inchon Landing: How Great Was the Risk?" *Joint Perspectives* 3 (summer 1982): 86–97.

Plehwe, Friedrich-Karl von, "Operation Sealion 1940." *RUSI: Journal of the Royal United Services Institute for Defence Studies* 118 (March 1973): 47–53.

Potter, E. B. *Nimitz.* Annapolis, Md.: Naval Institute Press, 1976.

———, ed. *Sea Power: A Naval History.* 2d ed. Annapolis, Md.: Naval Institute Press, 1981.

Reports of General MacArthur. Vol. 2, pt. 1. *Japanese Operations in the Southwest Pacific Area.* Washington, D.C.: Government Printing Office, 1966.

Richmond, Herbert W. *The Invasion of Britain: An Account of Plans, Attempts and Countermeasures from 1586 to 1918.* London: Methuen & Co., 1941.

Riegelman, Harold. *The Caves of Biak: An American Officer's Experience in the Southwest Pacific.* New York: Dial Press, 1955.

Rolf, Rudi. *Atlantic Wall Typology.* Beetsterzwag, The Netherlands: AMA, 1988.

———. *Der Atlantikwall: Perlenschnur aus Stahlbeton.* Beetsterzwag, The Netherlands: AMA, 1983.

Roskill, *The War at Sea.* Vol. 1, *The Defensive.* London: Her Majesty's Stationery Office, 1954.

Ruge, Friedrich. "The Invasion of Normandy." In *Decisive Battles of World War II: The German View,* edited by H. A. Jacobsen and J. Rohwer; translated by Edward Fitzgerald. New York: G. P. Putnam's Sons, 1965, 317–49.

———. *Rommel in Normandy.* Translated by Ursula R. Moessner. San Rafael, Calif.: Presidio Press, 1979.

———. "With Rommel before Normandy." *U.S. Naval Institute Proceedings* 80 (June 1954): 612–19.

Ryan, Cornelius. *The Longest Day, June 6, 1944.* New York: Simon & Schuster, 1959.

Savada, Andrea Matles, ed. *North Korea: A Country Study.* Washington, D.C.: Library of Congress, 1994.

Scheina, Robert L. "The Malvinas Campaign." *U.S. Naval Institute Proceedings Review* 1983: 98–117.

———. "Where Were Those Argentine Subs?" *U.S. Naval Institute Proceedings,* 110 (March 1984): 115–20.

Schenk, Peter. *Invasion of England 1940: The Planning of Operation Sealion.* London: Conway Maritime Press, 1990.

Schultz, Duane. *Wake Island: The Heroic, Gallant Fight.* New York: St. Martin's Press, 1978.

Sekistov, V. "Operation without a Risk." *Soviet Military Review* (December 1968): 45–47.

Senger und Etterlin, Fridolin von. *Neither Fear nor Hope.* Novato, Calif.: Presidio Press, 1989.

Shaw, Henry I., Jr., Bernard C. Nalty, and Edwin T. Turnbladh. *Central Pacific Drive.* Vol. 3, History of the U.S. Marine Corps Operations in World War II

Series. Washington, D.C.: Historical Branch, Headquarters Marine Corps, 1966.

Shulman, Milton. *Defeat in the West*. New York: E. P. Dutton & Co., 1948.

Simpson, Keith. "A Close Run Thing? D-Day, 6 June 1944: The German Perspective." *RUSI: Journal of the Royal United Services Institute for Defence Studies* 139 (June 1994): 60–71.

Skates, John Ray. *The Invasion of Japan: Alternative to the Bomb*. Columbia: University of South Carolina Press, 1994.

Skinner, Ian. "The Naval Threat on the Western Flank of Operation Neptune, June 1944." *Mariner's Mirror* 80 (May 1994): 178–90.

Smith, Julian C. "Tarawa." U.S. Naval Institute *Proceedings* 79 (November 1953): 1163–75.

Smith, Robert Ross. *The Approach to the Philippines*. United States Army in World War II Series. Washington, D.C.: Office of the Chief of Military History, Department of the Army, 1953.

Speidel, Hans. *Invasion 1944*. Translated by Theo R. Crevenna. New York: Paperback Library, 1968.

Spencer, John H. *The Battle of Britain Revisited*. Maxwell Air Force Base, Ala.: Air University, 1989.

Spurr, Russell. *A Glorious Way to Die: The Kamikaze Mission of the Battleship Yamato, April 1945*. New York: Newmarket Press, 1981.

Stacey, C. P. *The Canadian Army 1939–1945*. Ottawa: King's Printer, 1948.

Stockman, James R. *The Battle for Tarawa*. Washington, D.C.: Historical Section, Headquarters Marine Corps, 1947.

Summers, Harry G., Jr. *Korean War Almanac*. New York: Facts on File, 1990.

Tanaka, Raizo, with Roger Pineau. "Japan's Losing Struggle for Guadalcanal." U.S. Naval Institute *Proceedings* 82 (July 1956): 687–99; (August 1956): 815–31.

Thompson, Julian. *No Picnic: 3 Commando Brigade in the South Atlantic: 1982*. New York: Hippocrene Books, 1985.

Trevor-Roper, H. R., ed. *Blitzkrieg to Defeat: Hitler's War Directives 1939–1945*. New York: Rinehart & Winston, 1965.

———. "Why Hitler Did Not Invade England." *New York Times Magazine*, 6 June 1965, 22–23.

Trumpener, Ulrich. *Germany and the Ottoman Empire 1914–1918*. Princeton, N.J.: Princeton University Press, 1968.

———. "Liman von Sanders and the German-Ottoman Alliance." *Journal of Contemporary History* 1 (October 1966): 179–92.

"The Turkish General Staff History of the Campaign in Gallipoli." Pts. 1 and 2. *Army Quarterly* 11 (January 1926): 343–53; 12 (April 1926): 88–95.

Ugaki, Matome. *Fading Victory: The Diary of Admiral Matome Ugaki*. Edited by Donald M. Goldstein and Katherine V. Dillon; translated by Masataka Chihaya. Pittsburgh, Pa.: University of Pittsburgh Press, 1991.

Umezawa, Haruo, and Louis Metzger. "The Defense of Guam." *Marine Corps Gazette* 48 (August 1964): 36–43.

Updegraph, Charles L., Jr. *U.S. Marine Corps Special Units of World War II*. Washington, D.C.: Historical Division, Headquarters Marine Corps, 1972.

van Courtland Moon, John Ellis. "Project Sphinx: The Question of the Use of Gas in the Planned Invasion of Japan." *Journal of Strategic Studies* 12 (September 1989): 303–23.

van der Bijl, Nicholas, and Paul Hannon. *Argentine Forces in the Falklands*. Vol. 250 of Men-at-Arms Series. London: Osprey Publishing, 1992.

Vego, Milan. *Soviet Naval Tactics*. Annapolis, Md.: Naval Institute Press, 1992.

Villar, Roger. *Merchant Ships at War: The Falklands Experience*. Annapolis, Md.: Naval Institute Press, 1984.

Warlimont, Walter. *Inside Hitler's Headquarters 1939–45*. Translated by R. H. Barry. New York: Frederick A. Praeger, 1964.

Warner, Denis, and Peggy Warner. *The Scared Warriors: Japan's Suicide Legions*. New York: Van Nostrand Reinhold Co., 1982.

Weigley, Russell. *Eisenhower's Lieutenants: The Campaign of France and Germany*. Bloomington: Indiana University Press, 1981.

Westphal, Siegfried. *The German Army in the West*. London: Cassell, 1951.

Wheatley, Ronald. *Operation Sea Lion: German Plans for the Invasion of England 1939–1942*. Oxford: Clarendon Press, 1958.

Wilds, Thomas. "How Japan Fortified the Mandated Islands." U.S. Naval Institute *Proceedings* 81 (April 1955): 401–07.

Wills, Henry. *Pillboxes: A Study of UK Defences 1940*. N.p.: Leo Cooper, 1985.

Wilt, Alan F. *The Atlantic Wall: Hitler's Defenses in the West, 1941–1944*. Ames: Iowa State University Press, 1975.

Woodward, John F. *One Hundred Days: The Memoirs of the Falklands Battle Group Commander*. Annapolis, Md.: Naval Institute Press, 1992.

Yahara, Hiromichi. *The Battle for Okinawa*. Translated by Roger Pineau and Masatoshi Uehara. New York: John Wiley & Sons, 1995.

Yokoi, Toshiyuki. "Kamikazes in the Okinawa Campaign." In *The Japanese Navy in World War II: In the Words of Former Japanese Naval Officers*. Translated and edited by David C. Evans. Annapolis, Md.: Naval Institute Press, 1986.

Index

Abercrombie, HMS, 53
"absolute national defense sphere," Japanese, 134, 136, 158
active defense, 82
A-day (Philippines), 111
Admiralty Islands, 103
A-GO, Operation, 106, 136–37, 138; implemented at Battle of Philippine Sea, 140–41
Agrigento, 46
Aichi Baba, 13, 14
airborne operations: in Norway, 26; planned for Sea Lion, 27, 28, 31; at Sicily, 45, 47; at Salerno, 55; at Normandy, 70; not planned for invasion of Japan, 167–68. *See also* anti-airborne defenses
air superiority, 7, 133, 190, 207–8; for defense of Britain, 34; Allied not absolute in Italy, 56–57; Allied at Normandy, 74; Japanese at Wake Island, 85; related to defense of Wake and Midway Islands, 92; in SWPA, 102
air support: at Gallipoli, 20–21; Allied reliance on land-based support at Salerno, 51; at Normandy, 62, 70; Allied reliance on land-based support in SWPA, 102; Japanese reliance on land-based support in Philippines, 110
Alacrity, HMS, 196
Aleutian Islands, 88
Algiers, 40
Almond, Maj. Gen. Edward M., 176
Ambuscade, HMS, 199
amphibious demonstrations: at Gallipoli, 15–16; at Saipan, 138–40; at Tinian, 143; at Okinawa, 160. *See also* deception
amphibious doctrine, 79, 117, 208
amphibious operations: as most difficult of military operations, 1; small number repulsed, 1–2; naval character of, 132, 204–5
amphibious raids: Norway, 59–60; Dieppe, 60, 71; Makin Atoll, 118; Kunsan, 177
amphibious withdrawals: British at Gallipoli, 18–19; considered by Gen. Clark at Salerno, 53; Japanese at Guadalcanal, 101; U.S. at Hungnam, 183

249

amtracs. *See* LVT (landing vehicle, tracked)
Angaur, 148
anti-airborne defenses, 66, 169
anti-landing defense: three basic types of described, 2; complementary actions to, 6; German debate at Normandy, 65–66. *See also* defense at the water's edge; mobile defense; naval defense
anti-landing doctrine, 208; British lacking in 1940, 31; Germans lacking in Italy, 57; Germans lacking at Normandy, 65; U.S. Marine Corps, 79, 82–83, 87; impact of on defense of Wake and Midway Islands, 92; Japanese, 109, 135, 137, 143, 151, 168–69; lessons of Saipan and Peleliu incorporated into Japanese, 148; at Okinawa, 158
ANZAC. *See* Australia New-Zealand Army Corps
Anzac Cove, 14, 23
Anzio, 55–56, 64
Ardent, HMS, 198
Argentine Marine Corps, 187–88, 192
Argonaut, HMS, 196
Ariake Bay, 165, 167
Ari Burnu, 15, 16, 18
Arima, Rear Adm. Masabumi, 113
Ark Royal, HMS, 21
artillery, 140, 147, 155, 180
Ascension Island, 191, 194
Asiga Bay, 143
Assmann, Vice Adm. Kurt, 37–38
Ataturk, Kemal. *See* Kemal, Col. Mustafa
Atlantic Conveyor, 198–99
Atlantic Wall, 59–60; Gen. Ōshima's report on, 63
atomic bombs. *See* nuclear weapons

Attu, 154
Australia, 94
Australia, HMAS, 114
Australia-New Zealand Army Corps, 12, 15–16, 18
Autumn Voyage, Operation, 28

Babelthuap, 144
Badoglio, Marshal Pietro, 40
baka bombs, 163. *See also* suicide tactics, aviation
balanced defense, 6, 203–4
Balsa Air Force, 89
banzai attacks. *See* suicide tactics, ground
Base Defense Manual, 79
beaches, landing: at Gallipoli, 14; in Britain, 30; at Sicily, 44; at Guadalcanal, 97; at Tinian, 143; at Okinawa, 157; in Falkland Islands, 192; lacking at Inchon, 175–77
Bénouville, 72
Besika Bay, 15, 23
Betio, 120, 122. *See also* Tarawa
Biak, 103–6, 113, 138
Bismarck, 27
Bismarck Archipelago, 103
Blaskowitz, Col. Gen. Johannes, 62–63, 66
Blitz-Sperren (lightning minefields), 68–69
blockade, 7
"Blood-and-Iron-for-the-Emperor" units, 155
Blumentritt, Lt. Gen. Guenther, 63
Boise, USS, 47
Bonin Islands, 134
Bougainville, 102, 106, 120, 125, 166
Bouvet, 11
Bradley, Gen. Omar: on 1st Infantry Division at Normandy, 71; on

importance of naval gunfire at Sicily, 47; on threat of chemical warfare at Normandy, 77; on impact of nuclear weapons on amphibious warfare, 183–84
Breckinridge, Brig. Gen. James C., 79
Brilliant, HMS, 193, 199
Britain, battle of, 34
British Army units
—Constantinople Expeditionary Force, 12
—Home Forces, 28
—Eighth Army, 40, 42, 55
—2nd Battalion, Parachute Regiment, 191, 199
—3rd Battalion, Parachute Regiment, 191, 199
—1st Battalion, Welsh Guards, 200
—5 Infantry Brigade, 191, 198, 199
—IX Corps, 18
—X Corps, 53
—1st Airborne Division, 45
—29th Division, 12
—22nd Special Air Service Regiment (SAS), 191
Brooke, Gen. Alan, 29, 30, 33–34, 37
Buckner, Lt. Gen. Simon Bolivar, 160, 163
Bulair, 14, 15, 18
Butaritari, 118, 129

Cabo San Antonio, 187
Caen, 71–72
Canberra, 190, 198
Cape Torokina, 102, 103
Cap Gris-Nez, 35
Caroline Islands, 79, 117, 123, 134, 136, 156
Casablanca, 40
Castellano, Brig. Gen. Luis G., 189
casualties, 210–11; at Gallipoli, 23; at Omaha Beach, 71; at Wake Island, 87; at Peleliu, 146; at Leyte, 111; at Tarawa, 128–29; at Makin, 129–30; at Iwo Jima, 150; at Okinawa, 163–64; estimated for invasion of Japan, 170–71; at Inchon, 178; in Falkland Islands, 201; at Utah Beach, 201
cave warfare. *See* defense in depth
Charan Kanoa, 138
chemical warfare, 212; never employed at Gallipoli, 22; British plan for use in 1940, 34; absence of at Normandy, 76–77; *Tentative Manual for Landing Operations* on, 83; preparations for at Wake, 83; preparations for at Midway, 91; at Iwo Jima, 152; scares at Saipan and Peleliu, 152; not planned for defense of Japan, 172
Cherbourg, 72
Chiefs of Staff (British), 26–27
Cho, Lt. Gen. Isamu, 163
Churchill, Winston, 10, 42; on defense of Britain against invasion, 24, 31, 33–34
Clapp, Como. Michael C., 190, 191
Clark, Lt. Eugene F., 175
Clark, Gen. Mark W., 53–55, 203
coastal defense guns: at Cap Gris-Nez, 35; at Sicily, 41; debate over placement at Sicily, 43–44; at Salerno, 51; debate over placement at Normandy, 61; on Wake, 82; on Midway, 89; at Tarawa, 120–21, 123, 125; missing on Kwajalein, 131; positions unfinished at Saipan, 137; at Iwo Jima, 149; *See also* Atlantic Wall
coastal fortifications: Channel ports designated as fortresses, 60; prohibited on Pacific Islands by treaty, 80, 117; construction halted at Leyte, 109; unprecedented scale on Betio, 123–24; at

coastal fortifications (*continued*)
  Peleliu, 144; at Iwo Jima, 148;
  See also Atlantic Wall
code breaking, 88, 121. *See also* Ultra
combined (multinational) anti-landing operations: Turkish-German defense of Gallipoli, 12–13; Italian-German defense of Sicily, 41–42
combined (amphibious) operations: British usage, 9
command of amphibious operations, 75, 205–7; German plan for Sea Lion, 28; at Guadalcanal, 96; for recapture of Philippines, 108; for Gilberts operation, 119–20; for Falkland Islands landings, 191
command of anti-landing defenses, 151, 205–7; at Gallipoli, 13, 21; for the defense of Britain, 29, 37; at Sicily, 42; during the Italian campaign, 50, 57; at Normandy, 63–64, 75; at Wake Island, 81–82; at Midway, 89–90; at Guadalcanal, 96–97, 99–100; in Philippines, 108, 110, 115; in Marianas, 136; lessons from Saipan, 143; at Peleliu, 144; at Iwo Jima, 147, 151; for the defense of Japan, 165, 167; in Falkland Islands, 189–90
commando raids. *See* amphibious raids
Common Knowledge, Operation, 177
Conqueror, HMS, 195
Conrath, Maj. Gen. Paul, 41, 46, 48
Constantinople, 12
Coral Sea, battle of, 87–88, 90, 94
Corbett, Julian: on naval defense, 3
Corlett, Maj. Gen. Charles H., 76
Cornet, Operation, 167
Corsica, 40

counter-landing, 103, 127
culminating point, 7–8
Cunningham, Comdr. W. S., 81–82

Dakar, 2
Dardanelles, 11. *See also* Gallipoli
DD tank, 70–71
deception, 74, 177; at Gallipoli, 15; Operation Mincemeat, 40; First U.S. Army Group (FUSAG) at Normandy, 64; raid on Makin Atoll, 118; in Falkland Islands, 194
defense at the water's edge, 82; defined, 3–4; advantages and disadvantages, 4; at Gallipoli, 22; at Sicily, 43; discarded by Field Marshal Kesselring, 50; at Normandy, 65–67; at Wake Island, 83–84; planned at Midway, 91; at Tulagi, 98; at Tarawa, 122–25, 133; at Biak, 105; Japanese Army tactical doctrine militates against, 135; rejected at Iwo Jima, 148; Japanese cautioned against by Germans, 148; at Okinawa, 158; for the defense of Japan, 169; at Wonsan, 180; precluded in the Falkland Islands, 192
defense battalions, 79, 80; lack of infantry as a weakness of, 84. *See also* U.S. Marine Corps ground units
defense in depth: at Biak, 105–6; at Leyte, 109; precluded at Tarawa, 122; in Marianas, 134; lessons from Saipan, 142; at Peleliu, 145; at Iwo Jima, 149; at Okinawa, 158–59; for the defense of Japan, 169; in Falkland Islands, 192–93
DeForest, Lt. Cmdr. Donald C., 182
delay, impact on defense. *See* time as an aspect of defense

Index ~ 253

demonstration landings. *See* amphibious demonstrations
de Robeck, Vice Adm. John, 11
Devereux, Maj. James P. S., 80, 81, 83–84, 85, 91
Dieppe, 60, 71, 151
doctrine. *See* amphibious doctrine; anti-landing doctrine
Doenitz, Adm. Karl, 43
Dollman, Col. Gen. Friedrich, 62
Doolittle, Col. James H., 87
Dover, 28, 30
Dowding, Air Marshal Hugh, 34
Downfall, Operation, 167
Doyle, Rear Adm. James H., 176, 178, 180, 182
Dragon, 757
dual drive tank, 70–71
DUKW amphibious trucks, 47
Dulag, 110
Dunkirk, 26, 29

East Anglia, 30
Eighth Air Force (U.S.), 70
Eisenhower, Gen. Dwight D., 42, 75; on difficulty of amphibious operations, 1
elastic defense, 21
Empress Augusta Bay, battle of, 103, 125
Endurance, HMS, 193
English Channel, 30
Eniwetok, 132
Enterprise, USS, 95
Enver Pasha, 13
Exocet missiles, 189, 193, 194, 195, 199, 200
explosive motor boats, 64, 74. *See also* suicide tactics, naval

Falkland Islands, 186–202
fast attack craft, 20, 64, 69
Fearless, HMS, 186, 190

Fieldhouse, Adm. Sir John, 191, 198–99
First U.S. Army Group. *See* deception
Fisher, Adm. John: on naval gunfire against forts, 11
Fitzroy, 192, 199
flame weapons, 33, 67, 144, 169
Fleet Marine Force, 78
Fleet Training Publication No. 167, Landing Operations Doctrine, U.S. Navy, 79
fleet-versus-fleet battle, 79; Wake Island as a means of precipitating, 81; at Coral Sea, 87–88; at Midway, 87–88, 91; A-GO plan for, 106; Japanese hope to precipitate at Tarawa, 102–3; possibility of winning war, 107; at Leyte Gulf, 111–14, 116; Gilberts and Marshalls as bait to precipitate, 119, 122–23; Adm. Spruance on, 119; Imperial General Headquarters guidance on, 122
Fletcher, Rear Adm. Frank Jack, 85–87, 95
Florida Island, 98
Folkestone, 28
Formosa, 107, 109, 114, 154–55, 158, 159, 162
fortifications. *See* coastal fortifications
Fritz-X, 50–51, 55
Fuehrer Directives: No. 16 on invasion of Britain, 28; No. 40 on command relationships, 63
Fukudome, Rear Adm. Shigeru, 113
fukuryu suicide frogmen, 166
Fuller, J. F. C.: on importance of amphibious tactics in World War II, 1
FUSAG. *See* deception

Gallipoli, 10–23; significance of, 10; lessons of misunderstood by

Gallipoli (continued)
British, 24; U.S. Marine Corps studies, 79; compared with Falkland Islands, 191; See also Dardanelles
Galtieri, Gen. Leopoldo, 200
Galvanic, Operation, 120
gas warfare. See chemical warfare
Gavutu, 96–98
Geelvink Bay, 105
Gela, 46–47
General Belgrano, 189, 194–95
geography, impact on defense of. See terrain, impact on defense of
German Army units. See also Oberkommando der Wehrmacht
—Army Group B, 50, 62
—Army Group G, 63
—Panzer Group West, 65
—Seventh Army, 62, 66, 69
—Ninth Army, 28
—Tenth Army, 50, 51, 52
—Fifteenth Army, 62, 66, 71, 74
—Sixteenth Army, 28
— XIV Panzer Corps, 48, 52
—1st Parachute Division, 48
—16th Panzer Division, 51, 52, 53
—21st Panzer Division, 71–72
—26th Panzer Division, 53
—29th Panzer Division, 48
—15th Panzer Grenadier Division, 41, 44, 48
—29th Panzer Grenadier Division, 53
—276th Division, 63
—352nd Division, 71
—Division Sizilien, 41
—Kampfgruppe Schmalz, 46
—Panzer Lehr Division, 72
German-Japanese cooperation, 63, 148
German SS units
—I SS Panzer Corps, 72
—12th SS Panzer Division, 72
Geyr von Schweppenburg, Gen. of Panzer Troops Leo, 65–66, 76
Gilbert Islands, 102, 118–30, 134
Glamorgan, HMS, 200
Gneisenau, 27
Gold Beach, 70
Goliath, HMS, 20
Goose Green, 189, 196, 198, 199
Gorshkov, Adm. Sergei, 35, 76, 209; on reasons for success of World War II landings, 2
Goto, Col. Takashi, 138
Group Landwirt, 64
Guadalcanal, 118; battle for, 94–101, 201; lessons from, 119
Guam, 80, 82, 134, 137, 138, 140; invasion postponed, 141; battle for, 142–43
Guderian, Col. Gen. Heinz, 65
Gulf of Noto, 46
Guzzoni, Generale d'Armata Alfredo, 44, 46–48; as overall Axis commander on Sicily, 41, 42
gyokusai. See suicide tactics, ground

Hagushi, 157, 158, 160
Halder, Col. Gen. Franz: on Sea Lion as a river crossing, 30
Halsey, Vice Adm. William F., 81–82, 108, 110–11, 115
Hamilton, Gen. Ian, 12, 18
Hawaiian Islands, 80, 84, 94, 130
Hayate, 85
helicopters, 184, 188, 193, 213; first used for amphibious assault, 186; used by British to assault South Georgia, 193; employed during San Carlos landing in Falklands, 196; use during Falklands campaign affected by sinking of *Atlantic Conveyor*, 198–99

Helles, Cape, 14, 23
Henderson Field, 100
Henschel Hs 293a, 50–51
Herbstreise, Operation, 28
Hermann Goering Panzer Parachute Division, 41, 44, 46–47
Hermes, HMS, 187, 188, 190, 199, 202
Hersing, Lt. Otto, 20
Heye, Vice Adm. Helmuth, 64
Hill, Rear Adm. Harry W., 128
Hirohito, Japanese Emperor, 134, 171
Hiroshima, 173
Hiryu, 85
Hitler, Adolf: expects Allied landing on Sardinia or in Greece, 40; splits command of Italy, 50; infuriated by commando raids, 60; predicts location of invasion, 62; on flame warfare, 67; concerned about Pas-de-Calais, 74; releases reserves at Normandy, 72; on naval gunfire, 75
Home Defense Executive, 29
Home Fleet, Royal Navy, 29
Home Forces. *See* British Army units
Home Guard (Britain), 29
Home Guard (Okinawa), 155
Honshū, 164, 167
Hornet, USS, 87
Hosogaya, Vice Adm. Moshiro, 88
Hube, Gen. of Panzer Troops Hans Valentine, 48, 52
Hungnam, 183
Hyakutake, Lt. Gen. Seikichi, 94, 100

Ichiki, Col. Kiyonao, 88–89, 100
Ichimaru, Rear Adm. Toshinosuke, 147, 150
Imperial General Headquarters (Japanese), 96, 99–100, 109, 147; postpones offensive operations after Midway, 94; decides to evacuate Guadalcanal, 101; redraws central Pacific defense line, 123, 134; on U.S. naval gunfire, 142; on lessons from Saipan, 143; forces changes to Okinawa defense, 158–59; sets defense priorities for Japan, 164; abolishes Combined Fleet, 166–67
Inchon, 175–79
Inflexible, HMS, 11
Inoue, Lt. Gen. Sadae, 143–45
Inouye, Rear Adm. Shigeyoshi, 81, 84, 96
intelligence collection, 121, 130, 175
intelligence estimates: U.S. at Guadalcanal, 97; U.S. at Tarawa, 121; U.S. at Iwo Jima, 147; U.S. at Okinawa, 156–57; Japanese for invasion of Japan, 167; U.S. for invasion of Japan, 167
interdiction, 7
Intrepid, HMS, 186, 190
Invincible, HMS, 187, 188, 190, 199, 202
Ironside, Gen. Edmund, 32, 33, 37
Irresistible, HMS, 11
I-75, 129
Ishikawa, 157
Ismay, Gen. Hastings, 64
Italian armistice, 52
Italian Army units
—Sixth Army, 41, 42, 44, 48
—Seventh Army, 50
—XVI Corps, 46
—222nd Coastal Division, 51–52
—Livorno Division, 41, 46
—Napoli Division, 46
—Mobile Group E, 46
Ito, Vice Adm. Seichi, 162
Iwo Jima, 146–50

Japan, defense of, 107. *See also* Honshū; Kyūshū
Japanese Army units
—Air General Army, 165
—Kwantung Army, 164, 173
—Southern Army, 100, 107, 108
—8th Area Army, 100
—10th Area Army, 154
—14th Area Army, 109
—16th Area Army, 165, 169
—Fourteenth Army, 108
—Seventeenth Army, 94, 100
—Eighteenth Army, 100
—Thirty-first Army, 135, 136, 142, 143, 147
—Thirty-second Army, 154, 155, 156, 158, 159, 162–63
—Thirty-fifth Army, 108
—Fortieth Army, 165
—Fifty-sixth Army, 165
—Fifty-seventh Army, 165, 169
—Fourth Air Army, 108
—Sixth Air Army, 155, 161, 165
—5th Artillery Command, 154
—2nd Independent Mixed Brigade, 147
—44th Independent Mixed Brigade, 154, 157
—Ichiki Detachment, 88, 100
—"Ko" Detachment, 127
—9th Division, 154, 158
—14th Division, 143
—16th Division, 109, 113
—24th Division, 154
—29th Division, 136
—43rd Division, 136, 137, 138
—62nd Division, 154
—109th Division, 147
—8th Air Division, 155
—2nd Infantry Regiment, 144
—135th Infantry Regiment, 138
—136th Infantry Regiment, 140
—145th Infantry Regiment, 147
—9th Tank Regiment, 138, 140
—26th Tank Regiment, 147
—27th Tank Regiment, 154
—11th Shipping Group, 154, 155
Japanese-German cooperation. *See* German-Japanese cooperation
Japanese mandates, 96, 117, 134
Japanese Navy aviation units
—Third Air Fleet, 159
—Fifth Air Fleet, 155, 159–60, 163, 165
—Eleventh Air Fleet, 97
—24th Air Flotilla, 81, 84
—25th Air Flotilla, 97, 98
—26th Air Flotilla, 113
—201st Air Group, 113
—Yokohama Air Group, 96, 98
—Divine Wind Special Attack Force, 113
—*Kaigun Jinrai Butai* (Navy Thunder Gods Corps), 156
Japanese Navy units
—First Mobile Fleet, 138, 140
—Fourth Fleet, 81, 96, 97, 121, 135
—Sixth Fleet, 97, 129
—Eighth Fleet, 96, 97
—Central Pacific Area Fleet, 135
— Combined Fleet, 88, 96, 97, 102, 106, 108, 118, 135–35; fuel shortages affect, 107; plan for decisive fleet battle, 119; Adm. Koga assumes command of, 122; orders on island defense, 123; responsible for island defense, 135; abolished, 166–67
—First Carrier Striking Force, 88
—2nd Combined Special Landing Force, 88
—3rd Special Base Defense Force, 120
—Inner South Seas Force, 96
—Outer South Seas Force, 96–97
—Southeast Area Force, 97
—Navy General Command, 167

—Kure 3rd SNLF, 96, 98
—Sasebo 7th SNLF, 120
—Yokosuka 1st SNLF, 140
—Yokosuka 6th SNLF, 117, 118, 120
—14th Construction Unit, 98
—111th Construction Unit, 120
Jofre, Brig. Gen. Oscar L., 189
Johnson Island, 80
Joint Chiefs of Staff (U.S.), 95–96
joint operations, 8–9, 205
Joint Task Force 7, 177
Jomini, Baron Antoine Henri: on mobile defense, 5
Juno Beach, 70

Kadena, 157–58
Kahoolawe, 130
kaiten torpedoes, *See* suicide tactics, naval
kamikazes. *See* suicide tactics, aviation
Kanto Plain, 164, 167
Keitel, Field Marshal Wilhelm, 59
Kemal, Col. Mustafa, 16, 18
Kent, 30
Kerama Retto, 155, 160
Kesselring, Field Marshal Albert, 44, 50, 52; on mobile defense, 39; as German unified commander in Mediterranean, 42; on Allied delay after Tunisia, 43; countermands Gen. Guzzoni's order, 48; discards defense at the water's edge, 50; refines concept of mobile defense, 55; on naval gunfire, 214
Keyes, Adm. Roger J. B., 24
Kimmel, Adm. Husband E., 81, 85
Kinkaid, Vice Adm. Thomas C., 108
Kisaragi, 85
Kitchener, Field Marshal Horatio, 22
Kleinkampfverbände (KdK), 64, 74–75

Koga, Adm. Mineichi, 122–23, 125, 127, 135
Kondo, Vice Adm. Nobutake, 88
Kongo Maru, 85
KON operation, 106
Korea, 173–85, 186
Koror Island, 144
Koyanagi, Rear Adm. Tomiji, 94
Krancke, Adm. Theodor, 63–64
Krueger, Lt. Gen. Walter, 108, 167
Kum Kale, 15, 23
Kunsan, 174, 177
Kuribayashi, Lt. Gen. Tadamichi, 134, 147, 150
Kurita, Vice Adm. Takeo, 111–13, 115
Kuroda, Lt. Gen. Shigenori, 108, 109
Kushikino, 167
Kuzume, Col. Nauyuki, 105
Kwajalein, 127; capture of, 130–32
Kyūshū, 157, 159, 164–71

Lami Dozo, Gen. Basilio, 202
landing craft and ships, 187; impact of air-cushion landing craft (LCAC) on amphibious operations, 4, 213; *River Clyde* as an improvised landing ship, 17; LSTs allow rapid landing of tanks, 47; Germans test captured Allied, 67; LCI 1065 sunk by kamikaze, 114; Japanese developments, 103; rocket craft at Kwajalein, 131; shortage of LSTs for Inchon, 176
landings repulsed, 2; Japanese at Wake Island, 84–85
landmines: at Gallipoli, 15, 16; for the defense of Britain, 32; at Sicily, 44; at Salerno, 52, 53; at Normandy, 66; at Wake Island, 83; at Midway, 91; missing at Leyte, 109; at Tarawa, 123; not

landmines (*continued*)
emplaced at Eniwetok, 132; missing at Saipan, 137; at Peleliu, 144; at Iwo Jima, 149; largely missing in Japan, 169, 170; in Falkland Islands, 193
Lemnos, 12, 20
les Dunes-de-Varreville, 70
Leyte, 107, 109, 111, 113
Leyte Gulf, battle of, 110, 111–14
Licata, 46
Liddell Hart, B. H., 25, 217; on difficulty of amphibious operations, 1
Liman von Sanders, Field Marshal Otto, 12, 13, 16, 17; his estimate of Allied strength at Gallipoli, 12; concept of defense at Gallipoli, 14–15, 17; reaction to Suvla Bay landing, 18; on power of naval gunfire, 22, 214; on role of German Navy, 19
Lingayen Gulf, 114
Liscome Bay, USS, 129
Local Defense Volunteers, 29
Lombardo, Vice Adm. Juan J., 189
Luftwaffe, 43, 62; strength on Sicily, 42; air attacks at Sicily, 47; air attacks at Salerno, 55; strength at Normandy, 64
Luzon, 109, 157
LVT (landing vehicle, tracked), 127, 131, 187; Japanese defensive type, 166

MacArthur, General Douglas, 95, 108, 111, 171, 211, 216; Adm. Nimitz on strategy, 96; maintains objective of recapturing Philippines, 115; as ground commander for invasion of Japan, 167; as commander of UN forces in Korea, 174; selects force for Inchon landing, 175–76; plans another landing after Inchon, 179
Maginot Line: British anti-landing defenses compared with, 33
Maidos, 15
Majestic, HMS, 20
Makin, 118, 120, 122, 125, 129–30
Makino, Lt. Gen. Shira, 109, 111, 113
Maloelap, 130
Malvinas, 187. *See also* Falkland Islands
mandates. *See* Japanese mandates
Mannert L. Abele, USS, 163
maps: influence of on amphibious operations, 14, 97
Marcus Island, 125
Mariana Islands, 106–7, 117, 123, 134, 136–43, 148; as B-29 base, 147
Marshall, Gen. George, 76, 171, 172
Marshall Islands, 80, 82, 84, 117, 119, 134; outside main defense line, 123; capture of, 130–32; lessons from, 135
Maryland, USS, 125
Maugeri, Adm. Franco: on potential of naval defense at Salerno, 58
Menéndez, Brig. Gen. Mario, 186, 188, 189; evaluates possible landing sites in the Falkland Islands, 192–93; initially believes San Carlos landing is a diversion, 196; surrenders Falklands, 200
Messina, 48
midget submarines. *See* submarines
Midway, battle of, 91, 94, 100, 119
Midway Island, 80, 82, 88–92
Mikawa, Vice Adm. Gunichi, 96, 97, 98
Mille, 130
Milne Bay, 98; Japanese landing at repulsed, 2
Mincemeat, Operation, 40

Mindanao, 108, 116
mine countermeasures, 74, 177–78, 180–82, 213–14
mines, naval: at Gallipoli, 11, 19–20; at Sicily, 40; at Salerno, 52, 53; at Normandy, 68–69, 74; at Wake Island, 83; at Midway, 91; missing at Kwajalein, 131; at Eniwetok, 132, 213–14; planned at Okinawa, 160; at Inchon, 175, 177, 178–79; at Wonsan, 180–85; *See also* landmines
mixed defense, 32
Miyazaki, Capt. Shigetoshi, 94
Miyazaki Plain, 165, 167, 169
mobile defense, 82; defined, 5; advantages and disadvantages, 5–6; at Gallipoli, 14–15, 17–18, 22–23; for the defense of Britain, 32, 34, 35–37; at Sicily, 44; at Salerno, 51–53; Field Marshal Kesselring refines concept, 55; during Italian campaign, 57–58; at Normandy, 65, 71–72; debated before Normandy, 65–66; precluded at Wake Island, 83; on Guadalcanal, 99–100; precluded at Tarawa, 122; at Saipan, 138, 140; at Okinawa, 160–62; rejected in Falkland Islands, 192
mobility of naval forces, 5–6, 23, 47, 76
monitors, 20, 53
Montgomery, Field Marshal Bernard, 42, 52, 55
Moore, Maj. Gen. Jeremy, 191, 198, 199, 200
Morison, Samuel Eliot, 92
Morotai, 106
Morto Bay, 16
Muavenet-i-Millet, 20
Mudros, 20

Murai, Maj. Gen. Kenjiro, 144–46
Musashi, 106, 108, 111
Mussolini, Benito, 40–41

Nagasaki, 173
Nagumo, Vice Adm. Chuichi, 88, 135, 136, 142
Naha, 158, 161
Nakagawa, Col. Kunio, 144–46
Namur, 130–31
Naples, 51, 53, 60
Nauru, 119, 125
Nautilus, USS, 121
naval defense, 133; defined, 2; famous naval battles related to, 3; advantages and disadvantages of, 2–3; at Gallipoli, 21–22; Royal Navy's concept of for the defense of Britain, 24–25, 31–32; at Salerno, 53–55; during Italian campaign, 58; at Normandy, 67–69, 74–75; at Guadalcanal, 98–99; typical Japanese style of in SWPA, 103, 116; at Tarawa, 122; at Makin, 129–30; at Okinawa, 159–60; for defense of Japan, 169–70; in Falklands, 194, 196–98, 199–200; poor man's, 184; *See also* target priorities for naval defense
naval gunfire, general, 11, 76, 214–15; General Hamilton on, 22; Field Marshal Liman von Sanders on, 22; General Bradley on, 47; during Italian campaign, 58; Adolf Hitler on, 75; Japanese at Wake Island, 84–85; affect on Japanese anti-landing doctrine, 109; practice range established on Kahoolawe, 130; increased significantly at Kwajalein Atoll, 131; Imperial General Headquarters on, 142; Gen-

260 ~ Index

naval gunfire, general, *(continued)* eral Saito on, 142; in Falklands, 196, 200
naval gunfire against counterattacks, 58; at Gallipoli, 17, 23; at Sicily, 46–47; at Salerno, 53; at Saipan, 140
naval gunfire against fortifications: Adm. Fisher on, 11; at Normandy, 70; at Tarawa, 124–27; at Iwo Jima, 150
Navy Group West (German), 63–64
Nelson, Adm. Horatio, 11, 24
New Caledonia, 94, 157
New Guinea, 88, 94, 100, 101, 103, 118, 119; as possible site for decisive naval battle, 106
New Zealand, 94, 95
Nimitz, Adm. Chester, 88, 89–90, 108, 131, 132, 157; on time as a factor at Midway, 90; launches central Pacific drive, 117; wants Marine divisions for central Pacific, 119
Nishi, Lt. Col. Baron Takeichi, 147, 148
Nishida, Maj. Gen. Yoshima, 132
Noemfoor, 106
Nomura, Ambassador Kichisaburo, 152
Normandy, 59–77, 158, 201; Japanese debate over defending Philippines compared with German debate at, 109
North Korean People's Army (NKPA), 174, 175, 179
Norway, 26, 60
nuclear weapons, 172, 173, 183–84, 212–13

Obata, Lt. Gen. Hideyoshi, 135–38, 148
Oberkommando der Wehrmacht, 27–28, 72; directive on antilanding defense, 65; permission required to release reserves at Normandy, 66
obstacles, beach: at Gallipoli, 15, 16; for the defense of Britain, 32–33; at Sicily, 44; at Salerno, 52; at Normandy, 66–67, 71; at Wake Island, 83; at Midway, 91; missing at Leyte, 109; at Tarawa, 123–24; missing at Saipan, 137; at Peleliu, 144; at Iwo Jima, 149; largely missing in Japan, 169
Ocean, HMS, 11
Ochsner, Lt. Gen. Herman, 77
oka suicide bombs. *See* suicide tactics, aviation
Okinawa, 153, 154–64, 176, 178; compared with Falkland Islands, 193
OKW. *See* Oberkommando der Wehrmacht
Oldendorf, Rear Adm. Jesse B., 111
Olympic, Operation, 167, 170, 171–73
Omaha Beach, 70–71
Onishi, Vice Adm. Takijirō, 113
Oran, 40
Organization Todt, 60–61
Orne River, 62, 70, 71–72
Ōshima, Gen. Hiroshi, 63
Ota, Rear Adm. Minoru, 88, 155
Otero, Rear Adm. Edgardo A., 189
Ouistreham, 70
Overlord, Operation, 70. *See also* Normandy
Oyster mines, 68, 74
Ozawa, Vice Adm. Jisaburo, 110–11, 138, 140

Pachino Peninsula, 46
Palau Islands, 80, 106, 117, 136, 138; seizure of, 143–46
Palmyra, 80

Pandan, 2
Pantelleria, 45
paratroopers. *See* airborne operations
Pas-de-Calais, 62, 64, 74
"passive infiltration," 144–45
Patton, Lt. George S., Jr., 42, 51
Pearl Harbor. *See* Hawaiian Islands
Pebble Island, 189, 196
Pegasus Bridge, 72
Peleliu, 144–46, 148, 152, 166
Petroleum Warfare, Department of, 33
Philadelphia, USS, 55
Philippine Islands, 80, 102, 158; Japanese landing repulsed at, 2; recapture of, 107–13
Philippine Sea, battle of, 106, 140–41
Plan Y (for chemical warfare), 34
Plymouth, HMS, 200
Port Moresby, 88, 94
Port Pleasant, 200
Prince of Wales, HMS, 87
Pusan, 174–75, 179
Putnam, Maj. Paul A., 81

Rabaul, 94–95, 97; isolated instead of captured, 102; U.S. air attacks on, 103, 125
radio-controlled bombs, 50–51, 55, 75
Raeder, Adm. Erich, 27
RAF. *See* Royal Air Force
Raleigh, Sir Walter, 5–6, 203
Ramillies, HMS, 74
Ramsay, Vice Adm. Bertram, 34
reefs, 89, 121, 122, 127
Republic of Korea (ROK) Army, 174, 179, 180, 182
Republic of Korea (ROK) Marines, 176, 178
Repulse, HMS, 87
Richthofen, Field Marshal Wolfram von, 40

risk, 210–11
River Clyde, 17
Roi, 84, 130–31
Rommel, Field Marshal Erwin, 50, 60, 62, 72; on defense at the water's edge, 59; on need for time, 64; on naval gunfire, 214
Rommel's asparagus, 66
Rosario, Operation, 187–88, 192. *See also* Falkland Islands
Royal Air Force, 25–26, 29, 32
Royal Fleet Auxiliary, 190
Royal Marines, 177, 186, 190, 193
Royal Marine Units
—3 Commando Brigade, 191, 198–199, 200
—40 Commando, 191
—42 Commando, 191
—45 Commando, 186, 191, 199, 200
—Special Boat Squadron (SBS), 191
Royal Naval Division, 12
Royal Navy: role in antilanding defense, 31–32
Ruge, Adm. Friedrich, 65, 205
Rundstedt, Field Marshal Gerd von, 62, 63, 72; on Operation Sea Lion, 37; supports mobile defense at Normandy, 65
Rupertus, Maj. Gen. William H., 145
Ryukyu Islands, 134

Saint Lô, 71, 75
Saipan, 106, 134, 136–42, 152, 166; lessons from, 143
Saito, Lt. Gen. Yoshisugu, 138, 140; on naval gunfire, 142, 214
Salerno, 48–55, 60, 169
Salmuth, Col. Gen. Hans von, 62
San Bernardino Strait, 111
San Carlos, 192, 195–96, 199
San Jose, 111
San Luis, 195
Santa Fe, 193

Saratoga, USS, 85, 89, 95
Sardinia, 40
Saros Bay, 14, 15, 16, 17, 23
Satsuma Peninsula, 165, 167
Savannah, USS, 55
Savo Island, battle of, 99, 103
Scharnhorst, 27
Scoglitti, 46
S-day (Sea Lion), 31
sea control, 7, 133, 184, 190, 207–8; lack of by Germans during invasion of Norway, 26; impact on invasion of Britain, 35; related to defense of Wake and Midway Islands, 92; in SWPA, 102
Sea Lion, Operation, 62; final plan, 28; indefinitely postponed by Hitler, 35
Sedd el Bahr, 16
Seelöwe, Operation. *See* Sea Lion, Operation
Sele River, 51, 53
Senger und Etterlin, Lt. Gen. Fridolin von, 42, 61, 205, 214
Seoul, 175, 178
Shannon, Col. Harold D., 90–91
Sheffield, HMS, 195
Sherman, Adm. Forrest, 173, 183, 184
Shibasaki, Rear Adm. Keiji, 122–23, 133; assumes command in Gilberts, 120; on strength of Tarawa's defense, 125; killed at Tarawa, 128
Shikoku, 165, 167
SHO-GO operation: plans for, 107; SHO-1, 110–15
Shuri, 158
Sicily, 39–48
Simard, Comdr. Cyril T., 89
Sir Galahad, 200
Sir Tristram, 200
Slapton Sands, 69

"Slot," 101
Smith, Rear Adm. Allen E., 184
Smith, Lt. Gen. Holland M., 137, 141
Smith, Maj. Gen. Julian C., 128
Smith, Maj. Gen. Oliver P., 176, 178
Solomon Islands, 94–95, 100, 103, 118, 119
Sonoma, USS, 114
Soryu, 85
Souchon, Adm. Wilhelm, 13
South Georgia, 188, 190, 193
Southwest Pacific Area, 94–116
Sperrle, Field Marshal Hugo, 64
Spruance, Vice Adm. Raymond, 119, 137, 141
Stanley, 192, 198, 199, 201; airfield bombed by RAF, 193–94; capture of, 200
Stark, Adm. Harold R., 118
Stopford, Lt. Gen. Frederick, 18
stop lines, 32
strategy: Japanese during World War II, 79–80; Japanese in south Pacific, 94; U.S. in Pacific, 102
Struble, Vice Adm. Arthur D., 177–78, 179, 182
Student, Col. Gen. Kurt, 31
submarines, 98; German at Dardanelles, 19–20; Field Marshal Kitchener concerned about, 22; anti-invasion role at Normandy, 64, 74–75; deliver raiders to Makin, 118; impact on Japanese island defenses, 120, 136; periscope photography, 121; Japanese at Makin, 129; midgets at Okinawa, 155; mother ships for *kaiten* torpedoes, 156, 160; for defense of Japan, 165–66; Argentine in Falklands, 189, 195; British in the Falklands, 190, 191, 195; Argentine at South

Georgia, 193; *See also* suicide tactics, naval
suicide tactics, aviation: term kamikaze used by Japanese press, 113; initiated in Philippines, 113–15; results of attacks in Philippines, 114; *oka* bombs, 155–56; first *oka* attacks, 160; general attacks at Okinawa, 161–62; only ship sunk by *oka* bombs, 163; sorties at Okinawa, 163; land-launched *oka* bombs, 165; planned for defense of Japan, 165, 169–70
suicide tactics, ground: preview of at Tulagi, 98; by Col. Ichiki at Guadalcanal, 100; at Biak, 105–6; at Tarawa, 128; at Kwajalein, 131–32; at Saipan, 142; lessons from Saipan, 143; at Peleliu, 145–46; at Iwo Jima, 150; historical background, 153–54; banzai attacks (*gyokusai*), 154; for defense of Japan, 169
suicide tactics, naval: explosive motor boats, 155, 160, 165; *kaiten* torpedoes, 156, 160, 165; *Yamato* attack, 162; *fukuryu* suicide frogmen, 166; possibility of suicide boats at Wonsan, 180
Suribachi, Mount, 149, 150
Surigao Strait, 111
surprise: at Gallipoli, 18; at Salerno, 52; at Normandy, 70; at Guadalcanal, 98; at Okinawa, 160; versus need for naval gunfire at Inchon, 177
Suvla Bay, 14, 18
Suzuki, Lt. Gen. Sosaku, 108
Svenner, 74
Sword Beach, 70
SWPA. *See* Southwest Pacific Area
Syracuse, 46

Takagi, Vice Adm. Takeo, 129
Tanambogo, 96–98
Tanapag, 138, 142
Tanegashima, 167
Tangier, USS, 85, 89
tanks, 42, 70–71, 169; lack of at Wake, 87; at Midway, 89, 91; Japanese at Tarawa, 125; U.S. at Tarawa, 128; Japanese at Saipan, 138, 140; as major threat to Japanese, 143, 169
Tarawa, 102, 106, 201; lessons of not applied by Germans at Normandy, 65; defenses compared with those of Midway Island, 92; seized by Japanese, 118; U.S. assault on, 119–30
target priorities for naval defense, 3, 215–16; Adm. Nimitz's guidance on at Midway, 90; according to *Tentative Manual for Landing Operations*, 90; in Philippines, 110, 113, 116; Combined Fleet order on, 123; for the kamikazes in Japan, 169–70; in Falklands, 195, 196–98, 202
Tenaru River, 100
Tenedos, 21
Tentative Manual for Defense of Advanced Bases, 79
Tentative Manual for Landing Operations, 79, 82–83, 90–91; on destruction of enemy carriers, 92–93
Terauchi, Field Marshal Hisaichi, 108
terrain, impact on defense of: at Gallipoli, 13–14; for the defense of Britain, 30; at Sicily, 43; for Allied invasion of Europe, 62; at Wake Island, 82; at Midway, 90; at Guadalcanal, 97; in SWPA, 101–2, 116; at Biak, 105; in Gilberts

terrain, impact on defense of (*continued*)
    and Marshalls, 121–22, 130; in Marianas, 134–35; at Saipan, 141; at Peleliu, 145; at Iwo Jima, 149; at Okinawa, 157, 159; at Inchon, 175; in Korea, 175; in Falklands, 191–92
Third Air Fleet (Luftwaffe), 64
Thompson, Brig. Julian, 191, 198–99
tides: in Britain, 31; at Normandy, 64; at Tarawa, 127–33; at Inchon, 176–78
time as an aspect of defense, 132–33, 183–211; at Gallipoli, 14; for German invasion of Britain, 31, 37; impact of Allied delay before and after Sicily, 43, 52; during Italian campaign, 57; Field Marshal Rommel on, 64, 72; at Wake Island, 84; Adm. Nimitz on, 90; at Midway, 90; at Guadalcanal, 95, 97, 116; in Philippines, 107, 110, 116; at Tarawa, 119, 122; at Iwo Jima, 148, 152; Ambassador Nomura on, 152; at Okinawa, 157–58; at Inchon, 177, 179; in Falklands, 192, 198, 200, 201–2
Tinian, 137, 142–43
Tinian Town, 143
Togō, Adm. Heihachirō, 107, 116
Tojo, Hideki, 153
Tominaga, Lt. Gen. Kyoji, 108, 113
Tomonari, Rear Adm. Saichiro, 120
torpedo boats. *See* fast attack craft
Toyoda, Adm. Soemu, 116, 135, 138, 167
Trenchard, Marshal Hugh, 25
Triumph, HMS, 20
troop strengths: opposing at Gallipoli, 12–13; German at Normandy, 63; opposing at Normandy, 76; opposing at Guadalcanal, 96, 101; opposing in Philippines, 115; opposing at Tarawa, 120; Japanese in Marianas, 136; Japanese at Peleliu, 144; opposing at Iwo Jima, 147–48; Japanese at Okinawa, 154–55; U.S. at Okinawa, 157; North Korean at Inchon, 175
Truman, Harry S., 171, 174
Tsukahara, Vice Adm. Nishizo, 97
Tulagi, 94–98
tunnels. *See* defense in depth
Turkish Army, 12–13, 14, 15, 16, 18
Turner, Rear Adm. Richmond Kelly, 95, 119–20, 142

UDT. *See* underwater demolition teams
Uganda, HMS, 55
Ulithi, 156, 160
Ultra, 42, 50, 63, 74, 165, 167
underwater demolition teams, 131, 138, 149, 182. *See also fukuryu* suicide frogmen
unified command: lack of by defenders. *See* command of antilanding defenses
U.S. Army units
—Fifth Army, 51–53, 56
—Sixth Army, 108, 111, 167
—Seventh Army, 42
—Eighth Army, 174, 177, 179
—Tenth Army, 157, 160
—I Corps, 167
—II Corps, 47
—VI Corps, 53
—IX Corps, 167
—X Corps, 176, 179, 180, 182
—XI Corps, 167
—XXIV Corps, 157
—11th Airborne Division, 167
—82nd Airborne Division, 45, 55, 209

Index ~ 265

—1st Infantry Division, 47, 70, 71
—3rd Infantry Division, 210
—4th Infantry Division, 70, 201
—7th Infantry Division, 76, 157, 176, 179
—27th Infantry Division, 119, 129, 137, 141, 157
—41st Infantry Division, 106
—77th Infantry Division, 157, 160
—81st Infantry Division, 145, 157
—96th Infantry Division, 157
—1st Cavalry Division, 179
Usedom, Adm. Guido, 13
Ushijima, Lt. Gen. Mitsuru, 154, 155, 158–60, 163
U.S. Marine Corps aviation units
—1st Marine Aircraft Wing, 182
—VMF-211, 81–82, 83–84
—VMF-221, 85, 89
—VMSB-231, 89
U.S. Marine Corps ground units
—V Amphibious Corps, 157, 167, 170
—3rd Battalion, Fifth Marine Regiment, 178
—1st Defense Battalion, 80, 81, 84
—3rd Defense Battalion, 89
—4th Defense Battalion, 85
—6th Defense Battalion, 89, 91
—2nd Raider Battalion, 89, 118
—1st Marine Division, 95, 98, 119, 145, 157, 176, 179, 183, 210
—2nd Marine Division, 102, 119–20, 129, 133, 137, 138, 157, 160, 209
—3rd Marine Division, 102, 125, 148
—4th Marine Division, 137, 138, 143, 148, 210
—5th Marine Division, 148
—6th Marine Division, 157
—First Marine Regiment, 178
—Fifth Marine Regiment, 178
U.S. Navy units
—Third Fleet, 108, 110–11, 115

—Fifth Fleet, 130
—Seventh Fleet, 108
—Fifth Amphibious Force, 119–20
—Amphibious Group One, 176
Utah Beach, 70, 201
U-21, 20

Veinticinco de Mayo, 187, 189, 195
Vietinghoff, Gen. of Panzer Troops Heinrich von, 50, 52; selects mobile defense for Salerno, 51; incorrectly senses victory at Salerno, 53; withdraws from Salerno, 55
Vogelkop Peninsula, 106

Wake Island, 80–87
Walker, Lt. Gen. Walton H., 174
war games, anti-landing, 69, 107, 109, 160, 170
Warspite, HMS, 55, 74
Wasp, USS, 95
weapons: impact of improved types of, 211–13
weather, 30, 69–70, 85, 157–58; in Falklands, 191–92, 200
Westphal, Lt. Gen. Siegfried, 214
Wilkes Island, 84–85
Wilson, Brig. Tony, 199
withdrawals. *See* amphibious withdrawals
Wolmi-do, 175–79
Wonsan, 180–83, 184
Woodward, Rear Adm. John "Sandy," 190, 191; on selection of D-day, 192; keeps carriers out of range of Argentine air fields, 194; concerned about mines, 196; on U.S. Marine Corps, 201; on vulnerability of carriers, 202
Worcester, USS, 182
Wotje, 130

Yamamoto, Adm. Isoroku, 88, 122
Yamashita, Gen. Tomoyuki, 109
Yamato, 106, 108, 159, 162, 165
Yap, 144
YMS-516, 182
Yokoyama, Lt. Gen. Isamu, 165

Yonabaru, 158
Yontan, 157–58
Yo-Yo, Operation, 182

"Z" operation, 122–23, 125, 127

About the Author

Col. Theodore L. Gatchel retired from the U.S. Marine Corps in 1991 after a thirty-year career that included command of infantry units from the platoon to the battalion, two combat tours in Vietnam, and staff assignments at the regimental, Marine Expeditionary Brigade, and Fleet Marine Force/Marine Expeditionary Force level. His staff experience encompassed operations, personnel, and logistics. He taught amphibious warfare at the Naval War College, Newport, Rhode Island, and has lectured on the subject at many other institutions.

He has written extensively on the subject of amphibious warfare and has received awards for articles in both the *Marine Corps Gazette* and the U.S. Naval Institute *Proceedings*. He is a frequent contributor to the *Providence Journal-Bulletin* on military issues, and his op-ed pieces have appeared in newspapers around the country. *At the Water's Edge* is his first book.

The Naval Institute Press is the book-publishing arm of the U.S. Naval Institute, a private, nonprofit, membership society for sea service professionals and others who share an interest in naval and maritime affairs. Established in 1873 at the U.S. Naval Academy in Annapolis, Maryland, where its offices remain today, the Naval Institute has members worldwide.

Members of the Naval Institute support the education programs of the society and receive the influential monthly magazine *Proceedings* and discounts on fine nautical prints and on ship and aircraft photos. They also have access to the transcripts of the Institute's Oral History Program and get discounted admission to any of the Institue-sponsored seminars offered around the country.

The Naval Institute also publishes *Naval History* magazine. This colorful bimonthly is filled with entertaining and thought-provoking articles, first-person reminiscences, and dramatic art and photography. Members receive a discount on *Naval History* subscriptions.

The Naval Institute's book-publishing program, begun in 1898 with basic guides to naval practices, has broadened its scope in recent years to include books of more general interest. Now the Naval Institute Press publishes about 100 titles each year, ranging from how-to books on boating and navigation to battle histories, biographies, ship and aircraft guides, and novels. Institute members receive discounts of 20 to 50 percent on the Press's nearly 600 books in print.

Full-time students are eligible for special half-price membership rates. Life memberships are also available.

For a free catalog describing Naval Institute Press books currently available, and for further information about subscribing to *Naval History* magazine or about joining the U.S. Naval Institute, please write to:

Membership Department
U.S. Naval Institute
291 Wood Road
Annapolis, MD 21402
Telephone: (800) 233-8764
Fax: (410) 269-7940